BASEBALL SUPERSTARS

This is a CARLTON book

First published by Carlton Books Ltd, 2000

10 9 8 7 6 5 4 3 2 1

A CIP catalogue record for this book is available from the British Library

ISBN 1 84222 042 X

Project editor: Chris Hawkes
Project art direction: Brian Flynn
Picture research: Lorna Ainger
Production: Bob Bhamra

Printed and bound in Italy

Carlton Books Ltd
20 Mortimer Street
London W1N 7RD

BASEBALL SUPERSTARS

In the ballpark with the Major League's biggest stars

STEVE HERRICK

Contents

Introduction 6

The History of Baseball
1900s–1910s 8
1920s–1930s 10
1940s–1950s 12
1960s–1970s 14
1980s–1990s 16

Introduction 18
Albert Belle (Baltimore Orioles) 20
Pedro Martinez (Boston Red Sox) 22
Kevin Brown (Los Angeles Dodgers) 24
Greg Maddux (Atlanta Braves) 26
Gary Sheffield (Los Angeles Dodgers) 28
Bernie Williams (New York Yankees) 30
Barry Bonds (San Francisco Giants) 32
Randy Johnson (Arizona Diamondbacks) 34
Raul Mondesi (Toronto Blue Jays) 36
Sammy Sosa (Chicago Cubs) 38
Mark McGwire (St. Louis Cardinals) 40
Rafael Palmeiro (Texas Rangers) 42
Pat Hentgen (St. Louis Cardinals) 44
Ivan Rodriguez (Texas Rangers) 46
Ken Griffey Jr. (Seattle Mariners) 48
Juan Gonzalez (Detroit Tigers) 50
Roger Clemens (New York Yankees) 52
Andres Galarraga (Atlanta Braves) 54
Jim Thome (Cleveland Indians) 56
David Cone (New York Yankees) 58
Todd Stottlemyre (Arizona Diamondbacks) 60
Matt Williams (Arizona Diamondbacks) 62
John Smoltz (Atlanta Braves) 64
Kenny Lofton (Cleveland Indians) 66
Mo Vaughn (Anaheim Angels) 68
Mike Piazza (New York Mets) 70
Dante Bichette (Cincinnati Reds) 72
Alex Fernandez (Florida Marlins) 74
Tom Glavine (Atlanta Braves) 76
David Justice (Cleveland Indians) 78
Frank Thomas (Chicago White Sox) 80
Robin Ventura (New York Mets) 82
Ray Lankford (St. Louis Cardinals) 84
Roberto Alomar (Cleveland Indians) 86
Mike Mussina (Baltimore Orioles) 88
Jeff Bagwell (Houston Astros) 90
John Valentin (Boston Red Sox) 92
Cal Ripken Jr. (Baltimore Orioles) 94
Paul O'Neill (New York Yankees) 96
John Wetteland (Texas Rangers) 98
Scott Erickson (Baltimore Orioles) 100
Ron Gant (Philadelphia Phillies) 101
Craig Biggio (Houston Astros) 102
Roberto Hernandez (Tampa Bay Devil Rays) 103
Jay Bell (Arizona Diamondbacks) 104
Andy Benes (Arizona Diamondbacks) 105
Chuck Knoblauch (New York Yankees) 106
Moises Alou (Houston Astros) 107
Charles Nagy (Cleveland Indians) 108
Bobby Bonilla (New York Mets) 109
Pedro Astacio (Colorado Rockies) 110
Chuck Finley (Cleveland Indians) 111
Vinny Castilla (Tampa Bay Devil Rays) 112
Jeff Kent (San Francisco Giants) 113
Brady Anderson (Baltimore Orioles) 114
Travis Fryman (Cleveland Indians) 115
Greg Vaughn (Cincinnati Reds) 116
Aaron Sele (Texas Rangers) 117
Rod Beck (Chicago Cubs) 118
Eric Karros (Los Angeles Dodgers) 119
Tim Salmon (Anaheim Angels) 120
Steve Finley (Arizona Diamondbacks) 121
Todd Hundley (Los Angeles Dodgers) 122
Barry Larkin (Cincinnati Reds) 123
Scott Brosius (New York Yankees) 124
Bernard Gilkey (Arizona Diamondbacks) 125
Al Leiter (New York Mets) 126
Javy Lopez (Atlanta Braves) 127
Fred McGriff (Tampa Bay Devil Rays) 128
Larry Walker (Colorado Rockies) 129
Curt Schilling (Philadelphia Phillies) 130
Steve Trachsel (Chicago Cubs) 131
Carlos Delgado (Toronto Blue Jays) 132
Jeff Fassero (Seattle Mariners) 133
Andy Ashby (San Diego Padres) 134
Marquis Grissom (Milwaukee Brewers) 135
Derek Jeter (New York Yankees) 136
Dean Palmer (Detroit Tigers) 137
Kenny Rogers (New York Mets) 138
Kevin Appier (Oakland Athletics) 139
Jose Offerman (Boston Red Sox) 140
Trevor Hoffman (San Diego Padres) 141
Manny Ramirez (Cleveland Indians) 142
Tony Gwynn (San Diego Padres) 143
Mariano Riveira (New York Yankees) 144
Alex Rodriguez (Seattle Mariners) 145
Chipper Jones (Atlanta Braves) 146
Jeromy Burnitz (Milwaukee Brewers) 147
Brian Jordan (Atlanta Braves) 148
Shawn Green (Los Angeles Dodgers) 149
Brad Radke (Minnesota Twins) 150
Orlando Hernandez (New York Yankees) 151
Nomar Garciaparra (Boston Red Sox) 152
Jason Kendall (Pittsburgh Pirates) 153
Vladimir Guerrero (Montreal Expos) 154
Wade Boggs (Tampa Bay Devil Rays) 155
Matt Mantei (Arizona Diamondbacks) 156
Kevin Millwood (Atlanta Braves) 157
Scott Williamson (Cincinnati Reds) 158
Carlos Beltran (Kansas City Royals) 159
Picture Acknowledgments 160

7

Introduction

From its humble beginnings a century ago, baseball has become America's pastime and obsession. It's not melting snows that herald the coming of spring: it's the crack of the bat that signals the start of spring training exhibition games in March.

Fans from all over the country make pilgrimages down South and out West to see what their home team is sporting for the season. Even teams who have never witnessed the thrill of a playoff game hope their luck will change. Neither strikes nor escalating salaries nor scandals deter fans from rooting for their favorite teams.

The 20th century saw Babe Ruth save the integrity of the game following the Black Sox scandal of 1919. Even today—over 50 years after his death—Ruth is still the most memorable player the sport has given us.

The sport produced moments—both good and bad—that will never be forgotten.

The century gave us the likes of Ty Cobb, Joe DiMaggio, Willie Mays, Sandy Koufax and Hank Aaron. It also produced the fall of Pete Rose, the designated hitter, the cancellation of a World Series, shiny new ballparks and television coverage of games around the country.

The 21st century is upon us. And we know baseball will surely produce more memories.

History

The first basball stars

Cy Young won 511 games in his career. A modern starting pitcher would need to play 14 seasons just to make 511 starts.

The National League of Professional Base Ball Clubs was founded on February 2, 1876, a century after the founding of the United States. Although the game already had its share of ardent supporters, few would imagine that by the time another 100 years had passed, the sport would have turned into a billion-dollar a year business with 50 million paying spectators and players commanding multiyear contracts with salaries of more than $15 million a year.

The National League sported teams in Boston, Chicago, Cincinnati, St. Louis, Hartford, New York, Philadelphia and Louisville, all major cities with more than 75,000 potential paying customers. In 1899, former college baseball player and hard-nosed businessman Byron Bancroft Johnson, saw an opportunity to bring baseball to cities including Baltimore and Washington. By the turn of the century competition had sprung up between Johnson's brand-new American League and the National League.

The average ticket price was 25 cents. Fans came out to see Denton True (Cy) Young. With 511 victories and 316 defeats, Young became the winningest—and losingest—pitcher in Major League history. (Today, Major League

Baseball presents a Cy Young Award yearly to the top pitcher in each league.)

Teams often played by their own rules. New York Giants manager John McGraw, whom sportswriters dubbed "Little Napoleon", single-handedly wiped out the 1904 World Series. Miffed by a comment Ban Johnson made about his fiery temper, McGraw flatly refused to play against the American League representative, which that year meant facing the Boston Pilgrims.

Although the game maintained a rough and tough climate throughout the 1900s, there were men who were known as much for their virtue as their ability. One such player was Giants pitcher Christy Mathewson, who did more to improve the reputation of the game than any other player of his time. Matthewson's record was so spotless he upheld the promise he made to his mother never to play on Sunday. He went on to win 373 games, third on the all-time list.

The era had its share of hotheads and heroes. There was Detroit Tigers outfielder Ty Cobb. Hated by opposing players, fans and even some of his teammates, Cobb still was one of the best players in history. He ended his career in 1928 with a lifetime .360 batting average and 4,191 hits, a mark that would stand for 57 years.

Pitcher Walter Johnson was another dominant figure. In 21 seasons with the Washington Senators, he won 416 games, second to Young on the all-time list.

The celebrated combination of infielders Joe Tinker, Johnny Evers and Frank Chance made the 1906 Chicago Cubs legendary as one of the best teams in baseball history with 116 wins and 36 losses.

Two years later, fan enthusiasm reached a fever pitch that prompted vaudeville entertainer Jack Norworth and songwriter Albert von Tilzer to pen "Take Me Out to the Ball Game" which is played at almost every Major League game during the seventh-inning stretch.

But baseball's darkest hour was just dawning. The 1919 World Series between the Chicago White Sox and Cincinnati Reds appeared to be a shoe-in. The odds favored the mighty White Sox, but trouble brewed beneath the surface.

Several White Sox players had been upset for years because they felt they were grossly underpaid by team owner Charles Comiskey. Eight players agreed to throw the Series for $100,000. Suspicions arose that something was amiss as the Series unfolded and the Reds ultimately were victorious in eight games. Not only did the White Sox players lose the Series, they were double-crossed by the gamblers and didn't receive anything close to the amount of money they were promised.

In 1920, the White Sox were again in contention for the pennant when the scandal was uncovered and subsequently revealed in bold headlines around the country. Although no one went to jail, the eight players involved in the scheme were barred from baseball for life.

Joe Jackson, banned for life in 1920, has baseball's third highest batting average.

The most notable player kicked out of the game was Joseph Jefferson Jackson, one of the finest hitters to ever play. Jackson was nicknamed "Shoeless Joe" because he was once spotted playing in the minor leagues in his stocking feet because his shoes were too tight. Although he could neither read nor write, Jackson had a lifetime batting average of .356 when the Sox scandal broke. Jackson, whom Cobb called "the greatest hitter I ever saw", spent the rest of his career playing outlaw baseball on several Southern teams before opening a liquor store in his native South Carolina. He died a broken man in 1951.

Disenchanted with the game, the public began to stay away. Attendance waned. The game needed a catalyst to revitalize faith. It found such a savior in George Herman Ruth—the Babe.

Babe Ruth's heroics made baseball acceptable to the masses in the 1920s.

The era of the Babe

He was born George Herman Ruth on February 6, 1895, in Baltimore, the son of a saloonkeeper. The youth, who spent many of his formative years stealing from shopkeepers and warding off beatings by his father, would go down in history as one of the game's greatest players.

Ruth's parents felt the boy was uncontrollable and sent him to live at a reform school orphanage. It was there that he tried his hand at baseball and by age eight was playing on the varsity team with 12 year-olds. When Ruth was 19, he caught the eye of the Baltimore Orioles, who signed him. Within months the Red Sox bought his services as a pitcher.

The 6-foot-2-inch, 198-pound player's escapades off the field—which allegedly included wolfing down a dozen hot dogs at one sitting—earned him the nickname "Baby", which turned into "Babe". In the Red Sox's greatest years, the left-hander was the best pitcher in the American League, winning 89 games in six seasons. As his hitting ability became apparent, however, Ruth saw more action in the outfield. By the time he was sold to the New York Yankees in 1920, his days as a pitcher were pretty much a thing of the past.

The sale of Ruth is the most famous transaction in baseball history. The Red Sox haven't won the World Series since 1918 and Ruth's departure from Boston is still referred as "The Curse of the Bambino".

During that first season in New York, Ruth hit 54 home runs, 25 more than he had hit a year earlier, and one more than the rest of the team managed to hit. His slugging average was a mind-boggling .847. No one has come close to topping it since.

Ruth topped the 50-homer more four times in his career and hit 60 in 1927, a record that stood for 34 years. Expanding newspaper and magazine coverage made Ruth one of the most photographed and recognizable Americans of the decade.

The "Sultan of Swat" was released from the Yankees organization after the 1934 season and joined the Boston Braves as vice president, assistant manager and outfielder. He called it quits in 1935 after appearing in 28 games and hitting six

Lou Gehrig was named on more ballots for Major League Baseball's Player of the Century than any other man. The first baseman played in 2,130 consecutive games.

home runs. Ruth ended his career with 714 home runs, a record that lasted until 1974.

Ruth was the most beloved player of his time and the most famous in baseball history, but he wasn't the only Yankees' star. Lou Gehrig took over the team's first base job in 1925. He didn't take a day off for the next 14 years as the Yankees began the greatest dynasty in sports history, winning three World Series titles in the 1920s and five in the 1930s.

Meanwhile, many fans believed Gehrig was indestructible. He played in 2,130 consecutive games, but his career had a tragic ending. During the 1939 season, he was diagnosed with a deadly disease called amyotrophic lateral sclerosis. On July 4 of that season, a tribute was held for Gehrig at Yankee Stadium. He died two years later.

The 1920s was also marred by a tragedy which, to date, has not been repeated. On August 16, 1920, the Cleveland Indians were playing New York. With Tribe shortstop Ray Chapman batting, Yankees pitcher Carl Mays threw a fastball that slammed into Chapman's temple, crushing the side of his skull. He was carried from the field and died the next morning.

The beginning of the 1930s in the United States ushered in the worst years of the Great Depression. Attendance at Major League games hit an all-time low of 6.3 million. From 1932–1934, most clubs lost money, especially the National League's Braves and Phillies and the American League's Athletics, Browns and Senators. Financial differences between clubs caused great talent disparities, a cry that would still be heard 60 years later. In this decade the Yankees won four world titles.

To attract more fans, the novel concept of night games was spearheaded by Cincinnati general manager Larry MacPhail in 1935. To gain additional revenue, teams sold radio broadcasting rights and, in so doing, started a trend that would amount to 7.3 percent of Major League revenues by 1939. Concessions—particularly the sale of beer which gained in popularity after Prohibition was repealed—further increased profits.

As Ruth's star faded, new heroes rose through the ranks, including pitcher Johnny Vander Meer, who hurled two consecutive no-hit games in 1938; and young stars such as Joe DiMaggio and Ted Williams.

In June 1939, Major League Baseball celebrated its mythical centennial birthdate by opening the Baseball Hall of Fame in Cooperstown, New York, where, legend has it, West Point cadet Abner Doubleday invented the game. The tourist attraction is visited by more than 25,000 fans each year. Every summer the greatest players of all time are enshrined at the Hall, ensuring that their accomplishments will be forever revered.

From Di Maggio to Robinson

Joe DiMaggio's greatest feat was probably his 56-game hitting streak in 1941. He seamlessly took over the mantle of most famous Yankee from Lou Gehrig in 1939.

The 1940s began with two of the greatest seasons by hitters in Major League history. In 1941, Joe DiMaggio of the New York Yankees and Ted Williams of the Boston Red Sox thrilled fans all season. DiMaggio hit safely in a record 56 straight games, but Williams stole some of his thunder by hitting .406, the last Major Leaguer to bat .400 in a season. Many believe neither mark will be approached again.

Rebounding from the Depression, Major League Baseball was in the midst of a dramatic comeback when it was shaken to the core by World War II. More than 5,000 major and 3,500 minor leaguers were drafted into service. DiMaggio and Williams both missed time in the prime of their careers because of the war. Williams also served in the Korean War in the 1950s.

Although President Franklin Roosevelt gave the go-ahead to continue playing, teams had to cope with a shortage of players.

When DiMaggio returned from the war in 1946, he rejoined the Yankees. Although his average dropped below .300 that season, he helped the team become world champions and earned the third Most Valuable Player Award of his career. DiMaggio retired after the Yankees won yet another World Series in 1951.

The Yankees' dynasty continued in this era. They won four more World Series titles in the 1940s and six in the 1950s. The 1951 season featured one of the greatest pennant races of all-time. The New York Giants trailed the Brooklyn Dodgers by 13 games in August, but roared back. The teams were tied at the end of the season, forcing a three-game playoff. The teams split the first two games. In one of the most memorable moments in baseball history, the Giants won the deciding game on Bobby Thomson's home run off Ralph Branca in the ninth inning.

The postwar era brought a new set of challenges to Major League Baseball: integration and unionization. Although most team owners strongly resisted integration, Commissioner Happy Chandler favored it. So did Brooklyn Dodgers president Branch Rickey.

In 1946, Rickey signed Jackie Robinson to a contract and assigned him to the Dodgers' Montreal farm team. Although Robinson was a three-sport star at UCLA and served as an Army lieutenant during World War II, he was not accepted by most of his peers. He endured loneliness, verbal abuse and, as he wrote in his autobiography, "The knowledge that any mistake I made would be magnified because I was the only black man out there." In 1947, Robinson was called up to the Dodgers. He hit 12 home runs in 590 at-bats and ended the year with a batting average of .297, winning Rookie of the Year honors.

Robinson, along with outfielder Larry Doby, the American League's first black player that year with the Cleveland Indians, are credited to opening the doors to other black Americans.

Player unionism was also controversial. In 1946 a litany of player grievances led to the formation of the American Baseball Guild. Although the guild folded the same year it was founded, the players won concessions which included a pension plan, a minimum salary, payment for participation in spring training and the right to negotiate through elected player representatives.

When owners sought to abolish the pension plan in 1953, the players struck back by forming the permanent Major League Players Association. No one realized at the time how big a force the union would become.

This decade also saw financial strife for the owners of the National League Boston Braves, Philadelphia Athletics and St.Louis Browns, forcing them to sell to new owners who quickly relocated the clubs to other sites across the country. The Braves moved first—to Milwaukee in 1953. During the next two years, the Browns became the Baltimore Orioles and the Athletics transplanted to Kansas City. In 1958, the Brooklyn Dodgers and New York Giants shocked their fans by moving to Los Angeles and San Francisco respectively.

The medium of television was also transforming the game, pumping new revenues into team bank accounts. From $2.3 million in 1950, annual TV revenue rose to $12 million by 1960.

The ballpark building boom began, as the public financed brand-new homes for their teams. The new parks were located closer to heavily populated areas and were easily accessible by auto or public transportation. In 1959, it was decreed that all new parks constructed after that year must adhere to a minimum 325-foot distance from home plate to the right- and left-field fences.

Jackie Robinson became the Major Leagues' first black player of the 20th century.

Roger Maris' 61 home runs stood as a record for 37 years.

Maris sets new mark

The 1960s began with the breaking of one of the most cherished records of all-time. During the 1961 season—with the season now 162 games—New York Yankees outfielders Mickey Mantle and Roger Maris battled to be the first to break Babe Ruth's record of 60 home runs in one season. The stress-filled race was a close one as the season dragged into late summer. There was no doubt which player Yankee fans were pulling for: Mantle. The switch-hitting kid from Oklahoma had come up through the Yankees farm system and the fans thought it was time for him to take his rightful place in the team's storied history. Maris, meanwhile, wasn't even considered a true Yankee. He started his career with the Cleveland Indians and came to New York in a trade with the Kansas City Athletics.

While New York fans openly rooted for Mantle, the pressure got to Maris and his hair began to fall out. Finally, in mid-September, a litany of injuries caused Mantle to call it quits for the season with 54 home runs. On September 26—the Yankees 158th game of the season—Maris hit his 60th home run. Five days later, on the final game of the season, Maris belted one into the right-field bleachers. Even Maris' moment of glory was put down as many fans thought the record was tainted since Ruth hit his 60 homers in 154 games. Maris' record would stand for 37 years.

The 1960s saw the end of the Yankees' dynasty. New York reached the World Series five straight years from 1960–64 and won it in 1961 and 1962. However, their appearance in the '64 Series would be their last until 1976.

Despite the fact Ruth's record was broken, the 1960s was a decade dominated by pitching. Between 1961 and 1966 Sandy Koufax of the Los Angeles Dodgers won 129 games, including four no-hitters and one perfect game, while losing only 47. He became the first pitcher to strike out 300 batters in three different seasons, achieving a record 382 in 1965. The St. Louis Cardinals' Bob Gibson, meanwhile, struck out 17

Detroit Tigers in Game 1 of the 1968 World Series. During the 17 years he spent with the Cardinals, Gibson's other career highlights included more than 3,000 career strikeouts and a 1.12 earned run average in 1968. The 1968 season also Denny McLain of the Detroit Tigers win 31 games.

In an attempt to beef up hitting opportunities, rules makers in 1969 shortened the strike zone and lowered pitching mounds.

The 1960s also was a decade of expansion. The American League started franchises in Washington and Los Angeles in 1961 while the National League followed in 1962 with teams in Houston and New York. Baseball expanded again in 1969 with Montreal—the first team outside the United States to be in the Majors—and San Diego joining the National League and Kansas City and Seattle joining the American League.

By adding two new clubs to each league and subdividing them into six-team East and West divisions, major-league owners discovered a successful format that is the forerunner to today's three-division leagues. The new format kept a 162-game regular season, but added a postseason best-of-five League Championship Series. This strategy focused fan attention on their favorite divisional race, with more teams being in the playoffs.

The 1960s saw player salaries escalate, courtesy of the union. By the end of the decade, salaries averaged $20,000. In 1966, Sandy Koufax and Don Drysdale paved the way for the hefty paychecks to come by using a lawyer in contract negotiations. Umpires also became a more powerful force when their union, the Major League Umpires Association, gained recognition as a bargaining agent.

Another Ruth record fell as baseball headed into the 1970s. Atlanta Braves slugger Hank Aaron hit the 713th home run of his career—one short of Ruth's record—on the last day of the 1973 season. Aaron hit his 714th home run on Opening Day of the 1974 season. On April 8, Aaron homered off Los Angeles' Al Downing to finally pass Ruth. Aaron returned to Milwaukee—where he started his career with the Braves—for the final two years of his career and finished with 755 homers, a record that still stands.

Tragedy also hit the 1970s. Three months after collecting his 3,000th major-league hit on September 30, 1972, Pittsburgh Pirates great Roberto Clemente lost his life in trying to help mankind. He and four others were killed when a cargo plane carrying food, clothing and medicine to earthquake-stricken Nicaragua crashed minutes after leaving San Juan, Puerto Rico.

The 1970s also saw two outstanding teams take their place in baseball history. The Oakland Athletics won three straight World Series from 1972–74 while the Cincinnati Reds, known as the "Big Red Machine", won the Series in 1975 and 1976.

Henry Aaron clasps the ball he hit into the Braves bullpen for home run 715.

Records, controversies and scandals

The last two decades of the 20th century will be known as much for what happened off the field as what happened on it.

The ongoing problems between the owners and the players' union escalated. The 1981 season was interrupted by a players strike that lasted from mid-June to the end of July. Players agreed to strike in response to owners' demands for a ceiling on salaries and compensation for players lost by clubs annually in re-entry drafts. Repercussions of the 50-day work stoppage included owners losing their demand for a salary cap, but winning compensation for lost free agents.

The decade also saw the greatest and the worst moments in the career of Pete Rose, perhaps the most popular player ever. Rose had long pursued the all-time career record of 4,191 hits held by Ty Cobb. On September 11, 1985, Rose finally passed Cobb with a single off San Diego pitcher Eric Show. A sellout crowd jammed Cincinnati's Riverfront Stadium to cheer the hometown hero, who began managing the Reds in 1984. Rose retired with 4,256 hits and a sure spot in the Baseball Hall of Fame, or so it seemed.

However, late in the decade the office of baseball commissioner A. Bartlett Giamatti began investigating stories about Rose's gambling habits and betting on baseball, in particular.

The investigation discovered telephone records of calls Rose had made to bookies, betting slips made out in Rose's handwriting and testimony from several of Rose's associates. Late in the 1989 season, Giamatti concluded Rose had bet on baseball and barred the all-time hit king from the game indefinitely. The decision caused great debate around the country, with Rose vehemently denying he bet on the game he loved. A few days after the announcement, Giamatti died of a heart attack.

Rose, who subsequently served a jail sentence for tax evasion, is ineligible for election into the Hall of Fame. He still maintains his innocence, but baseball has made little movement toward lifting the ban.

As if the Rose scandal wasn't enough, baseball fans saw several star players suspended for drug use as the 1980s

Pete Rose turns for second at the only speed he knew—flat out. Baseball's all-time leader in safe base hits will, however, be better remembered for his indefinite ban.

Mark McGwire (left) and Sammy Sosa brought baseball back into the world media spotlight with their home run duels in 1998 and 1999.

dragged into the early 1990s. However, the biggest bombshell for fans was yet to come.

Tensions between the owners and players escalated into the 1990s. A showdown finally came during the 1994 season. The players, still battling against the owners' claim they needed a cap on salaries, went on strike in early August. Most fans hoped the two sides would come to their senses and end the nonsense in a week or two. It never happened and, a month later, Commissioner Bud Selig did the unthinkable: He canceled the World Series. Baseball's most sacred event had gone on through America's involvement in four wars and the Great Depression, but it couldn't survive the fact the two sides couldn't figure out a way to split up the billions of dollars generated by the sport.

The following spring another unthinkable thing happened. The strike was still going on, so the owners decided to open spring training camps with replacement players. Teams actually broke camp with these players, but the strike was finally settled the weekend before the regular season was to begin. Camps opened again—this time with the real Major Leaguers—and the season started a month late.

The strike did irreparable harm to the game. Baseball needed something to bring the fans back, and it finally happened in 1998. Roger Maris' record of 61 home runs in a season had stood since 1961, and no player had come close to breaking it. That changed when not one, but two players, made a charge at the record. Mark McGwire of the St. Louis Cardinals and Sammy Sosa of the Chicago Cubs battled throughout the summer. The nightly highlight shows became a must for fans, who were captivated by the duel.

The Cardinals and Cubs met for a series in St. Louis' Busch Stadium in early September. With Maris' children in the stands and Sosa standing in right field, McGwire first tied Maris' record and broke it the following night. McGwire finished the season with an incredible 70 homers while Sosa had 66.

The two almost did it again in 1999, with McGwire hitting 66 and Sosa hitting 63.

The end of the 1990s also saw the return of the Yankees. New York won the World Series three time in four years between 1996 and 1999. That gave the Yankees a record 25 World Series titles.

The Players

At no other time in baseball history have fans had so many superstars to cheer for.

From ace pitchers to slugging position players, this is the greatest era of stars the game has ever seen.

There are ace pitchers who are working on Hall of Fame careers. There's Randy Johnson with his intimidating presence on the mound and his 100-mile-per-hour fastball. There's Greg Maddux, who gets by on guile and smarts. And then there's Pedro Martinez, simply the best pitcher in the game today.

In this era of offense, there are plenty of superstars to cheer for. Mark McGwire and Sammy Sosa seem intent on making the race for the home run record an annual event. Ken Griffey Jr. and Barry Bonds, who have already built Hall of Fame careers, are still going strong.

Then there's a core of young superstars, including Bernie Williams, Ivan Rodriguez, Manny Ramirez and Vladimir Guerrero, who put up good numbers every year and should only get better.

There's also the great shortstop debate about whoís the best between Derek Jeter, Alex Rodriguez and Nomar Garciaparra. All three combine their outstanding offensive and defensive skills as they redefine the position.

Other stars who have been thrilling fans for years, such as Cal Ripken Jr. and Roger Clemens, are heading toward the twilight of their careers.

Baseball fans love their stars, both young and old, and will continue to cheer them into the next century.

Albert Belle

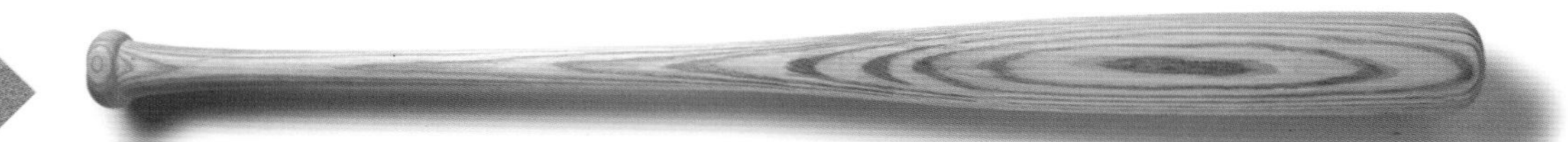

Profile

Name: Albert Jojuan Belle
Height: 6–2 **Weight:** 210
Throws: Right **Bats:** Right **Position:** Right field **Born:** August 25, 1966, Shreveport, La. **Drafted:** Selected by the Cleveland Indians in the second round of the 1987 free-agent draft **Acquired:** Signed as a free agent by the Baltimore Orioles on December 1, 1998
Pre-Majors highlights: Led Louisiana State to the College World Series in 1986
Personal information: Has been suspended five times during his career

"There's no doubt what Albert Belle can do for a lineup. He's the most dangerous hitter in the game today. He makes everyone around him better."

Former Baltimore manager Ray Miller

Career milestones

1987 Got his first major-league hit, an RBI single off Nolan Ryan.

1992 Hit three home runs in one game. Accomplished the feat again in 1995

1995 In strike-shortened season, he hit 52 home runs and 50 doubles in only 143 games. Was named Sporting News Player of the Year

1996 Signed as a free agent with the Chicago White Sox following the season. Played with the Sox the next two seasons

1997 Had a 27-game hitting streak (May 3–June 1, 1997)

1998 Led American League with 399 total bases, 15 sacrifice flies and .655 slugging percentage

Albert Belle remains one of the most feared sluggers in baseball today. Belle makes headlines both on the field, where he is one of the game's top hitters, and off the field, where he makes news with his controversial behavior.

Despite his off the field problems, Belle's talent is still in great demand. He was the highest paid player in baseball in 1999 after signing with the Baltimore Orioles as a free agent in December 1998. Belle signed a five-year contract that will pay him $65 million.

In his first season with the Orioles, Belle batted .297 with 37 home runs and 117 RBIs. When Belle signed with Baltimore, there was speculation he might threaten Mark McGwire's record of 70 home runs in one season by playing in hitter-friendly Camden Yards. That didn't happen, but Belle still put up solid numbers in what otherwise was a disappointing 1999 season for the Orioles.

As he usually does, Belle also made news off the field. His problems with the media continued after a clubhouse tirade in spring training was reported, which led to Belle boycotting reporters for most of the season, which is his usual practice. Belle also had a dugout confrontation with former Orioles manager Ray Miller after failing to run out a ground ball.

Controversy is nothing new with Belle, who played for the Cleveland Indians from 1989–96, the Chicago White Sox from 1996–98 and the Orioles last season. His stellar college career at Louisiana State ended when he was suspended by his coach during his senior season. The suspension cost him his first-round draft status. He was taken by the Indians in the second round in 1987.

Belle has been suspended by the American League five times for offenses ranging from throwing a baseball at a heckling fan to charging the mound to corking his bat. Belle also has feuded with managers, coaches and teammates.

There's no disputing, however, what Belle can do for a lineup. He has put up huge numbers wherever he's been. Belle has had 101 or more RBIs and 30 or more home runs in the last eight seasons. He has led the American League in RBIs three times—in 1993 (129), in 1995 (126) and in 1996 (148). Belle's career high came in 1998 when he drove in 152 with the White Sox.

Belle played a key role in the resurgence of the Indians, who had gone 41 years without being in the postseason before winning the American League Central Division in 1995. Between 1992 and 1996, he averaged 41 home runs and 123 RBIs.

Batting

Year	G	AB	R	H	HR	RBI	BB	SO	SB	CS	OBP	SLG	AVG
1999	**161**	**610**	**108**	**181**	**37**	**117**	**101**	**82**	**17**	**3**	**.400**	**.541**	**.297**
Career	**1398**	**5294**	**903**	**1569**	**358**	**1136**	**631**	**893**	**88**	**36**	**.372**	**.573**	**.296**

Fielding

Year	Posn	G	GS	TC	PO	A	E	DP	FLD%
1999	**OF**	**154**	**154**	**273**	**252**	**17**	**4**	**2**	**.985**
Career		**1201**	**1197**	**2577**	**2431**	**83**	**63**	**16**	**.976**

88

Pedro Martinez

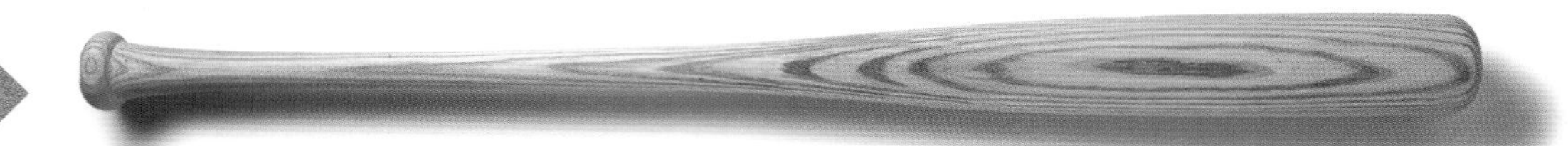

Profile

Name: Pedro Martinez
Height: 5-11 **Weight:** 170
Throws: Right **Bats:** Right
Position: Pitcher **Born:** October 25, 1971, Manoguayabo, Dominican Republic **Drafted:** Signed by Los Angeles as a free agent in June 1988
Acquired: Traded from Montreal on November 18, 1997
Pre-Majors highlights: Named The Sporting News Minor League Player of the Year in 1991, with combined 18 wins and 192 strikeouts at three levels **Personal information:** Brother Ramon also pitches for the Red Sox

"He couldn't even pick up a ball two days ago, and was almost in tears. He's just the most unbelievable pitcher I've ever seen." **Boston pitcher Bret Saberhagen, after Martinez beat Cleveland in the playoffs**

Career milestones

1992 Made Major League debut with Los Angeles on September 24
1993 Traded from Los Angeles to Montreal, November 19.
1997 National League Cy Young Award winner and ERA leader
1997 Led National League with 1.90 ERA and 13 complete games
1998 First pitcher with 300 strikeouts and an ERA under 2.00 (1.90) since Steve Carlton in 1972 (310 K, 1.97 ERA)
1999 All-Star Game MVP Cy Young winner

There's no doubt Pedro Martinez is the most dominant pitcher in baseball.

Almost single-handedly, Martinez led the Boston Red Sox to the 1999 wild card playoff berth in the American League, an upset win over the Cleveland Indians in the Division Series and an appearance against the New York Yankees in the American League Championship Series.

Martinez's numbers say it all. The righthander finished the 1999 season with a 23–4 record and a 2.07 earned run average. In 213.1 innings, he allowed just 160 hits, struck out 313 and issued only 37 walks. Opponents batted a microscopic .205 against Martinez and he gave up nine home runs all season.

In baseball's offense-happy era, Martinez's numbers are unheard of. Considering they came in the league where pitchers don't hit, they're even more amazing.

Martinez's accomplishments earned him the American League Cy Young Award and serious consideration for the league's Most Valuable Player Award.

Martinez saved his best for the playoffs, where he overcame overwhelming odds to be dominant again. A back injury forced him to leave Game 1 of the Division Series against the hard-hitting Indians, even though he was working on a shutout at the time. It looked like Martinez and the Red Sox were finished. Boston lost the first two games of the best-of-five series and even the Red Sox thought Martinez's back would keep him out for the rest of the series.

How wrong they were. After Boston won the next two games at Fenway Park to tie the series, the decisive fifth game moved back to Cleveland. Martinez's status was still uncertain, but he warmed up before the game and told Red Sox manager Jimy Williams he was available if needed.

With the score tied 8–8 in the fourth inning, the Red Sox needed him, and the Indians were finished. Martinez held the highest-scoring offense in baseball hitless over the final six innings, striking out eight and walking three. The Indians didn't come close to scoring and the Red Sox rallied for a 12–8 win.

After the game, Martinez was mobbed by his teammates, who carried their ace pitcher off the field.

"Once I got in, that's all I needed. I wouldn't come out," Martinez said. "I wasn't going to let go. I wasn't going to."

Martinez's heroics weren't over. In Game 3 of the ALCS against the Yankees, he pitched seven scoreless innings while holding New York to two hits. Martinez struck out 12 and walked two in the only game of the series Boston won.

How great is Martinez? Even though he wasn't close to 100 percent, he threw 17 shutout innings against the best teams in baseball in the playoffs.

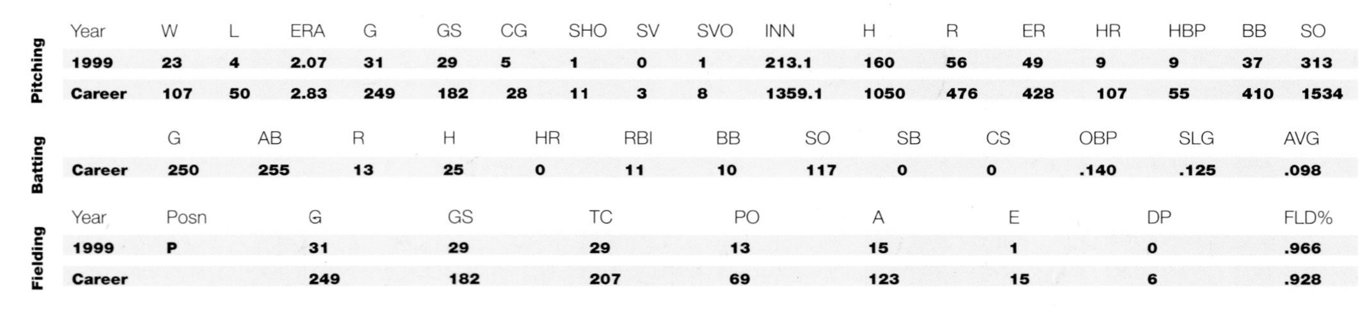

Pitching

Year	W	L	ERA	G	GS	CG	SHO	SV	SVO	INN	H	R	ER	HR	HBP	BB	SO
1999	**23**	**4**	**2.07**	**31**	**29**	**5**	**1**	**0**	**1**	**213.1**	**160**	**56**	**49**	**9**	**9**	**37**	**313**
Career	**107**	**50**	**2.83**	**249**	**182**	**28**	**11**	**3**	**8**	**1359.1**	**1050**	**476**	**428**	**107**	**55**	**410**	**1534**

Batting

	G	AB	R	H	HR	RBI	BB	SO	SB	CS	OBP	SLG	AVG
Career	**250**	**255**	**13**	**25**	**0**	**11**	**10**	**117**	**0**	**0**	**.140**	**.125**	**.098**

Fielding

Year	Posn	G	GS	TC	PO	A	E	DP	FLD%
1999	**P**	**31**	**29**	**29**	**13**	**15**	**1**	**0**	**.966**
Career		**249**	**182**	**207**	**69**	**123**	**15**	**6**	**.928**

Kevin Brown

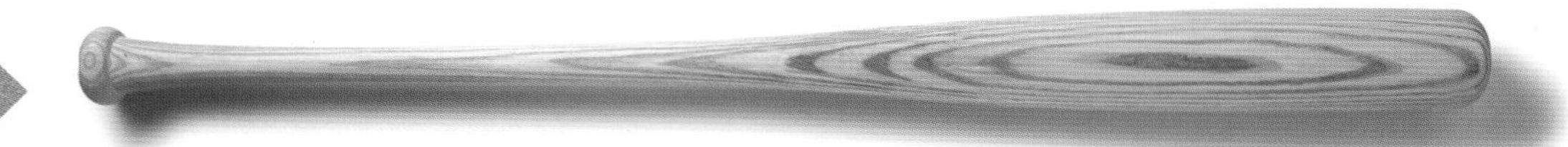

Profile

Name: James Kevin Brown **Height:** 6–4 **Weight:** 195 **Throws:** Right **Bats:** Right **Position:** Pitcher **Born:** March 3, 1965, McIntyre, Georgia **Drafted:** Selected by the Texas Rangers in the first round (fourth overall) of the 1986 free-agent draft **Acquired:** Signed as a free agent on December 12, 1998 **Pre-Majors highlights:** Made only six appearances in the minors before being called up by Texas in 1986 **Personal information:** After making the baseball team at Georgia Tech as a walk-on, Brown recorded 28 wins and 249 strikeouts, both school records

"They brought him in to be a No. 1 starter, and that's what he has been."

Los Angeles first baseman Eric Karros.

Career milestones

1993 Had best overall season, leading American League with 21 wins and 265.2 innings while pitching for Texas

1996 Runner-up in National League Cy Young voting in 1996, posting 17–11 record, but leading league with 1.89 ERA

1997 Went 16–8 with a 2.69 ERA in 33 starts for the World Champion Florida Marlins

1997 Pitched no-hitter against San Francisco on June 10

1998 Set San Diego single-season record with 257 strikeouts

1999 Went 18–9 with a 2.78 ERA in first season with Los Angeles

The terms "No. 1 starter" and "ace pitcher" are used a lot these days. A lot of pitchers try to fit those roles, but in this day and age, very few succeed.

Kevin Brown is an exception. The righthander fits both titles very well. Any team looking for a pitcher who will post a lot of wins, throw a ton of innings and take the ball for big games would be wise to sign up Brown.

And a team that does sign up Brown has a good chance at improving. Brown has posted 15 or more wins in six of the last eight seasons. There have been times in the last four seasons that he has been almost unhittable. Just ask the Florida Marlins and the San Diego Padres. Brown signed with the Marlins before the 1996 season and went 17–11 with a 1.89 earned run average A year later, Brown finished with a 16–8 record and a 2.69 ERA while pitching Florida to the World Series title. Traded to the Padres after that season when the Marlins slashed their payroll, Brown quickly elevated San Diego to the top of the baseball world. He went 18–7 with a 2.38 ERA as the Padres stunned baseball by advancing to the 1998 World Series.

Brown's efforts made him the plum of the free-agent market following the 1998 season. It paid off with a five-year, $65 million contract from the Los Angeles Dodgers. Brown's presence didn't mean as much to the Dodgers as it did to the Marlins and Padres. Los Angeles finished a disappointing 77–85 and in third place in the National League West, but it certainly wasn't Brown's fault. He went 18–9 with a 3.00 ERA in one of the few bright spots in LA's bleak 1999 season.

Brown has developed into one of baseball's top workhorses. Over the last four seasons, he is 69–35 with a 2.70 while averaging 245 innings.

Some pitchers these days are satisfied with getting into the sixth or seventh inning and turning the game over to the bullpen. Brown, one of the most intense competitors in the game today, feels much differently.

"I take a lot of pride in my ability to take the ball and pitch a lot of innings," said Brown. "I think that's what a starting pitcher is supposed to do."

Brown showed early in his career that he was going to be something special. After being drafted by Texas in the 1986 free-agent draft, he made just six appearances in the minors before the Rangers called him up. Brown was in the big leagues to stay by 1989. His best season with the Rangers came in 1992 when he finished 21–11, a league-high in wins, with a 3.32 ERA and a league-leading 265.2 innings pitched.

Pitching

Year	W	L	ERA	G	GS	CG	SHO	SV	SVO	INN	H	R	ER	HR	HBP	BB	SO
1999	**18**	**9**	**3.00**	**35**	**35**	**5**	**1**	**0**	**0**	**252.1**	**210**	**99**	**84**	**19**	**7**	**59**	**221**
Career	**157**	**108**	**3.27**	**349**	**347**	**66**	**16**	**0**	**0**	**2430.2**	**2313**	**1015**	**882**	**140**	**108**	**683**	**1701**

Batting

Year	G	AB	R	H	HR	RBI	BB	SO	SB	CS	OBP	SLG	AVG
Career	**353**	**308**	**10**	**40**	**0**	**20**	**17**	**106**	**0**	**0**	**.175**	**.146**	**.130**

Fielding

Year	Posn	G	GS	TC	PO	A	E	DP	FLD%
1999	**P**	**35**	**35**	**93**	**41**	**46**	**6**	**2**	**.935**
Career		**348**	**346**	**782**	**312**	**436**	**34**	**30**	**.957**

LA
Dodgers
27

Greg Maddux

Profile

Name: Gregory Alan Maddux **Height:** 6–0 **Weight:** 175 **Throws:** Right **Bats:** Right **Position:** Pitcher **Born:** April 14, 1966, San Angelo, Texas **Drafted:** Selected by the Chicago Cubs in the second round of the 1984 free-agent draft **Acquired:** Signed as a free agent by the Atlanta Braves on December 9, 1992 **Pre-Majors highlights:** Made minor league all-star teams in 1985 and 1986 **Personal information:** Brother Mike has pitched in the majors for 14 years

"He has the ability to move the ball around and that makes it tough. He's been doing this for years. He's one of the best."

St. Louis Cardinals manager, Tony LaRussa

Career milestones

1986 Made first Major League start, for the Chicago Cubs on September 7.
1992 Won National League Cy Young Award
1993 Won National League Cy Young Award and led league in earned run average
1994 Won National League Cy Young Award and led league in earned run average
1995 Won National League Cy Young Award and led league in earned run average
1997 Posted 10th consecutive season with 15-or-more wins and 200 innings pitched
1998 National League leader in earned run average

Some pitchers, such as Randy Johnson, do it with a 100 mile-per-hour fastball. Others, like Pedro Martinez, dominate hitters with the best stuff in the game.

So how has Greg Maddux become one of the top pitchers in baseball today?

Let Tony Gwynn, one of the best hitters to ever play the game, tell it.

"He ties me up in knots—fastball in, change-up, fastball away, change-up, change-up," Gwynn said. "I know how well he works both sides of the plate. I just try to take a defensive approach to facing him."

Maddux makes almost every hitter in baseball feel defensive. He doesn't have Johnson's fastball or Martinez's dominating stuff. Standing six-feet tall and weighing only 175 pounds, Maddux looks more like an accountant or a librarian than he does a big-league pitcher, but he wins more than any pitcher in the game today.

Even in what has to be considered an off-season—at least for him—Maddux went 19-9 with a 3.57 earned run average, the highest ERA of his career, as his Atlanta Braves made it to the World Series for the fifth time in the 1990s.

Most baseball people think the 300-win plateau is unattainable, but Maddux, who will turn 34 in April 2000, has an outside shot if he stays healthy. He goes into the 2000 season with a 221–126 career record. Maddux needs five or six solid seasons to reach 300 wins, but his chances shouldn't be dismissed. He has won at least 15 games and pitched at least 202 innings in each of the last 12 seasons. So Maddux has both success and durability on his side.

Maddux helps himself win with his defense. He was named the National League's Gold Glove pitcher from 1990–98.

Maddux's legend grew even larger in the 1999 season. He pitched the last six weeks of the season with a broken bone in his right wrist, an injury suffered in late August. After missing only one start, Maddux returned to the rotation and pitched seven shutout innings against the Cincinnati Reds.

The performance stunned everyone, especially the Reds.

"No way," said Reds first baseman Sean Casey when told Maddux was pitching with the injury. "I can't believe his wrist is broken. I didn't see anything different. He's nasty. His ball moves all over the place, but he always knows where it's moving."

Maddux has had 12 consecutive seasons with at least 15 wins. He made the National League Cy Young Award his personal property by winning the award four straight seasons from 1992–95. Still, seeing the Braves winning is more important than individual success to him. "I want a (World Series) ring more than a Cy Young," he said.

Pitching

Year	W	L	ERA	G	GS	CG	SHO	SV	SVO	INN	H	R	ER	HR	HBP	BB	SO
1999	**19**	**9**	**3.57**	**33**	**33**	**4**	**0**	**0**	**0**	**219.1**	**258**	**103**	**87**	**16**	**4**	**37**	**136**
Career	**221**	**126**	**2.81**	**436**	**432**	**93**	**28**	**0**	**0**	**3068.2**	**2761**	**1104**	**959**	**157**	**80**	**691**	**2160**

Batting

Year	G	AB	R	H	HR	RBI	BB	SO	SB	CS	OBP	SLG	AVG
Career	**445**	**990**	**75**	**176**	**4**	**52**	**24**	**269**	**4**	**2**	**.199**	**.215**	**.178**

Fielding

Year	Posn	G	GS	TC	PO	A	E	DP	FLD%
1999	**P**	**33**	**33**	**91**	**29**	**58**	**4**	**3**	**.956**
Career		**436**	**432**	**1119**	**378**	**702**	**39**	**55**	**.965**

MADDUX
31

Gary Sheffield

Profile

Name: Gary Antonian Sheffield
Height: 6–0 **Weight:** 190
Throws: Right **Bats:** Right **Position:** Left Field
Born: November 18, 1968, Tampa, Florida
Drafted: Selected by the Milwaukee Brewers in the first round (sixth overall) of the 1986 free-agent draft
Acquired: Traded from the Florida Marlins on May 15, 1998 to Los Angeles **Pre-Majors highlights:** Led California League with 103 RBIs in 1987 **Personal information:** Cousin of Major-League pitcher Dwight Gooden

"You can learn a lot from a guy like that. I talk to him all the time. Gary is a winner and I'll always listen to him."

Los Angeles third baseman, Adrian Beltre

Career milestones

1992 Traded from Milwaukee to San Diego on March 27
1993 Traded from San Diego to Florida on June 24. Made history when he was voted onto the National League All-Star team, making him the first player from an expansion team to start an All-Star Game
1996 Had best season with Marlins, hitting .314 with 42 homers, 120 RBIs and 142 walks
1997 Helped lead Marlins to World Series title in franchise's fifth year of existence
1998 Traded from Marlins to Los Angeles on May 15.

It's true Gary Sheffield is a well-traveled player. He's played for four teams in his career, including three in a five-year period.

There's also something else that's true about Sheffield. If numbers are what you're looking for, he's definitely your man.

Playing left field for the Los Angeles Dodgers, Sheffield put together another solid season in 1999. He hit .301 with 34 home runs and 101 runs batted in. How good was Sheffield's season? He joined Dodgers legend and Hall of Famer Duke Snider as the only players in franchise history to hit at least .300 with 30 homers, 100 RBIs, 100 runs and 100 walks in a single season.

The big numbers are nothing new. When Sheffield is healthy, his production is as good as any of the other power hitters in baseball.

Sheffield, one of the key members of the World Series champion Florida Marlins in 1997, was involved in one of the biggest trades in baseball history on May 16, 1998. The Marlins sent Sheffield, along with catcher Charles Johnson, outfielders Jim Eisenreich and Bobby Bonilla and pitcher Manuel Barrios to the Dodgers in exchange for catcher Mike Piazza and third baseman Todd Zeile.

The trade made huge headlines. In this day and age, it's rare that players of such stature are traded for one another. Such deals also put a lot of pressure on the players involved, but Sheffield has lived up to it since putting on a Dodgers uniform. He hit .316 with 16 homers and 57 RBIs in 90 games after the trade in 1998 and followed that with another big year last season.

Sheffield left Florida as the Marlins all-time leader in homers (122), runs (365), walks (424) and hit-by-pitches (43).

Considering how long he's been in the big leagues and how long he's been putting up big numbers, it's hard to believe Sheffield is only 31 years old. He has had stardom written all over him since the Milwaukee Brewers drafted him in the first round in 1986. Sheffield was in the big leagues by 1988 when he came to the Brewers as a shortstop. He was bothered by injuries most of his career with the Brewers, however, and missed most of the 1991 season.

Sheffield's career took off after he was traded to San Diego before the 1992 season. He hit 33 homers, drove in 100 runs and hit .330 while being voted the Major League Player of the Year and the Comeback Player of the Year by The Sporting News.

Sheffield, who has made the National League All-Star team five times, was also a big force for the Marlins in the 1997 playoffs. He batted .556 as the Marlins swept the San Francisco Giants in the Division Series and batted .292 with a home run and five RBIs in the seven-game World Series win over the Cleveland Indians.

Batting

Year	G	AB	R	H	HR	RBI	BB	SO	SB	CS	OBP	SLG	AVG
1999	**152**	**549**	**103**	**165**	**34**	**101**	**101**	**64**	**11**	**5**	**.407**	**.523**	**.301**
Career	**1308**	**4645**	**779**	**1345**	**236**	**807**	**757**	**550**	**156**	**71**	**.392**	**.501**	**.290**

Fielding

Year	Posn	G	GS	TC	PO	A	E	DP	FLD%
1999	**OF**	**145**	**145**	**249**	**235**	**7**	**7**	**1**	**.972**
Career		**1272**	**1268**	**2936**	**1623**	**1179**	**134**	**126**	**.954**

LA
Dodgers

Profile

Name:
Bernabe Figueroa Williams
Height: 6–2 **Weight:** 205 **Throws:** Right **Bats:** Both **Position:** Center field
Born: September 13, 1968, San Juan, Puerto Rico
Acquired: Signed by the New York Yankees as a non-drafted free agent on September 13, 1985
Pre-Majors highlights: Led Carolina League in hitting, 1988 with .335 average **Personal information:** Won four gold medals at an international track meet at the age of 15

Bernie Williams

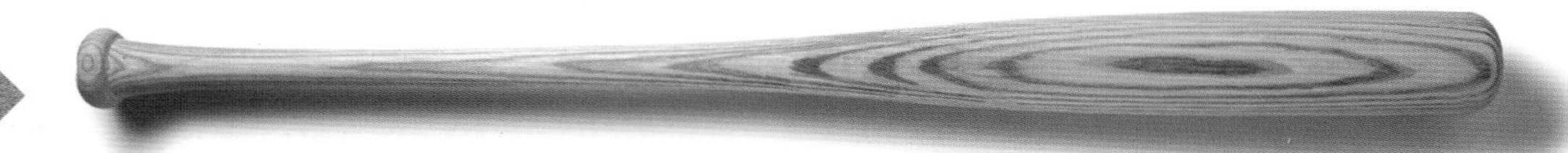

"When you think of complete players, Bernie Williams' name has to go right at the top of the list."

New York Yankees owner, George Steinbrenner

Career milestones

1991 Made Major League debut on July 7
1995 Led American League center fielders in putouts and total chances
1996 MVP of American League Championship Series
1997 Won American League Gold Glove
1997 Hit .329 against right-handers and .326 against left-handers
1998 Won American League batting championship and Gold Glove

If there's such a thing as an underrated superstar, it's Bernie Williams.

The New York Yankees center fielder can do it all on the baseball field. Williams hits for a high batting average. He hits for power. He drives in runs. He scores runs. He walks. He steals bases. He's a Gold Glove defensive player. He's one of the top switch-hitters in the game and can hit just about anywhere in the lineup.

And he's been a key member of a Yankee team that's won the World Series three times in the last four years.

Despite all of his accomplishments, Williams doesn't seem to get the recognition the other top players, such as Ken Griffey Jr., Barry Bonds and Sammy Sosa receive. Williams doesn't get a lot of commercial endorsements and his face doesn't appear on the cover of sports magazines. While others get more headlines, Williams puts together good seasons year after year and helps his team stay on top of the baseball world.

"Bernie goes about his business and puts up the numbers," said Yankees manager Joe Torre. "That's just the way he is."

Williams had another outstanding season in 1999. He batted .342 with 25 home runs and 115 RBIs. The batting average and home run totals are career highs.

Consistency is the biggest part of Williams' game. He has hit .300 or better in five consecutive seasons. The streak started in 1995, when Williams batted .307. He followed that by batting .305 in 1996, .328 in 1997 and .339 in 1998, when he won his first American League batting title, edging Boston's Mo Vaughn on the last day of the season by two points.

Williams' streak coincides with the Yankees' resurgence as the best team in baseball. New York won the World Series in 1996, 1998 and 1999. The Yankees won an amazing 125 games in 1998 and have won 12 consecutive World Series games.

"Winning is what it's all about," said Williams. "Whatever I can do to help us win is all that matters."

The Yankees know how important Williams is to their success. He was a free agent after the 1998 season and was one of the most sought-after players on the free-agent market. For a while, it looked like he would sign with the Boston Red Sox, but at the last minute Williams decided to stay with the Yankees, who signed him to a seven-year deal for $87.5 million.

Although he's not a prototype cleanup hitter, that's where Williams has been hitting for the Yankees. He has responded by averaging 25 home runs and 104 RBIs the last four seasons.

Considering Williams is still only 31 years old, there's a good chance his best days are still ahead of him.

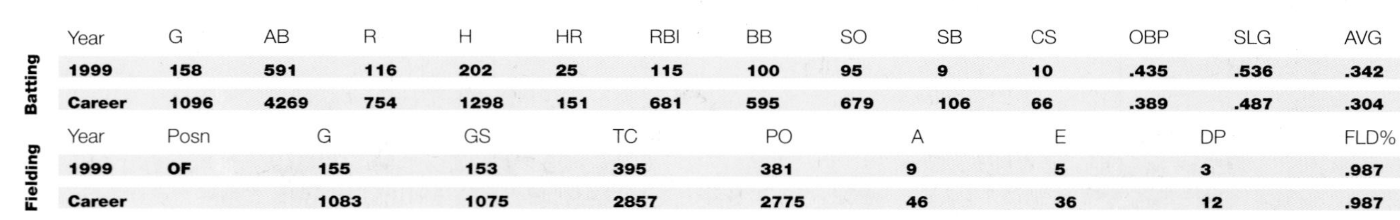

Batting

Year	G	AB	R	H	HR	RBI	BB	SO	SB	CS	OBP	SLG	AVG
1999	**158**	**591**	**116**	**202**	**25**	**115**	**100**	**95**	**9**	**10**	**.435**	**.536**	**.342**
Career	**1096**	**4269**	**754**	**1298**	**151**	**681**	**595**	**679**	**106**	**66**	**.389**	**.487**	**.304**

Fielding

Year	Posn	G	GS	TC	PO	A	E	DP	FLD%
1999	**OF**	**155**	**153**	**395**	**381**	**9**	**5**	**3**	**.987**
Career		**1083**	**1075**	**2857**	**2775**	**46**	**36**	**12**	**.987**

Barry Bonds

Profile

Name: Barry Lamar Bonds **Height:** 6–1 **Weight:** 185 **Throws:** Left **Bats:** Left **Position:** Left field **Born:** July 24, 1964, Riverside, California **Drafted:** Selected by the Pirates in the first round (sixth overall) of the 1985 free-agent draft **Acquired:** Signed by the San Francisco Giants as a free agent on December 8, 1992 **Pre-Majors highlights:** Played only 115 minor league games before being called up to the majors in 1986 **Personal information:** Son of former Major League outfielder Bobby Bonds. Barry and Bobby have more home runs, RBIs, and stolen bases than any other father-son combo in Major League history.

"What's significant about his 2,000 career hits is the number of walks (1,430) he's had in-between and the number of home runs he's had (445). He's a power hitter." **San Francisco Giants manager, Dusty Baker**

Career milestones

1990 Was named National League Most Valuable Player and won first Gold Glove

1992 Was named National League Most Valuable Player

1993 Was named National League Most Valuable Player. Led league in home runs, RBIs and won Gold Glove

1996 Hit .308 with 42 homers, 129 RBI, 151 walks, and 40 stolen bases

1998 Hit his 400th career homer on August 23 at Florida

1999 Collected 2,000th career base hit on September 11 vs. Atlanta, a fourth inning double off Tom Glavine

The minute Barry Bonds retires, the folks in Cooperstown, New York, can start getting ready for him.

The San Francisco Giants star has Hall of Fame numbers right now. The rest of his career will merely be putting the finishing touches on the final masterpiece.

It's difficult to judge which one of Bonds' accomplishments is the most impressive. He became the first player in Major League history to surpass both 400 home runs and 400 stolen bases. Bonds has scored more runs, driven in more runs, and drawn more walks than any other player this decade.

Bonds, an eight-time All-Star and winner of seven Gold Gloves, was named Player of the Decade for the 1990s by The Sporting News and has won three National League Most Valuable Player Awards. His numbers for the 1990s speak for themselves. Bonds batted .302 with 1,091 runs scored, 299 doubles, 42 triples, 361 home runs, 1,076 RBIs and 343 stolen bases in 1,434 games.

Bonds, 35, ended the 1999 season with 445 home runs and 460 stolen bases. He also picked up his 2,000th career hit off Atlanta Braves ace Tom Glavine. That led Braves manager Bobby Cox to make a comment many managers have felt over the years.

"I thought he had more than that," said Cox. "It feels like he's had 1,000 against us."

Only three other players have reached the 300 mark in homers and steals: Willie Mays, Andre Dawson and Bonds' father, Bobby. Bonds has reached the 30-home run, 30-stolen base plateau five times in his career (1990, 1992, 1995 and 1996). He joins his father (1969, 1973, 1975, 1977 and 1978) as the only five-time 30-30 men in ML history

Bonds was named the Most Valuable Player in the National League in 1990, 1992 and 1993. The first two came while he was playing for the Pittsburgh Pirates. That accomplishment puts Bonds, who signed with the Giants following the '92 season, in some truly Hall of Fame company. He joins Jimmie Foxx (1932, 1933 and 1938), Joe DiMaggio (1939, 1941 and 1947), Stan Musial (1943, 1946 and 1948), Roy Campanella (1951, 1953 and 1955), Yogi Berra (1951, 1954 and 1955), Mickey Mantle (1956, 1957 and 1962) and Mike Schmidt (1980, 1981 and 1986) as one of only eight players in baseball history to win the MVP award three times.

Despite being bothered by knee, elbow and groin injuries that limited him to 102 games, Bonds hit 34 home runs in 1999. He finished the season with 445 career home runs, which puts him 22nd on the all-time list.

There's no doubt Bonds' name belongs in the truly elite company of baseball greats. There's also no doubt his name will be there forever when his career is over.

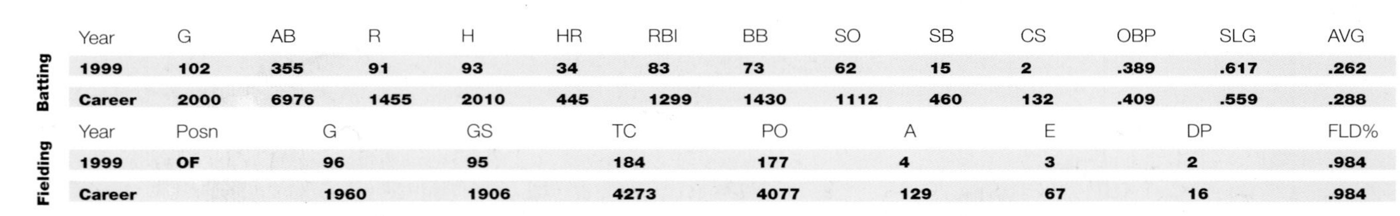

Batting

Year	G	AB	R	H	HR	RBI	BB	SO	SB	CS	OBP	SLG	AVG
1999	**102**	**355**	**91**	**93**	**34**	**83**	**73**	**62**	**15**	**2**	**.389**	**.617**	**.262**
Career	**2000**	**6976**	**1455**	**2010**	**445**	**1299**	**1430**	**1112**	**460**	**132**	**.409**	**.559**	**.288**

Fielding

Year	Posn	G	GS	TC	PO	A	E	DP	FLD%
1999	**OF**	**96**	**95**	**184**	**177**	**4**	**3**	**2**	**.984**
Career		**1960**	**1906**	**4273**	**4077**	**129**	**67**	**16**	**.984**

BONDS
FILA

Randy Johnson

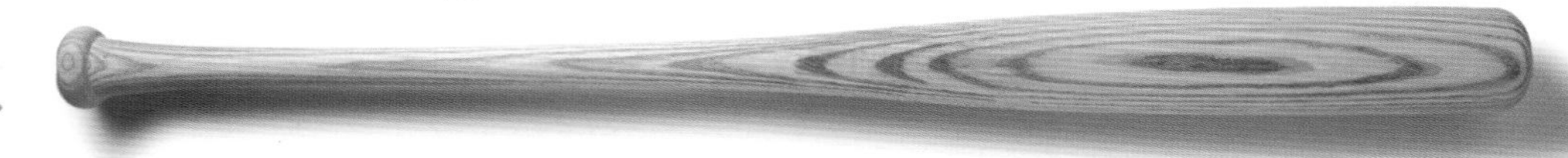

Profile

Name: Randall David Johnson **Height:** 6–10 **Weight:** 225 **Throws:** Left **Bats:** Right **Position:** Pitcher **Born:** September 10, 1963, Walnut Creek, California **Drafted:** Selected by the Montreal Expos in the second round of the 1985 free-agent draft **Acquired:** Signed by the Arizona Diamondbacks as a free agent, December 10, 1998 **Pre-Majors highlights:** Led Double-A Southern League in strikeouts, 1987 **Personal information:** Attended college at the University of Southern California

"You really don't appreciate how great he is until he's on your team and you see him every day and what he brings to your club."

Arizona manager, Buck Showalter.

Career milestones

1989 Traded from Montreal Expos to Seattle Mariners on May 25

1990 Threw no-hitter against the Detroit Tigers on June 2

1995 American League Cy Young Award winner and led league in strikeouts

1997 Struck out 19 in a 4-1 loss to Oakland, setting an American League mark for strikeouts in a game by a left-handed pitcher

1998 Traded by Seattle Mariners to Houston Astros on July 31

1999 Major League leader in strikeouts and won Cy Young Award in National League

Whether it's in the American League or the National League, it doesn't matter to Randy Johnson.

Dubbed "The Big Unit", the 6-foot-10, 225-pound left-hander is the most feared pitcher in baseball.

Unfortunately for National League hitters, they got to experience the fear of facing Johnson throughout the 1999 season. Signed as a free agent by the Arizona Diamondbacks on December 1, 1998, Johnson had another brilliant season. He led the Diamondbacks to the 1999 National League West title in the franchise's second year of existence.

"What we accomplished was a very special thing," said Johnson. "I signed to play here to be close to family. The fact we were able to do what we did made for a very special season."

Once again, Johnson was near the top of several pitching categories. He finished the season with a 17–9 record and a 2.48 earned run average. Johnson led the Major Leagues with a career-high 364 strikeouts while also establishing career highs in complete games (12) and innings pitched (271.2). He also led the Majors in the latter two categories.

Appropriately enough, Johnson was on the mound when the Diamondbacks wrapped up the 1999 division title, the fastest an expansion team has reached the playoffs in baseball history. After allowing three unearned runs in the first inning against the San Francisco Giants on September 24, Johnson pitched shutout ball the rest of the way in an 11–3 win.

"If you would have written a script, it couldn't have been any better than that," said Johnson.

Johnson's dominance reached a new level in 1999. He registered 23 double-figure strikeout games, tying Nolan Ryan's record for most in a season and two more than the previous National League mark set by Sandy Koufax in 1965. Johnson also set a record by being the fastest pitcher to reach 300 strikeouts in a season when he fanned Florida's Keith Millar on August 26 in his 29th start.

With a little more support from his teammates, Johnson's record would have looked better. He tied a Major League record by coming up on the short end of four straight shutouts by opposing teams from June 25 to July 10. Pitchers threw a no-hitter, a one-hitter, a two-hitter and a three-hitter at the Diamondbacks in those games. Johnson allowed five earned runs in 32 innings and struck out 54 in that stretch.

The 1999 season was the first full year Johnson, a six-time All-Star, spent in the National League since 1989, the year he was traded from Montreal to Seattle. Johnson became the Mariners' all-time leader in wins (130), shutouts (19) and strikeouts (2,162) before being traded to Houston during the 1998 season. He helped the Astros win the National League West title before signing with the Diamondbacks after the season.

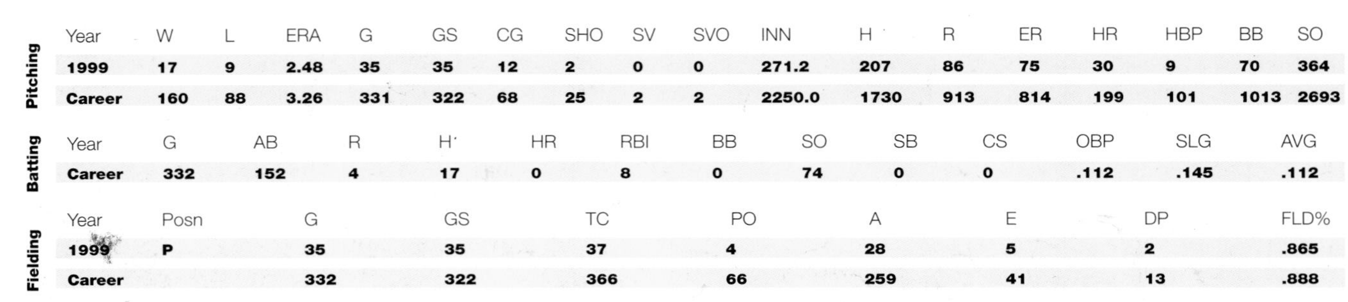

Pitching

Year	W	L	ERA	G	GS	CG	SHO	SV	SVO	INN	H	R	ER	HR	HBP	BB	SO
1999	**17**	**9**	**2.48**	**35**	**35**	**12**	**2**	**0**	**0**	**271.2**	**207**	**86**	**75**	**30**	**9**	**70**	**364**
Career	**160**	**88**	**3.26**	**331**	**322**	**68**	**25**	**2**	**2**	**2250.0**	**1730**	**913**	**814**	**199**	**101**	**1013**	**2693**

Batting

Year	G	AB	R	H	HR	RBI	BB	SO	SB	CS	OBP	SLG	AVG
Career	**332**	**152**	**4**	**17**	**0**	**8**	**0**	**74**	**0**	**0**	**.112**	**.145**	**.112**

Fielding

Year	Posn	G	GS	TC	PO	A	E	DP	FLD%
1999	**P**	**35**	**35**	**37**	**4**	**28**	**5**	**2**	**.865**
Career		**332**	**322**	**366**	**66**	**259**	**41**	**13**	**.888**

Raul Mondesi

Profile

Name: Raul Mondesi
Height: 5–11 **Weight:** 202
Throws: Right **Bats:** Right
Position: Right field **Born:** March 12, 1971, San Cristobal, Dominican Republic **Drafted:** Signed by the Los Angeles Dodgers as a non-drafted free agent, June 6, 1988 **Acquired:** Traded from the Los Angeles Dodgers to the Toronto Blue Jays on November 9, 1999 **Pre-Majors highlights:** Was named the top prospect in the Texas League in 1992 **Personal information:** Hit .291 in 42 games after being called up by the Los Angeles Dodgers in 1993

"We feel Raul Mondesi is one of the top talents in the game today. He'll be a big part of our team."

Toronto general manager, Gord Ash

Career milestones

1994 Was named the National League Rookie of the Year
1995 Won the National League Gold Glove
1997 Became the first player in Dodger franchise history to hit 30 homers and steal 30 bases in the same season
1997 Won the National League Gold Glove
1998 Led the Dodgers in nearly every major offensive category, including at-bats (580), runs (85), hits (162), total bases (288), doubles (26), triples (five), home runs (30) and RBI (90)

American League fans will now get a look at one of the best all-around players in the game.

In one of the biggest trades of the offseason, the Toronto Blue Jays picked up outfielder Raul Mondesi from Los Angeles in a deal that sent outfielder Shawn Green to the Dodgers.

Mondesi comes to the Blue Jays with an impressive list of credentials. He'll still only be 29 years old on Opening Day 2000, but he has already achieved a lot in his career. Mondesi made an immediate impact in the Major Leagues when he won the National League Rookie of the Year Award in 1994. He's been impressing people ever since.

There's no doubt Mondesi is a multi-tool player. He can hit for a high batting average. He can hit for power. He can steal bases. He is a good defensive player with one of the best throwing arms in baseball.

"He's an exciting player," said Toronto general manager Gord Ash. "You don't find too many players with his kind of talent."

Mondesi will bring the total package to the Blue Jays. In 1997, he hit 30 home runs and stole 32 bases to become the first 30-30 man in Dodgers history. He led Los Angeles in almost every major offensive category in 1998. Mondesi also won the National League Gold Glove for his defensive play in 1995 and 1997.

"He'll add a lot to the middle of our lineup and he'll add a lot to our outfield," said Ash.

Mondesi's batting average dipped to .253 in 1999, but his production was still there as he hit 33 home runs with 99 runs batted in. The Dodgers had been expected to challenge for the World Series. Instead they went 77–85, a miserable return for a massive investment.

The 1999 season produced some controversy for Mondesi. After being benched for a couple of games, he criticized Dodgers general manager Kevin Malone and manager Davey Johnson and demanded a trade. That's why he excited about joining the Blue Jays.

"I don't like talking bad about anybody or any team," Mondesi said. "It's not the way I am. I did have some difficulties with the team but there are things I would really not want to discuss. I look at this more as a new beginning. I want to focus more on being a Blue Jay."

"We've satisfied ourselves that more is made of the reputation than is deserved," Ash said.

The Blue Jays thought enough of Mondesi to pick up the option years in his contract for the 2002 and 2003 seasons. It's hard to find many players who have put up these kind of consistent numbers in only seven years in the big leagues. The Blue Jays want to make sure Mondesi puts up those numbers in Toronto for a long time.

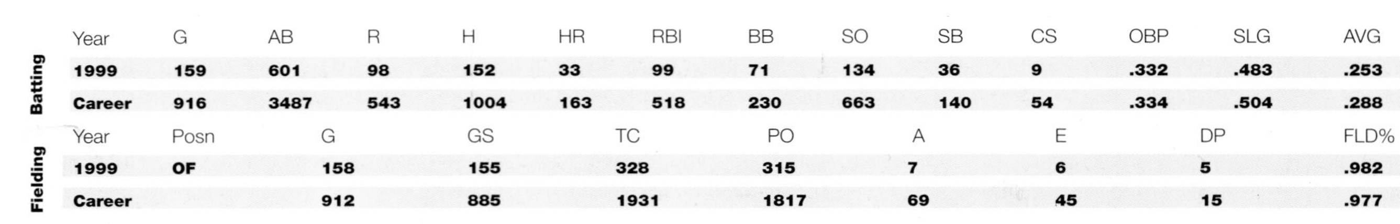

Batting

Year	G	AB	R	H	HR	RBI	BB	SO	SB	CS	OBP	SLG	AVG
1999	**159**	**601**	**98**	**152**	**33**	**99**	**71**	**134**	**36**	**9**	**.332**	**.483**	**.253**
Career	**916**	**3487**	**543**	**1004**	**163**	**518**	**230**	**663**	**140**	**54**	**.334**	**.504**	**.288**

Fielding

Year	Posn	G	GS	TC	PO	A	E	DP	FLD%
1999	**OF**	**158**	**155**	**328**	**315**	**7**	**6**	**5**	**.982**
Career		**912**	**885**	**1931**	**1817**	**69**	**45**	**15**	**.977**

43

Sammy Sosa

Profile

Name: Samuel Sosa
Height: 6–0 **Weight:** 185
Throws: Right **Bats:** Right **Position:** Right field **Born:** November, 12, 1968, San Pedro De Macoris, Dominican
Drafted: Signed as a free agent by the Texas Rangers, July 30, 1985 **Acquired:** Traded by the Chicago White Sox to the Chicago Cubs, March 30, 1992
Pre-Majors highlights: Named to South Atlantic League All-Star, 1987
Personal information: Brother Jose played in the Cubs organization

"Nobody was thinking Mark (McGwire) and I had the opportunity to do it again. You just never know in this game." **Chicago Cubs right fielder, Sammy Sosa**

Career milestones

1989 Made Major League debut for Texas Rangers on June 16. Traded from Texas to Chicago White Sox on July 29
1996 Despite playing in only 124 games because of a broken hand, he hit 40 homers with 100 RBIs
1997 Played all 162 games, hitting 36 homers, scoring 90 runs and driving in 119
1998 National League Most Valuable Player and RBI Leader
1999 Won Hank Aaron Award in the National League

Sammy Sosa has come a long way in his baseball career. And no one knows that better than Sosa.

"My first year, 1990, I hit 15 home runs with the White Sox and I thought I was Babe Ruth," Sosa said during the 1999 season.

At the time, Sosa was regarded as an up-and-coming star. Little did anyone, particularly Sosa, realize at the time that one day he would be smashing some of Ruth's most storied records.

One year after smashing 66 home runs, Sosa hit 63 in 1999 in yet another storybook season for the Chicago Cubs right fielder. Not only did he become the first player in Major League history to reach the 60-home run mark twice, he did it in back-to-back seasons.

Sosa's accomplishments have had everyone in baseball talking.

"He's one of the real treasures we have in the game now," said Jim Lefebvre, who was Sosa's first Cubs manager in 1992 and managed the Milwaukee Brewers for the last two months of the 1999 season. "People ask me if I saw greatness in Sammy. I saw a five-tool guy with three outstanding traits—a great body type, he is absolutely fearless and he wanted to be great. He worked hard at it. But to think he'd hit 60—and twice—I couldn't have predicted that."

For the second straight season, Sosa and St. Louis Cardinals slugger Mark McGwire captivated baseball fans all over the world with their race for home run supremacy. And for the second straight season, McGwire, who belted 66 homers, edged out Sosa. McGwire beat Sosa, 70–66 in 1998.

Sosa knows what the home run battles have meant to people. As far as he's concerned, it's a matter of giving the people what they want.

"Basically, the name of the game now is home runs," Sosa said. "All the people come to the park to see us hit them. That was one of the reasons why Mark and I brought baseball back last year."

Until Sosa came along, Ruth had come the closest to two 60-homer seasons. He hit 59 in 1921 and became the first to reach the mark in 1927, when he finished with 60 in a 154-game season. Roger Maris hit 61 homers in a 162-game season in 1961. No one else reached 60 until 1998, when McGwire and Sosa took center stage.

Sosa's performance was one of the few bright spots for the Cubs in 1999. He batted .288, drove in 141 runs and had a slugging percentage of .635. Sosa, who made his third All-Star team, also was named National League Player of the Month for May after batting .321 with 13 HR and 27 RBIs.

What will the year 2000 hold for Sosa? No one knows, but you can be sure baseball fans around the world will be watching.

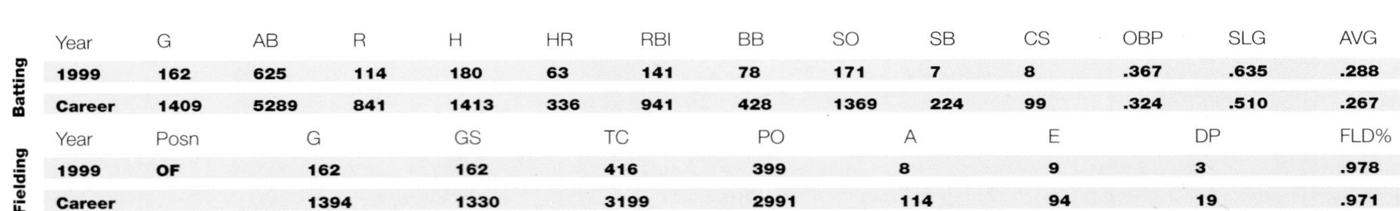

Batting

Year	G	AB	R	H	HR	RBI	BB	SO	SB	CS	OBP	SLG	AVG
1999	162	625	114	180	63	141	78	171	7	8	.367	.635	.288
Career	1409	5289	841	1413	336	941	428	1369	224	99	.324	.510	.267

Fielding

Year	Posn	G	GS	TC	PO	A	E	DP	FLD%
1999	OF	162	162	416	399	8	9	3	.978
Career		1394	1330	3199	2991	114	94	19	.971

SOSA
21

Mark McGwire

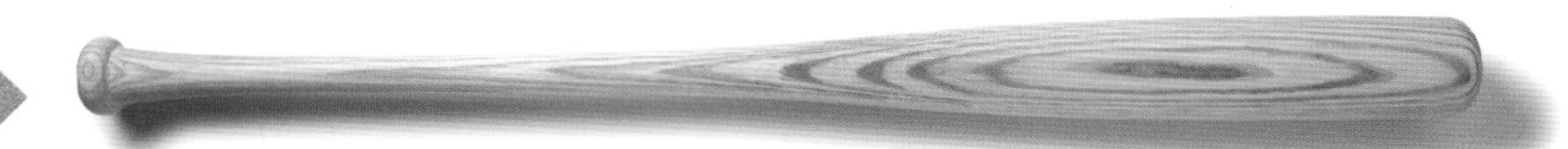

"He maintained intense concentration for six months, which is almost impossible to do, unless you're Superman. I think sometimes he's Superman."

St. Louis Cardinals manager, Tony La Russa.

Career milestones

1984 Selected in the first round of the free agent draft by Oakland.
1987 American League Rookie of the Year after hitting .289 with 49 HR and 118 RBI. Became only the second player to win the award unanimously since Carlton Fisk in 1972. His 49 HRs were a single-season club record and a Major League record for a rookie.
1991 Hits his 200th home run
1996 Hits his 300th home run
1998 Breaks Roger Maris' legendary home-run record and ends to end the season with 70, and becomes the 26th player in baseball history to hit 400 career home runs
1999 Hits his 500th home run. Ends season with 522 homers and is 10th on the all-time list.

A year after making history, Mark McGwire ruled baseball again in 1999.

No, the St. Louis Cardinals star didn't break the home run record he set in 1998 when he hit 70, but blasting 65 wasn't a bad encore.

After leading Sammy Sosa for nearly all of 1998, McGwire took a different approach in 1999. He trailed Sosa for most of the season, but homered six times in the final seven games to move past the Chicago Cubs slugger, who ended the season with 63. McGwire pulled away from Sosa late in the 1998 season by homering five times in the last three games.

McGwire also led the National League with 147 RBIs, which matched the career high he had set the previous year. He also became the first player in history to finish with more RBIs than hits (145) in a season.

McGwire also is moving beyond single-season accomplishments. He's quickly moving up on the all-time home run list. His 1999 effort moved him past Hall of Famers Ted Williams and Willie McCovey into 10th place on the career list with 522 home runs.

McGwire, a certain Hall of Famer himself, has topped the 50 home run mark in four straight seasons, 1996–99, a baseball record. He hit 52 while playing for Oakland in 1996, 58 in 1997 while splitting the season between Oakland and St. Louis, 70 in 1998 and 65 last season.

Going into the 1998 season, most baseball fans thought Roger Maris' record of 61 home runs was an unreachable mark. After shattering that mark two seasons in a row, McGwire, who turned 36 in October, could actually reach another mark that has been hailed as untouchable. He trails all-time leader Hank Aaron, who hit 755 career homers, by 233. Seeing that McGwire has hit 245 home runs the last four seasons, Aaron's mark might not be as unattainable as originally thought.

After all he has achieved in the 1998 and '99 seasons, McGwire is downplaying his accomplishments. He doesn't think he can reach Aaron's record. If he fails, his nightmarish spell of injuries in the early 1990s will be to blame.

"It's too far away," McGwire said. "The logical answer if anybody wants to talk about somebody who's going to break the record would be Ken Griffey Jr."

Aaron, for one, disagrees. He thinks McGwire has a legitimate chance at breaking his record.

"The way he's hitting home runs, he could break the record next year," Aaron said in late 1999. "He's hitting them in bunches. 70 home runs? He might hit 80 some year. Whew! That's a lot of home runs."

Injuries will be the key to McGwire's chances. "It all comes down to health," he said. "I think the biggest concern for me as far as longevity is my back. If my back holds up, I can play for a few more years."

Batting

Year	G	AB	R	H	HR	RBI	BB	SO	SB	CS	OBP	SLG	AVG
1999	**153**	**521**	**118**	**145**	**65**	**147**	**133**	**141**	**0**	**0**	**.424**	**.697**	**.278**
Career	**1688**	**5652**	**1059**	**1498**	**522**	**1277**	**1185**	**1400**	**11**	**8**	**.394**	**.587**	**.265**

Fielding

Year	Posn	G	GS	TC	PO	A	E	DP	FLD%
1999	**1B**	**151**	**150**	**1274**	**1181**	**80**	**13**	**119**	**.990**
Career		**1608**	**1568**	**14368**	**13244**	**1017**	**107**	**1301**	**.993**

Rafael Palmeiro

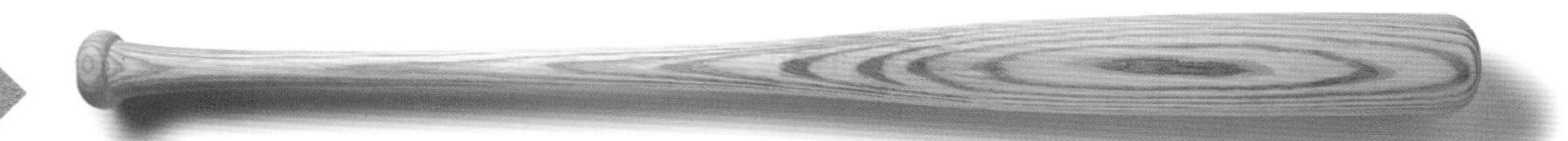

Profile

Name: Rafael Corrales Palmeiro **Height:** 6–0 **Weight:** 190 **Throws:** Left **Bats:** Left **Position:** First base/Designated hitter **Born:** September 24, 1964, Havana, Cuba **Drafted:** Selected by the Chicago Cubs in the first round (22nd overall) of the 1985 free-agent draft **Acquired:** Signed as a free agent by the Texas Rangers, December 4, 1998 **Pre-Majors highlights:** Led the Eastern League with 95 RBIs in 1986 **Personal information:** Cousin, Orlando Palmeiro, is an outfielder for the Anaheim Angels

"Raffy is a steady player. That's the best way to describe him. He does his job and puts up the numbers every year." **Texas Rangers manager, Johnny Oates**

Career milestones

1987 Hit .276 with 14 homers for Cubs in his rookie season

1988 Traded from Chicago Cubs to Texas Rangers, December 5

1997 Won first American League Gold Glove. Also won award in 1998

1998 American League Silver Slugger and Gold Glove winner. Also earned the Baltimore Orioles Most Valuable Player Award

1999 Made All-Star team for fourth time and won The Sporting News Player of the Year Award

Who's the top player in baseball in the 1990s? It might surprise a lot of people to see Rafael Palmeiro's name near the top of the list.

When it comes to durability, Palmeiro is at the top. He led the Majors with 1,527 games played in the 1990s. When it comes to production, he's right there, too. Palmeiro was second, behind the Chicago Cubs' Mark Grace, with 1,747 hits.

The 1999 season was Palmeiro's best, and he overcame some big obstacles to achieve it. Despite a pair of arthroscopic knee surgeries in February and March, his durability and production didn't suffer. While many players would have taken their time getting back in the lineup, Palmeiro pushed himself like a rookie fighting for a roster spot.

The lefthanded hitter led Texas in games played (158), homers (47) and RBIs (148). He also batted .324 with a slugging percentage of .630. The knee problems forced him out of his usual role at first base, where he has won two Gold Gloves, and into the designated hitter spot for most of the year, but he more than made up for that with his numbers. The home run and RBI totals were career highs as the Rangers won their second straight American League West title.

The season earned Palmeiro the honor of being named *The Sporting News*' Player of the Year. That award is one of the most prestigious in baseball because it's voted on by Major League Players.

"I'm shocked, really stunned about it," said Palmeiro. "It's not something I ever thought I'd win. I know I can be pretty hard on myself at times, but this is amazing. To be honored by your peers makes it special."

Last season was quite a homecoming for Palmeiro, who played with the Rangers from 1989–93. He left Texas as a free agent following the '93 season and signed with the Baltimore Orioles, where he put in five solid seasons. Palmeiro hit .289 or better in four of the five years in Baltimore. He averaged 40 homers and 119 RBIs in his last four seasons with the Orioles. Palmeiro became the first player in Orioles' history to drive in 100 or more runs in four straight years.

Those kind of numbers don't come without a professional approach to the game. Palmeiro, who started his career with the Chicago Cubs in 1986, has played in at least 152 games in 10 of his 14 big-league seasons.

"That's something I take a lot of pride in," he said. "It's important to make every effort to be in the lineup every day."

With that kind of attitude and such good numbers, it's easy to see why Palmeiro has the respect of his peers around baseball.

Batting

Year	G	AB	R	H	HR	RBI	BB	SO	SB	CS	OBP	SLG	AVG
1999	**158**	**565**	**96**	**183**	**47**	**148**	**97**	**69**	**2**	**4**	**.420**	**.630**	**.324**
Career	**1940**	**7281**	**1157**	**2158**	**361**	**1227**	**832**	**906**	**86**	**37**	**.369**	**.513**	**.296**

Fielding

Year	Posn	G	GS	TC	PO	A	E	DP	FLD%
1999	**1B/DH**	**28**	**28**	**275**	**261**	**13**	**1**	**23**	**.996**
Career		**1752**	**1710**	**14641**	**13381**	**1171**	**89**	**1269**	**.994**

Profile

Name: Patrick George Hentgen
Height: 6–2 **Weight:** 200 **Throws:** Right **Bats:** Right **Position:** Pitcher
Born: November 13, 1968, Detroit, Michigan
Drafted: Selected by the Toronto Blue Jays in the fifth round of the 1986 June free-agent draft. **Acquired:** Traded by Toronto Blue Jays to the St. Louis Cardinals on November 11, 1999 **Pre-Majors highlights:** Pitched a combined no-hitter with two other pitchers for Class A Dundein in 1988

Pat Hentgen

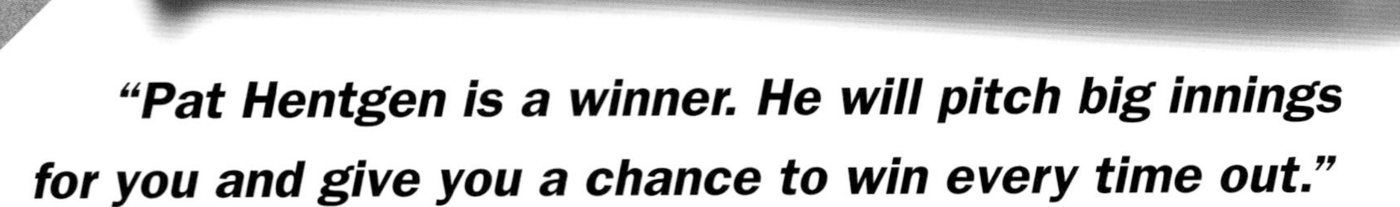

"Pat Hentgen is a winner. He will pitch big innings for you and give you a chance to win every time out."

Gord Ash, Toronto Blue Jays general manager

Career milestones

1991 Had 2.45 ERA in three games for Blue Jays in 1991 in Major League debut
1993 Named to American League All-Star team for first time. Also made team in 1994 and 1997
1996 Won American League Cy Young Award. Finished season with 20–10 record (second Toronto pitcher ever to have a 20-win season) and 3.22 ERA in 35 starts
1997 Tied for American League lead in shutouts, complete games, and innings pitched
1998 Had sixth consecutive winning season, going 12–11 with a 5.17 ERA in 29 starts.
1999 Traded to the St. Louis Cardinals

You might call Pat Hentgen a throwback. The former Toronto Blue Jays' right-hander is an exception in this day and age of mediocre starting pitching. Before finishing the 1999 season with an 11–12 record, Hentgen posted winning seasons six times in seven years. He finished that stretch with an 89–62 record and a 4.00 earned run average.

Hentgen topped the 200 inning mark four times in that stretch. He led the league twice, pitching 265.2 innings in 1996 and 264 innings in 1997.

Those back-to-back seasons were the best of Hentgen's career, which began in 1991 when he appeared in three games for the Blue Jays. He won the American League Cy Young Award in 1996, when he went 20–10 with a 3.22 ERA. Finishing what he started, Hentgen led the league with 10 complete games and three shutouts.

The 1997 season produced similar results. Hentgen had a 15–10 record with a 3.68 ERA. Starting a league-high 35 games (the same number he started the previous year), Hentgen again led the league with nine complete games and three shutouts.

Hentgen has developed a reputation for taking the ball every time his manager has given it to him. He made 183 straight starts from April 17, 1983 to August 24, 1998. That streak was stopped by shoulder tendinitis late in the '98 season, which limited him to 29 starts. Since joining the Blue Jays' rotation during the 1993 season, Hentgen has averaged 31 starts the last seven seasons.

Hentgen's numbers in 1999 were off, thanks to the shoulder injury that began bothering him the previous season. The injury affected his control and cut down on his strikeouts. Hentgen tried to counter that with a split-finger pitch to go along with his fastball and the results improved as the season went along.

In his first full season in the Major Leagues in 1993, Hentgen was a key member of Toronto's last World Series championship team. He finished the season with a 19–9 record and a 3.87 ERA while picking up a win in the World Series against Philadelphia. He held the Phillies to one run and five hits in six innings while striking out six and walking three to win Game 3.

For Hentgen, the individual awards are nice, but he's more concerned with the big picture—winning.

"My whole career I've been a team player and I want to continue to do that," he said. "I just want to win. There's no substitute for the adrenaline rush when there are only four or five teams left."

Now he has a new challenge. Hentgen was traded to the Cardinals in November 1999. National League hitters had better watch out.

Pitching

Year	W	L	ERA	G	GS	CG	SHO	SV	SVO	INN	H	R	ER	HR	HBP	BB	SO
1999	**11**	**12**	**4.79**	**34**	**34**	**1**	**0**	**0**	**0**	**199.0**	**225**	**115**	**106**	**32**	**3**	**65**	**118**
Career	**105**	**76**	**4.14**	**252**	**222**	**31**	**9**	**0**	**1**	**1555.2**	**1587**	**783**	**716**	**191**	**37**	**557**	**995**

Batting

Year	G	AB	R	H	HR	RBI	BB	SO	SB	CS	OBP	SLG	AVG
Career	**252**	**18**	**0**	**1**	**0**	**0**	**0**	**8**	**0**	**0**	**.056**	**.056**	**.056**

Fielding

Year	Posn	G	GS	TC	PO	A	E	DP	FLD%
1999	**P**	**34**	**34**	**40**	**15**	**22**	**3**	**4**	**.925**
Career		**252**	**222**	**281**	**96**	**175**	**10**	**19**	**.964**

Profile

Name: Ivan Rodriguez
Height: 5–9 **Weight:** 205
Throws: Right **Bats:** Right
Position: Catcher **Born:** November 30, 1971, Manati, Puerto Rico **Drafted:** He was signed by the Texas Rangers as a non-drafted free agent in 1988 **Pre-Majors highlights:** Was named Top Prospect in Florida State League in 1990 **Personal information:** Was only 19 years old when called up by the Texas Rangers in 1991

Ivan Rodriguez

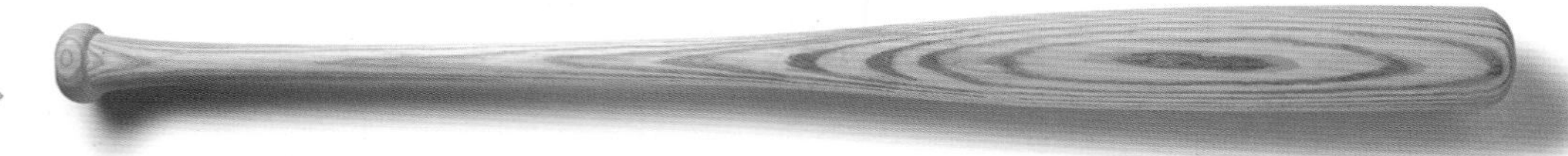

"He's become more than just a good catcher. He's one of the best all-round players in the game when you consider what he can do offensively and defensively."

Texas Rangers manager, Johnny Oates

Career milestones

1991 Made Major League debut, June 20
1992 Won first American League Gold Glove. Has won the award eight straight years
1996 Had 47 doubles, a Major League record for doubles by a regular catcher
1998 Led the Rangers with a career-high .321 average. Also set career-highs in home runs (21) and RBIs (91). Recorded his 1,000th career hit on May 10

Baseball experts all agree that Ivan "Pudge" Rodriguez is the best catcher in the game today. By the time Rodriguez's career is finished, he'll go down as one of the all-time greats at the position.

Even though he's only 28 years old, Rodriguez, who catches for the Texas Rangers, has achieved feats most players can only dream about. He has been named to the American League All-Star team eight years in a row and has won eight straight Gold Glove Awards for his outstanding defensive play behind home plate.

How impressive is the Gold Glove total? Only Hall of Famer Johnny Bench has won more with 10.

There aren't many catchers who can dominate a game, but Rodriguez has been doing so for years. Because of his strong arm behind the plate, he completely shuts down the running game of opposing teams. Even the top basestealers in the game don't try to run against Rodriguez for fear of taking their teams out of big innings. It's impossible to quantify how many runs a season Rodriguez saves his team.

"His presence behind the plate takes teams out of their games," said Texas manager Johnny Oates. "They don't run when he's behind the plate. It's an overlooked part of the game, but it means so much to our team. It's so important."

Rodriguez threw out a career-best 52.8 percent of runners who tried to steal against him in 1999, his third consecutive season above 50 percent.

Rodriguez was called up by the Rangers when he was 19 years old, making him the youngest player in the Major Leagues in both 1991 and 1992. Early in his career, most of the headlines he made came because of his defense. In his first two years in the big leagues, he drove in 27 runs in 1991 and 37 runs in 1992. His offensive game has improved every year since then. By 1995, he was batting .303 with 12 homers and 67 RBIs. Rodriguez's production went up steadily each season. He batted .300 with 19 homers and 86 RBIs in 1996, hit .313 with 20 homers and 77 RBIs in 1997 and batted .321 with 21 homers and 91 RBIs in 1998.

Rodriguez exploded in 1999. In helping the Rangers win their second straight American League West title, he batted .332 with 35 home runs and 113 RBIs.

"I just try to get better every year," said Rodriguez. "I try to work as hard as I can and keep improving. I don't want to be satisfied with what I've done. I went to keep getting better every year."

Considering his age and his talent, there's a good chance Rodriguez will keep getting better. And that's bad news for opposing pitchers and baserunners.

Batting

Year	G	AB	R	H	HR	RBI	BB	SO	SB	CS	OBP	SLG	AVG
1999	**144**	**600**	**116**	**199**	**35**	**113**	**24**	**64**	**25**	**12**	**.356**	**.558**	**.332**
Career	**1169**	**4443**	**649**	**1333**	**144**	**621**	**237**	**571**	**60**	**28**	**.337**	**.465**	**.300**

Fielding

Year	Posn	G	GS	TC	PO	A	E	DP	FLD%
1999	**C**	**141**	**141**	**940**	**850**	**83**	**7**	**13**	**.993**
Career		**1133**	**1096**	**7494**	**6773**	**645**	**76**	**75**	**.990**

27
3
24
T
TEXAS RANGERS
BASEBALL CLUB

Ken Griffey Jr.

Profile

Name: George Kenneth Griffey Jr. **Height:** 6–3 **Weight:** 205 **Throws:** Left **Bats:** Left **Position:** Center field **Born:** November 21, 1969, Donora, Pennsylvania **Drafted:** Selected by the Seattle Mariners in the first round (first overall) of the 1987 free-agent draft **Pre-Majors highlights:** Named to Carolina League All-Star Team, 1988 **Personal information:** Son of former Major League outfielder Ken Griffey Sr.

"Watching Junior play every day is truly a pleasure. He's one of the most gifted players to ever play the game." **Seattle Mariners manager, Lou Piniella**

Career milestones

1987 First pick of draft

1991 With father Ken Sr. became the first father-son duo to hit back-to-back homers in a game

1992 Won American League Gold Glove, led league in RBIs and was named All-Star Game Most Valuable Player

1994 Led American League in home runs and won Gold Glove

1997 Named Most Valuable Player in American League and led league in home runs

1998 Led American League in home runs and won Gold Glove

When a baseball fan sits down to watch the nightly highlight show, there's a good chance he's going to see a clip of Ken Griffey Jr. doing something special.

The man simply known as "Junior", might be hitting a tape-measure home run. Or he might be robbing a hitter of a homer with one of his patented leaping grabs at the fence. Or he might be killing an opposing team's rally by gunning down a runner at the plate.

Sometimes it seems like there isn't anything the Seattle Mariners center fielder can't do on a baseball field. "Junior can win a game in so many different ways," said Mariners manager Lou Piniella. "He can win a game with his bat or his speed or his defense. There aren't many guys who can do all those things."

Griffey completed another outstanding season in 1999. He belted 48 home runs to lead the American League for the third straight season, and for the fourth time in the last six years. Griffey's defensive play earned him his 10th straight Gold Glove.

Griffey has hit 40 or more homers in five of the last six years and has blasted at least 48 in four straight seasons. Had it not been for an act of God, Griffey would have been the first player in Major League history to hit 50 home runs three straight years. He finished the 1996 season with 49, but lost a home run that he hit in a game that was rained out before it became an official contest. Griffey followed that with back-to-back seasons of 56 in 1997 and 1998.

The most remarkable thing about Griffey's production is his age. He turned 30 years old in November 1999. One can only speculate how many records he'll break if he plays another 10 years. Griffey hit his 300th career home run on April 13, 1998. He was 28 years and 143 days old at the time, making him the second youngest player in Major League history to reach the milestone. Griffey became the seventh youngest player to reach 200 homers in 1996. The six players above him are in the Baseball Hall of Fame. He goes into the 2000 season two homers shy of the 400 mark for his career.

"I try not to pay much attention to that stuff," Griffey said, "but once in awhile I look at the names and just start laughing out loud."

Griffey is the most recognized player in baseball today. He made the American League All-Star team for the 10th time in 1999. He led the league in voting for the seventh time and led the Major Leagues in voting for the fifth time.

Griffey does have one big advantage over most Major Leaguers. His arrival in the "bigs" was not a novelty. His father Ken Griffey Sr. was a long-time Major Leaguer and Junior grew up in and around baseball clubhouses, especially in Cincinnati. Ken Sr. and Jr, even had a brief spell playing together in Seattle.

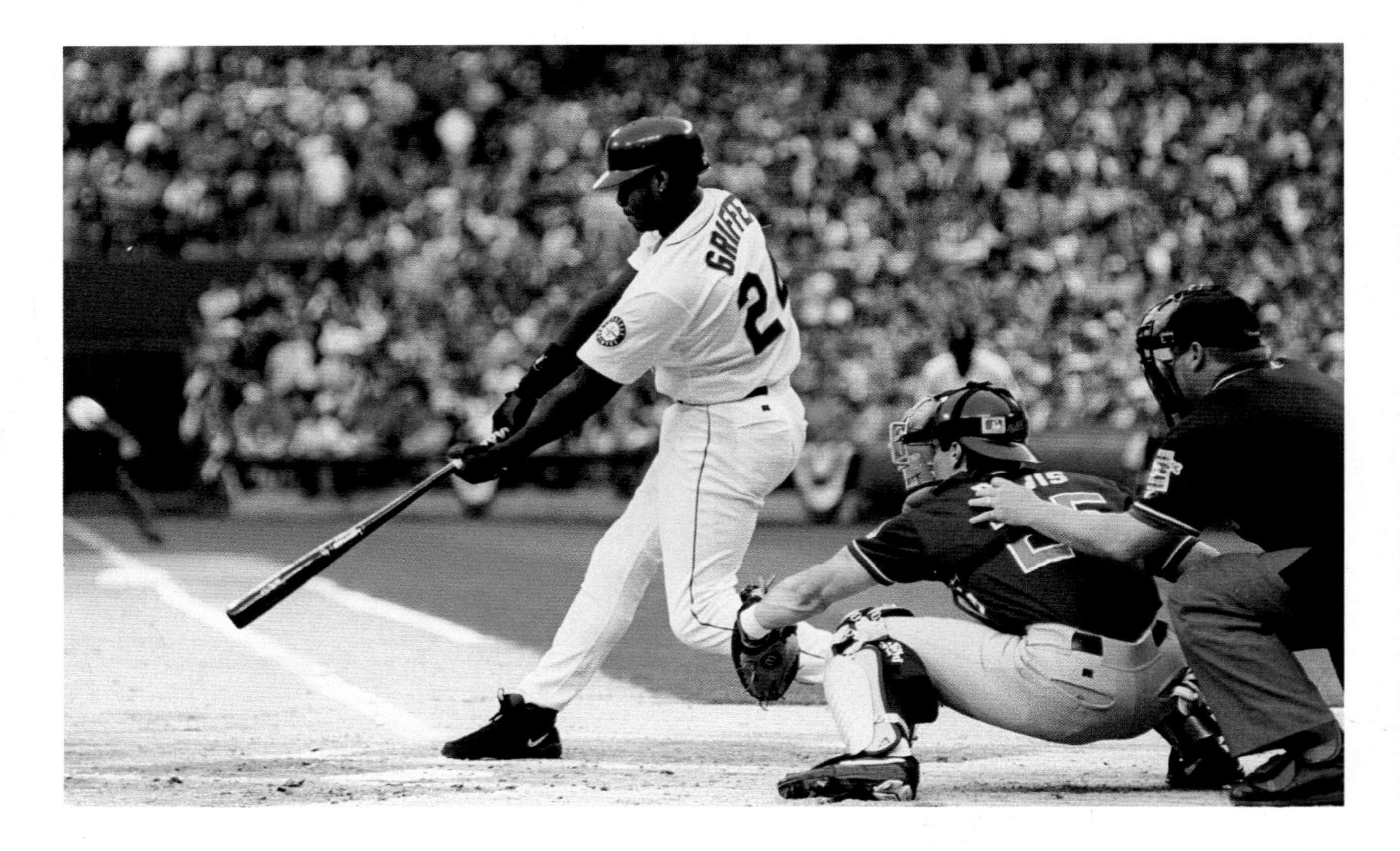

Batting

Year	G	AB	R	H	HR	RBI	BB	SO	SB	CS	OBP	SLG	AVG
1999	**160**	**606**	**123**	**173**	**48**	**134**	**91**	**108**	**24**	**7**	**.384**	**.576**	**.285**
Career	**1535**	**5832**	**1063**	**1742**	**398**	**1152**	**747**	**984**	**167**	**60**	**.380**	**.569**	**.29**[illegible]

Fielding

Year	Posn	G	GS	TC	PO	A	E	DP
1999	**OF**	**158**	**154**	**406**	**387**	**10**	**9**	**5**
Career		**1486**	**1458**	**3805**	**3642**	**108**	**55**	**34**

Profile

Name: Juan Alberto Vazquez Gonzalez **Height:** 6–3 **Weight:** 215 **Throws:** Right **Position:** Right field **Born:** October 16, 1969, Aricebo, Puerto Rico **Drafted:** Signed by the Texas Rangers as a free agent in May, 1986 **Acquired:** Traded by the Texas Rangers to the Detroit Tigers, November 2, 1999 **Pre-Majors highlights:** Led American Association in homers and RBIs, 1990 **Personal information:** Married singer Olga Tanon in December, 1998

Juan Gonzalez

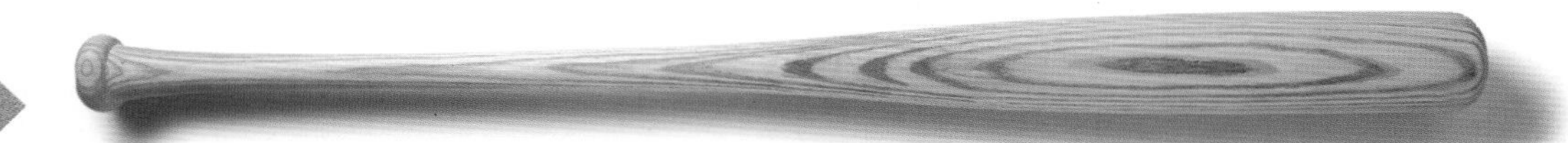

"Juan is the kind of hitter who can carry a team for a long time. Just having him in the middle of our lineup will make us a better team."

Detroit general manager, Randy Smith

Career milestones

1989 Got first Major League hit, September 4

1992 Led American League in home runs

1993 Led American League in home runs

1996 Named American League Most Valuable Player

1998 Named American League Most Valuable Player and led league in RBIs. Had 101 RBIs by All-Star break, second-best mark in Major League history.

The Detroit Tigers will open a new era with one of the top players in baseball on their side.

In a blockbuster trade on November 2, the Tigers acquired Gonzalez, a two-time winner of the American League Most Valuable Player Award, from the Texas Rangers in a nine-player deal.

The trade gives Tigers the marquee player they wanted for the opening of their new ballpark, where they will begin play in 2000. Gonzalez, who turned 30 during the 1999 playoffs, is a proven slugger who hits for high average. In helping the Rangers win their second straight American League West title in 1999, Gonzalez hit .326 with 39 homers and 128 RBIs. In developing into one of the most feared sluggers in the game, he averaged 43 homers and 140 RBIs in the past four seasons.

While the Tigers are adding one of the game's top players, the trade is a risk for Detroit. The Tigers traded left-hander Justin Thompson, Gabe Kapler, a center fielder with star potential, and rookie Francisco Cordova, a promising reliever. Gonzalez can be a free agent after the 2000 season and the Tigers haven't been able to lure star players to stay in Detroit. If the Tigers don't sign Gonzalez to a long-term contract, it means they traded a good package of young players for someone who stayed only one season.

"You have to dare to be good," Detroit general manager Randy Smith said. "If you're dealing with premier players, there's always the risk they may walk. Once they find out what kind of place Detroit is to play in and live, we think we have an equal chance to keep them."

Gonzalez isn't sure what he'll do. He wants to play the 2000 season with the Tigers before deciding if he'll hit the free-agent market next winter.

"I need to see it before I decide anything," he said. "I'm a new member of the Tigers family. I'm happy. Life continues. I'll be there trying the best I can for my new team. I'm happy."

Even if Gonzalez stays in Detroit for only one season, Tigers fans will see one of the top sluggers in the game. He was named the league's MVP in 1996 and 1998, led the league in home runs in 1992 and 1993 and in RBIs in '98.

Gonzalez hit .318 with 45 home runs, 50 doubles and 157 RBIs in 1998. Despite playing in only 133 games because of a torn ligament in his left thumb in 1997, he finished the season with 42 homers and 131 RBIs.

The Tigers hope Gonzalez will be a big part of their future. If not, they will be counting on him to start their new era on the right foot.

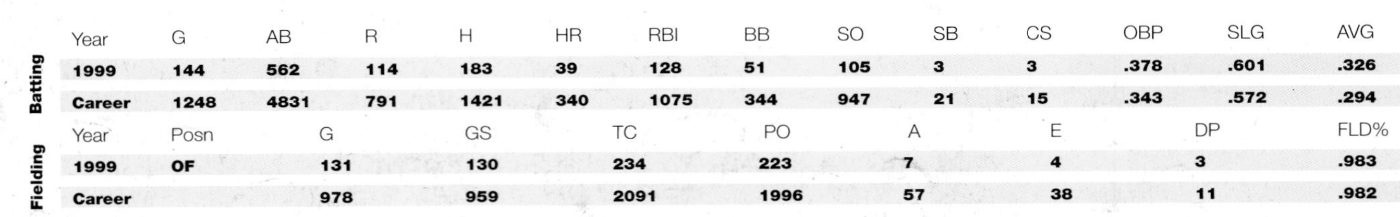

Batting

Year	G	AB	R	H	HR	RBI	BB	SO	SB	CS	OBP	SLG	AVG
1999	**144**	**562**	**114**	**183**	**39**	**128**	**51**	**105**	**3**	**3**	**.378**	**.601**	**.326**
Career	**1248**	**4831**	**791**	**1421**	**340**	**1075**	**344**	**947**	**21**	**15**	**.343**	**.572**	**.294**

Fielding

Year	Posn	G	GS	TC	PO	A	E	DP	FLD%
1999	**OF**	**131**	**130**	**234**	**223**	**7**	**4**	**3**	**.983**
Career		**978**	**959**	**2091**	**1996**	**57**	**38**	**11**	**.982**

T
TEXAS

Roger Clemens

Profile

Name:
William Roger Clemens
Height: 6–4 **Weight:** 230
Throws: Right **Bats:** Right **Positions:** Pitcher **Born:** August 4,1962, Dayton, Ohio
Drafted: Selected by the Red Sox in the first round (19th pick overall) ofthe 1983 free-agent draft
Acquired: Traded by the Blue Jays to the Yankees on February 18, 1999 **Pre-Majors highlights:** Had a 25–7 record in two All-American seasons at University of Texas. Pitched Texas to the win in the 1983 College World Series Championship Game
Personal information:
Married with four children

"Roger Clemens is a non-stop Hall of Famer. What he's done in his career has been incredible."

New York Yankees manager, Joe Torre

Career milestones

1986 American League Most Valuable Player, Cy Young Award winner, earned run average leader and All-Star Game Most Valuable Player
1987 American League Cy Young Award winner
1991 American League Cy Young Award winner, earned run average leader and strike out leader
1997 American League Cy Young Award winner, earned run average leader and strikeout leader
1998 American League Cy Young Award winner, earned run average leader and strikeout leader

The 1999 season wasn't a typical Roger Clemens year. After going 41–13 the previous two years for the Toronto Blue Jays, Clemens, traded to the New York Yankees in spring training, saw his numbers decline. He finished with a 14–10 record and his earned run average, which was 2.05 in 1997 and 2.65 in 1998, shot up to 4.60.

None of that mattered to Clemens, who has won a record five American League Cy Young Awards and was named the league's Most Valuable Player in 1986. What mattered to Clemens was more important than any individual awards. For the first time in his storied career, the right-hander was part of a World Series championship team. The Yankees won the American League East title, swept the Texas Rangers in the Division Series, beat the Boston Red Sox in five games in the American League Championship Series and swept the Atlanta Braves in the World Series.

Clemens, who turns 38 in 2000, has been in the Major Leagues since 1983, and nothing will beat the feeling of winning his first World Series.

"We don't put a lot of stock in it," he said of the individual awards. "You get a handshake, a pat on the back. All the individual stuff is great, but it really doesn't make a difference unless you get to this point."

Appropriately enough, Clemens was the winning pitcher the night the Yankees wrapped up the World Series. He held the Braves to one run and five hits in 7.2 innings in the Yankees' 4–1 win. "This is the moment I've been waiting for since I came here," said Clemens. "This is why I wanted to come here, to share in this moment with such a special team and a special group of guys."

The list of Clemens' individual accomplishments is endless. He won the Cy Young Award in 1986, 1987, 1991, 1997 and 1998. The fact he won the award 10 years apart is a testimony to his talent and his durability.

Clemens has won 20 games five times. He led the league in wins in 1986, when he went 24–4 with Boston, and in 1987, when he was 20–9. Proving he was getting better with age, he did it again in 1997, going 21–7 with the Blue Jays, and in 1998, when he went 20–6. He has led the league in earned run average and in shutouts six times and in strikeouts five times. He also holds the Major's record of 20 strikeouts in a nine-inning game, doing it in 1986 and '99.

"He's a guy who, year-in-and-year-out, is a bottom-line success," said Yankees general manager Brian Cashman. "He's a perennial Cy Young Award winner."

The only place left for Clemens is his future residence in the Baseball Hall of Fame.

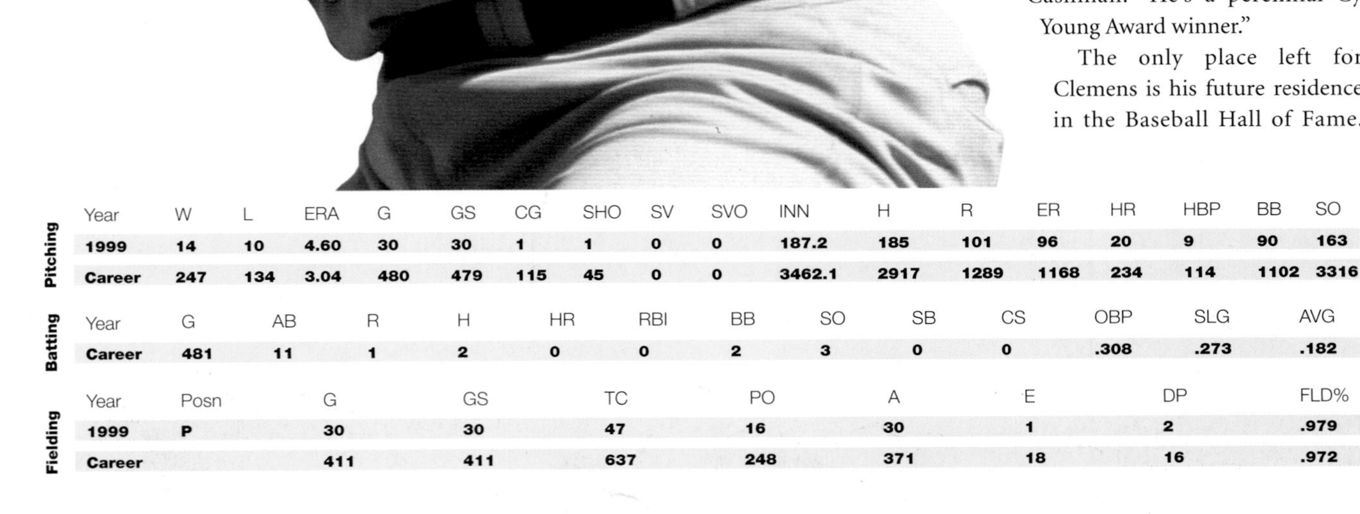

Pitching

Year	W	L	ERA	G	GS	CG	SHO	SV	SVO	INN	H	R	ER	HR	HBP	BB	SO
1999	**14**	**10**	**4.60**	**30**	**30**	**1**	**1**	**0**	**0**	**187.2**	**185**	**101**	**96**	**20**	**9**	**90**	**163**
Career	**247**	**134**	**3.04**	**480**	**479**	**115**	**45**	**0**	**0**	**3462.1**	**2917**	**1289**	**1168**	**234**	**114**	**1102**	**3316**

Batting

Year	G	AB	R	H	HR	RBI	BB	SO	SB	CS	OBP	SLG	AVG
Career	**481**	**11**	**1**	**2**	**0**	**0**	**2**	**3**	**0**	**0**	**.308**	**.273**	**.182**

Fielding

Year	Posn	G	GS	TC	PO	A	E	DP	FLD%
1999	**P**	**30**	**30**	**47**	**16**	**30**	**1**	**2**	**.979**
Career		**411**	**411**	**637**	**248**	**371**	**18**	**16**	**.972**

W YORK

Profile

Name:
Andres Jose Galarraga
Height: 6-3 **Weight:** 235 **Throws:** Right **Bats:** Right **Position:** First Base
Born: June 18, 1961, Caracas, Venezuela
Drafted: Signed by the Montreal Expos as an undrafted free agent, January 19, 1979
Acquired: Signed a free agent contract with Atlanta on November 21, 1997 after leaving Colorado
Personal information: Missed the 1999 season after being diagnosed with cancer

Andres Galarraga

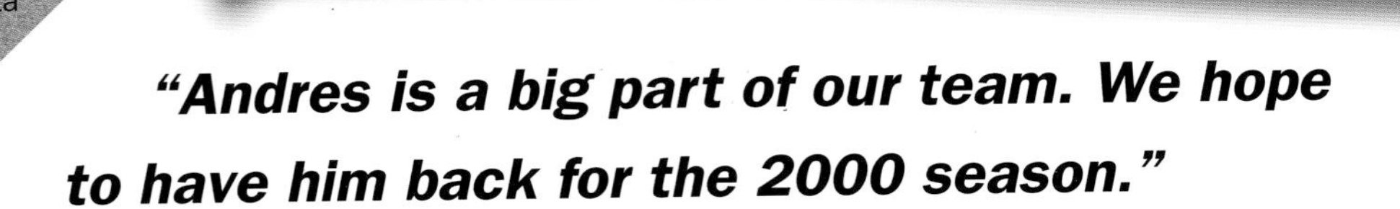

"Andres is a big part of our team. We hope to have him back for the 2000 season."

Atlanta Braves manager, Bobby Cox

Career milestones

1989 Won National League Gold Glove Award
1990 Won National League Gold Glove Award
1993 Won National League batting title
1996 Led National League in home runs and runs batted in
1997 Led National League in runs batted in
1998 Led the Atlanta Braves in home runs (44) and runs batted in (121)

Andres Galarraga has won a National League batting title, led the league in homers and runs batted in, won two Gold Gloves and made four All-Star teams, but his biggest battle came in 1999.

Galarraga, the star first baseman of the Atlanta Braves, was diagnosed with cancer and missed the entire season. As the season ended, it looked like Galarraga had beaten the disease and the Braves were hopeful he would make a full recovery and return to the field in 2000.

Galarraga has been one of the best all-around first basemen in baseball since coming to the Major Leagues in 1985 with the Montreal Expos. He was named the National League Gold Glove winner at first base in 1989 and 1990 and led the league in total chances for first baseman from 1995–97. His quick movement around the bag earned him the nickname "The Big Cat".

Galarraga has batted over .300 seven times in his career, has topped the 100 runs batted in mark four times and has hit over 30 home runs five times.

Galarraga played for the Expos from 1985–91 before he was traded to the St. Louis Cardinals. He played one season for the Cardinals before signing with the Colorado Rockies after the 1992 season.

His career took off with the Rockies. The 1993 season started a string of six straight outstanding seasons. Galarraga led the National League with a .370 batting average while hitting 22 homers with 98 RBIs and won the league's Comeback Player of the Year Award from The Sporting News. The batting average was the highest by a right-handed hitter since Joe DiMaggio hit .381 in 1939.

Galarraga had back-to-back 31-homer seasons in 1994 and 1995. The '95 season included a three-homer game on June 25 and a six-hit game on July 3. He was a key member of the Rockies' team that won the National League wild card in the franchise's third season of existence to become the fastest team ever to make the playoffs. He led the league with 47 homers and 150 RBIs in 1996 and led the league again in RBIs with 140 the following season.

The first baseman, who has nine career grand slams, signed with the Braves following the 1997 season and proved his numbers in Colorado weren't just the result of Denver's high altitude. He batted .305 with 44 home runs and 121 RBIs in his first season with the Braves. Atlanta made it to the World Series in 1999, but could have used Galarraga's bat when they were shut down in the four-game sweep by the New York Yankees.

Galarraga and the Braves are both optimistic he'll return next season, which could lead to one of baseball's best comeback stories.

Batting

Year	G	AB	R	H	HR	RBI	BB	SO	SB	CS	OBP	SLG	AVG
Career	**1774**	**6629**	**1011**	**1921**	**332**	**1172**	**467**	**1615**	**121**	**68**	**.347**	**.504**	**.290**

Fielding

Year	Posn	G	GS	TC	PO	A	E	DP	FLD%
Career	**1B**	**1749**	**1679**	**16852**	**15515**	**1197**	**140**	**1373**	**.992**

Jim Thome

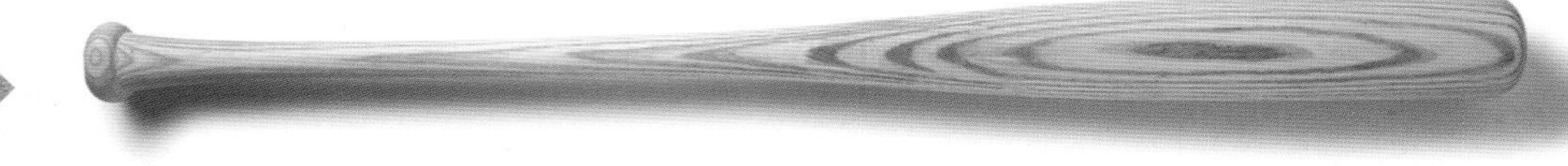

Profile

Name: James Howard Thome
Height: 6–4 **Weight:** 225
Throws: Right **Bats:** Left **Position:** First Base
Born: August 27, 1970, Peoria, Illinois
Drafted: Selected by the Cleveland Indians in the 13th round of the 1989 free-agent draft
Pre-majors highlight: Led the International League with .332 average and 102 runs batted in in 1993
Personal information: Active in the Cleveland community, serving as honorary co-chairman of the United Way Home Run Derby the last three years.

"Jimmy is a solid hitter. You don't find too many hitters with his kind of talent and ability."

Cleveland Indians manager, Charlie Manuel

Career milestones

1991 Hit first Major League home run on October 4 off New York's Steve Farr

1994 Led American League third basemen with 20 home runs

1995 Hit career-high .314 with 25 homers and 73 runs batted in

1997 Became the first Indians player to ever hit 40 homers and draw 100 walks in a season

1998 Hit 30 home runs to become the first left-handed hitter in Indians' history to hit 30 homers in three straight seasons

Even though he's only been an every-day player in the Major Leagues since 1994, it hasn't taken Jim Thome long to rack up impressive numbers.

The slugging first baseman has been a key figure for a team that has won five straight American League Central Division titles and appeared in two World Series since 1995.

Since breaking into the Indians' lineup, Thome has hit .293 and averaged 31 home runs and 92 runs batted in over the last six seasons.

Thome has quickly worked his way up the Indians' all-time home run list. After hitting 33 in 1999, he has 229 career homers and is second behind Albert Belle, who hit 242 as an Indian.

Thome is also making a run at postseason history. He hit four home runs in 1999's Division Series against Boston and has 16 playoff homers in his career. Thome passed Babe Ruth with that effort and trails only Mickey Mantle and Reggie Jackson, who have 18.

"We have a lot of pride in what Jimmy has done," said Indians general manager John Hart. "He's come up through our farm system and is one of our home-grown talents. He has played a big role in what we have accomplished here."

Thome has belted 30 or more homers four straight seasons and has topped the 100 RBI mark three times in the last four years. A broken bone in his hand limited him to 123 games in 1998, limiting his RBI total to 85.

"The numbers are nice, but I really don't pay attention to them that much," said Thome. "It's special to be up there with some of those names, but to me, it's more about the team winning. That's what is really special to me. Our goal is to win the World Series. It would be special to bring that to the fans of Cleveland."

In 1999, Thome batted .277 with 33 homers and 108 RBIs. He's one of the rare power hitters who is patient at the plate. Thome led the American League with 127 walks. He also led the league with 171 strikeouts to become the first player since Mantle (1958) to lead the league in walks and strikeouts.

"Jimmy is one of the strongest hitters I've ever seen," said Indians manager Charlie Manuel. "He can drive the ball out of any part of the ballpark."

He showed off his strength last season by blasting a 511-foot home run to dead center field at Cleveland's Jacobs Field off Kansas City's Don Wengert.

Thome has been a big part of the Indians' resurgence. Not 30 until August 2000, he and the team both have a very bright future.

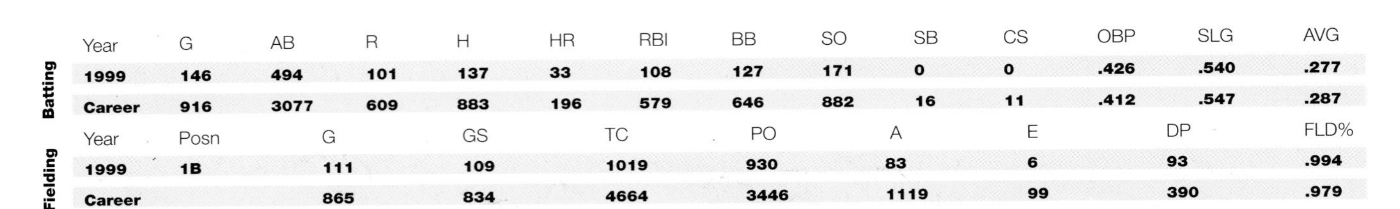

Batting

Year	G	AB	R	H	HR	RBI	BB	SO	SB	CS	OBP	SLG	AVG
1999	146	494	101	137	33	108	127	171	0	0	.426	.540	.277
Career	916	3077	609	883	196	579	646	882	16	11	.412	.547	.287

Fielding

Year	Posn	G	GS	TC	PO	A	E	DP	FLD%
1999	1B	111	109	1019	930	83	6	93	.994
Career		865	834	4664	3446	1119	99	390	.979

25

Profile

Name: David Brian Cone
Height: 6–1 **Weight:** 190 **Throws:** Right **Bats:** Left **Position:** Pitcher
Born: January 2, 1963, Kansas City, Missouri
Drafted: Selected by the Kansas City Royals in the third round of the 1981 free-agent draft **Acquired:** Re-signed by the Yankees as a free agent on Dec. 21, 1995
Pre-Majors highlight: Finished 16-3 while splitting 1982 season between Class A Charleston and Class A Fort Myers
Personal information: Established David Cone Charitable Gift Fund in 1996 to benefit worthwhile charities and non-profit organizations nationwide

David Cone

"David Cone is a warrior. You look at what he's been through in his career and it's amazing what he has accomplished."

New York Yankees manager, Joe Torre

Career milestones

1988 Finished with a 20–3 record for the New York Mets
1990 Led National League in strikeouts
1991 Led National League in strikeouts. Tied league record with 19 strikeouts, October 6
1994 Won American League Cy Young Award
1998 Finished with a 20–7 record for the New York Yankees

David Cone's numbers show why he has had a truly remarkable career.

The New York Yankees right-hander has been one of the top pitchers in this era. In his 14-year Major League career, Cone has achieved a record of 180–102, pitched on four World Series championship teams and been named to five All-Star teams.

Another highlight of Cone's career came in 1999 when he helped the Yankees win their third World Series in the last four years by going 12–9 with a 3.44 earned run average. The pinnacle came on July 18 when he pitched a perfect game against the Montreal Expos in a 6–0 win at Yankee Stadium. The gem was even more special because it came on Yogi Berra Day and ex-Yankee Don Larsen, the only pitcher to ever throw a perfect game in the World Series, threw out the first pitch.

"What an honor," said Cone. "All the legends were here. It makes you stop and think about Yankee magic and the mystique of this place."

Cone's longevity is the most telling aspect of his career. In his first full season in the Majors with the New York Mets in 1988, he finished with a 20–3 record and a 2.22 earned run average. A decade later in 1998, he had a 20–7 record and a 3.55 ERA for the New York Yankees. That broke the Major League record for the longest stretch between 20-win seasons.

Many people thought Cone's career was over in 1996 when he developed circulatory problems in his right arm on May 8, 1996. He had surgery two days later to remove an arm aneurysm. Cone, however, came back and helped the Yankees in the postseason. He won a game against the Atlanta Braves in the World Series and helped the Yankees win their first championship since 1978.

Cone came back strong in 1997 to go 12-–6 with a 2.82 ERA, but his shoulder was still bothering him. After a poor outing against Cleveland in the Division Series, Cone underwent surgery on October 17 and missed the early part of the 1998 season. When he finally came back, he looked like the Cone of old in registering the second 20-win season of his career. He was among the league leaders in wins, winning percentage, strikeouts and ERA while opposing batters hit .205.

Cone was drafted by the Kansas City Royals in 1981 and was in the big leagues four years later. In one of the most lopsided trades in baseball history, Cone and catcher Chris Jelic were traded to the Mets for catcher Ed Hearn and pitchers Rick Anderson and Mauro Gozzo on March 27, 1987.

The trade turned out to be a steal for the Mets. Cone went on to record a 75–42 record with the Mets before being traded to Toronto on August 27, 1992. The Blue Jays picked up Cone for the stretch drive and he helped the Blue Jays win their first World Series. He's been synonymous with championship teams ever since.

Pitching

Year	W	L	ERA	G	GS	CG	SHO	SV	SVO	INN	H	R	ER	HR	HBP	BB	SO
1999	12	9	3.44	31	31	1	1	0	0	193.1	164	84	74	21	11	90	177
Career	180	102	3.19	390	361	56	22	1	0	2590.0	2144	1011	918	212	87	985	2420

Batting

Year	G	AB	R	H	HR	RBI	BB	SO	SB	CS	OBP	SLG	AVG
Career	391	404	28	62	0	22	16	88	0	1	.191	.176	.153

Fielding

Year	Posn	G	GS	TC	PO	A	E	DP	FLD%
1999	P	31	31	20	7	12	1	1	.950
Career		379	361	460	197	239	24	17	.948

Todd Stottlemyre

Profile

Name: Todd Vernon Stottlemyre **Height:** 6–3 **Weight:** 200 **Throws:** Right **Bats:** Left **Positions:** Pitcher **Born:** May 20, 1965, Yakima, Washington **Drafted:** Selected by the Toronto Blue Jays in the secondary phase of the 1985 free-agent draft **Acquired:** Signed as a free agent by the Arizona Diamondbacks, December 2, 1998 **Pre-Majors highlight:** Led International League in games started, 1987 **Personal information:** Father, Mel Sr., is a former Major League pitcher and is pitching coach for the New York Yankees

"Every start is a new gift. To be able to put on a major-league uniform and go out and compete at this level. That's all I want to do, to compete and be able to pitch the way I did before." **Arizona Diamondbacks pitcher, Todd Stottlemyre**

Career milestones

1988 Made Major League debut, May 6

1992 Threw 3.2 scoreless relief innings for Toronto against Atlanta in the World Series

1997 Posted 100th career victory, May 25, joining his father Mel as the only father-son tandem to each post 100 Major League victories.

1999 Defeated the New York Mets in Game 2 of the National League Division Series

Most pitchers making $8 million a season who tear their rotator cuffs in May would be perfectly content to sit out the rest of the year and attempt a comeback the next season.

Todd Stottlemyre proved in 1999 that he is not most pitchers.

That's why Stottlemyre was still able to help the Arizona Diamondbacks win the National League West in just their second year of existence and make the playoffs quicker than any expansion team in Major League history.

Arizona signed Stottlemyre on December 2, 1998 with the hope he would stabilize their rotation behind ace Randy Johnson. For the first six weeks of the season, that's exactly what happened. Stottlemyre got off to a quick 4–1 start, but suffered a setback on May 17 when he injured his right shoulder in the fifth inning against the San Francisco Giants. The injury was later diagnosed as a torn right rotator cuff, the worst kind of an injury for a pitcher.

Luckily for Stottlemyre, he only suffered a partial tear and he made the decision to bypass surgery, which would have ended his season hoping instead the shoulder would get better through rehabilitation work.

After three months of hard work, Stottlemyre's decision turned out to be the right move. He was back in the Diamondbacks' rotation by August 20 and recorded his first win since the injury by holding Florida to two runs and five hits in a 7–2 win. He went on to pitch well down the stretch as Arizona clinched the division and qualified for the playoffs. Stottlemyre got the victory in the Diamondbacks' only win over the New York Mets in the Division Series in Game 2.

Stottlemyre, who has a career record of 129–113 in 12 seasons, has a knack for ending up on playoff teams. He helped the Toronto Blue Jays reach the postseason in 1989, 1991, 1992 and 1993. The Blue Jays won the World Series in the '92 and '93 seasons. He also helped the St. Louis Cardinals reach the National League Championship Series in 1996 and was a member of the Texas Rangers team that won the American League West title in 1998.

Stottlemyre's success and his toughness come from his bloodlines. His father, Mel Sr., was a pitcher for the New York Yankees from 1964–74 and is now the Yankees' pitching coach. His brother, Mel Jr., pitched for the Kansas City Royals in 1990.

Stottlemyre credits his father for helping him through the injury.

"When I first got injured, he said, 'One thing about it is it will take a lot of hard work, and you like to work,'" Stottlemyre said. "That's how I've taken it. It's a challenge, and somehow—with the help of the trainers and my family—we'll find a way to beat it."

Pitching

Year	W	L	ERA	G	GS	CG	SHO	SV	SVO	INN	H	R	ER	HR	HBP	BB	SO
1999	**6**	**3**	**4.09**	**17**	**17**	**0**	**0**	**0**	**0**	**101.1**	**106**	**51**	**46**	**12**	**6**	**40**	**74**
Career	**129**	**113**	**4.22**	**349**	**317**	**25**	**6**	**1**	**3**	**2076.0**	**2076**	**1058**	**973**	**224**	**81**	**773**	**1499**

Batting

Year	G	AB	R	H	HR	RBI	BB	SO	SB	CS	OBP	SLG	AVG
Career	**350**	**207**	**17**	**44**	**0**	**7**	**24**	**77**	**1**	**1**	**.294**	**.246**	**.213**

Fielding

Year	Posn	G	GS	TC	PO	A	E	DP	FLD%
1999	**P**	**17**	**17**	**21**	**8**	**12**	**1**	**1**	**.952**
Career		**349**	**317**	**419**	**161**	**241**	**17**	**18**	**.959**

32

Matt Williams

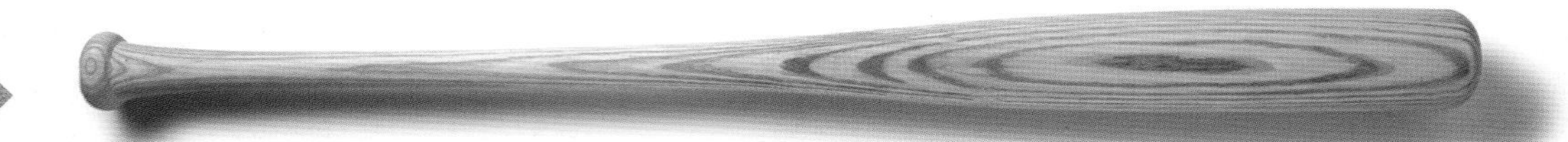

Profile

Name: Matthew Derrick Williams **Height:** 6–2 **Weight:** 214 **Throws:** Right **Bats:** Right **Position:** Third Base **Born:** November 28, 1965, Bishop, California **Drafted:** Selected by the San Francisco Giants in the first round of the 1986 free-agent draft **Acquired:** Traded from the Indians to the Diamondbacks, December 1, 1997 **Pre-Majors Highlights:** Named an NCAA All-America at shortstop **Personal Information:** His grandfather, Bart Griffith, played for the Brooklyn Dodgers and Washington Senators from 1922-24

"Matt plays hard all the time. That's the most impressive thing about him. He runs out every ground ball no matter what the situation." **Arizona Diamondbacks manager, Buck Showalter**

Career milestones

1990 Led National League in runs batted in

1991 Won National League Gold Glove

1993 Won National League Gold Glove

1994 Won National League Home Run title. Finished second in the MVP voting behind Jeff Bagwell

1997 Won American League Gold Glove

1999 Finished with at least 20 homers for the 10th consecutive season

Steady. Consistent. Dangerous hitter. Smooth fielder. Smart player.

Those are several of the adjectives that can be used to describe Arizona Diamondbacks third baseman Matt Williams. They all add up to show that Williams is one of the top players of the 1990s.

Williams had another outstanding all-around season in 1999 and played a key role as Arizona won the National League West title in only its second year of existence. He batted .303 with 35 home runs and a team-high 142 runs batted in while making 10 errors at third base.

Solid seasons are nothing new to Williams. He has hit at least 20 home runs in 10 consecutive seasons, has passed the 100-RBI mark four times, has won four Silver Sluggers and four Gold Gloves and been selected to five All-Star teams.

"Matt puts up the numbers every season," said Arizona manager Buck Showalter. "He helps you win in so many ways."

Had it not been for the players' strike that ended the 1994 season, Williams might have made headlines for breaking the single-season record for home runs long before Mark McGwire and Sammy Sosa did. Williams had a career-high 43 homers in 115 games when the season ended and was on pace to pass Roger Maris' record of 61. His 40 home runs through July 31 had already set a National League record. Williams' chances of breaking Maris' record went out of the window when the strike began in early August and the season was canceled in September. He still set an all-time franchise record for most home runs by a third baseman.

In 1995, Williams batted a career-high .336 with 23 homers and 65 RBIs, but was limited to just 76 games due to injury.

Williams was traded by the Giants to the Cleveland Indians following the 1996 season. He batted .263 with 32 homers and 105 RBIs as the Indians came within two outs of winning the World Series. Williams also was named to the American League's Silver Slugger and Gold Glove teams.

That turned out to be his only season in the American League. After he requested a trade close to the West Coast so he could be near his family, the Indians dealt Williams to the expansion Diamondbacks for third baseman Travis Fryman and pitcher Tom Martin. In his first year with Arizona, Williams missed almost a month with a stress fracture in his foot, but still hit 20 homers with 71 RBIs.

"I felt it was important to be close to my family," said Williams. "As far as I'm concerned, this is a perfect situation for me."

Arizona management believed Williams was the perfect player to build a new team around. Judging from the results of the first two years, it looks like they were right.

Batting

Year	G	AB	R	H	HR	RBI	BB	SO	SB	CS	OBP	SLG	AVG
1999	**154**	**627**	**98**	**190**	**35**	**142**	**41**	**93**	**2**	**0**	**.344**	**.536**	**.303**
Career	**1560**	**5872**	**850**	**1575**	**334**	**1050**	**390**	**1175**	**48**	**32**	**.316**	**.496**	**.268**

Fielding

Year	Posn	G	GS	TC	PO	A	E	DP	FLD%
1999	**3B**	**153**	**151**	**432**	**123**	**299**	**10**	**30**	**.977**
Career		**1543**	**1498**	**4664**	**1347**	**3152**	**165**	**337**	**.965**

ARIZONA
DIAMOND
BACKS
EASTON

John Smoltz

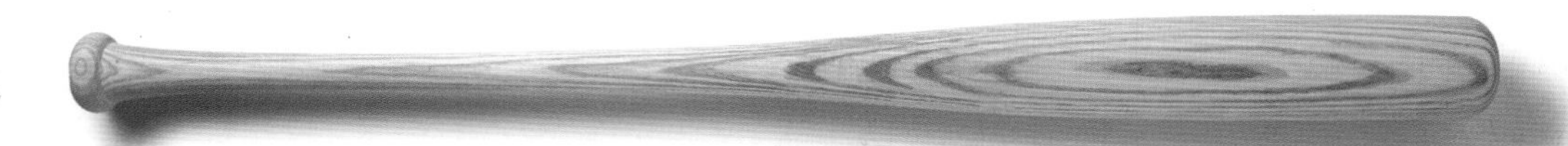

"It's unfair he's throwing the knuckleball. It should be against the law. I'll have to talk to the league president about this." **Florida Marlins manager, John Boles**

Profile

Name: John Andrew Smoltz **Height:** 6–3 **Weight:** 220 **Throws:** Right **Bats:** Right **Position:** Pitcher **Born:** May 15, 1967, Warren, Michigan **Drafted:** Selected by the Detroit Tigers in the 22nd round of the 1985 free-agent draft **Acquired:** Traded by the Detroit Tigers to the Atlanta Braves, August 12, 1987 **Personal Information:** Played on USA Junior Olympic team and in National Sports Festival (won Gold and Silver) **Pre-Majors highlight:** Went 10–5 with a 2.79 ERA at Class AAA Richmond in 1988

Career milestones

1992 Led National League in strikeouts and was named Most Valuable Player of National League Championship Series
1996 Won National League Cy Young Award and led league in wins, strikeouts, innings pitched, and winning percentage
1997 Led National League in innings pitched
1998 Had only 26 starts but posted a 17–3 record and 2.90 earned run average

On August 12, 1987, the Atlanta Braves traded veteran pitcher Doyle Alexander to the Detroit Tigers for a young pitching prospect named John Smoltz.

In the ensuing weeks, the biggest news of the trade came when Alexander went undefeated down the stretch and helped pitch the Tigers to the American League East title. Little mention was made of Smoltz, Detroit's 22nd round pick in the 1985 free-agent draft, who had posted an 11–18 record in two minor-league seasons in the Tigers' farm system.

Time can change a lot of perceptions. Twelve years later, the trade might have been the best the Braves have ever made. Smoltz was one of the dominant pitchers of the 1990s. He went 143-95 in the 10-year period. As a central figure in the best rotation in baseball, Smoltz won at least 14 games eight times and took home the National League Cy Young Award in 1996.

With the exception of the 1994 season when the players' strike canceled the postseason, the Braves won the National League divisional title every year since 1991 and made five appearances in the World Series. Their one title came in 1995.

"Getting John was one of the key acquisitions as we started to build our team," said Braves manager Bobby Cox. "He, obviously, has been a huge part of what we have accomplished here and what we have done."

"It's been a big thrill to be a part of all this," said Smoltz. "We have a chance to get to the World Series every year. That's what all players hope for. As a player, that's all you can ask."

Smoltz showed the Braves early on he could be counted on in big games. As Atlanta completed its worst-to-first ascent in the NL East in 1991, Smoltz was 12–2 with a 2.62 ERA in second half of the season.

Smoltz's best season came in his Cy Young year in 1996. He was 24–8 with a 2.94 ERA while leading the league in innings pitched (253.2) and strikeouts (276).

Smoltz also has proven he can make adjustments in his game as his career has gone on.

While going 11–8 with a 3.19 ERA in 1999, Smoltz was limited to 29 starts because of elbow problems that eventually forced him into a low three-quarters delivery. He adjusted to the new delivery quickly and even developed a knuckleball and a change up. Not only has the new approach confused hitters, it's also hard for Smoltz to explain.

"If you asked me to scout myself, it would be impossible," he said. "I'm sure hitters are not seeing (my pitches) as well."

It doesn't look like the ensuing decade is going to be any easier for hitters than the 1990s were with Smoltz around.

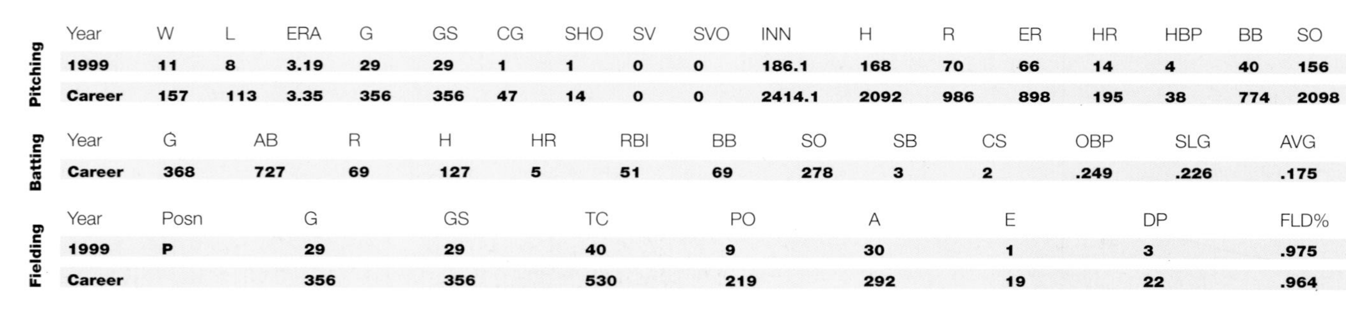

Pitching

Year	W	L	ERA	G	GS	CG	SHO	SV	SVO	INN	H	R	ER	HR	HBP	BB	SO
1999	**11**	**8**	**3.19**	**29**	**29**	**1**	**1**	**0**	**0**	**186.1**	**168**	**70**	**66**	**14**	**4**	**40**	**156**
Career	**157**	**113**	**3.35**	**356**	**356**	**47**	**14**	**0**	**0**	**2414.1**	**2092**	**986**	**898**	**195**	**38**	**774**	**2098**

Batting

Year	G	AB	R	H	HR	RBI	BB	SO	SB	CS	OBP	SLG	AVG
Career	**368**	**727**	**69**	**127**	**5**	**51**	**69**	**278**	**3**	**2**	**.249**	**.226**	**.175**

Fielding

Year	Posn	G	GS	TC	PO	A	E	DP	FLD%
1999	**P**	**29**	**29**	**40**	**9**	**30**	**1**	**3**	**.975**
Career		**356**	**356**	**530**	**219**	**292**	**19**	**22**	**.964**

Atlanta

Profile

Name: Kenneth Lofton **Height:** 6–0 **Weight:** 190 **Throws:** Left **Bats:** Left **Position:** Center Field **Born:** May 31, 1967, East Chicago, Indiana **Drafted:** Selected by the Astros in the 17th round of the 1988 free-agent draft **Acquired:** Signed by the Indians as a free agent, December 8, 1997 **Pre-Majors Highlights:** Didn't play varsity baseball until his junior season **Personal Information:** Was the sixth man on the University of Arizona Wildcats basketball team that advanced to the Final Four in 1989 and was starting point guard the following season

Kenny Lofton

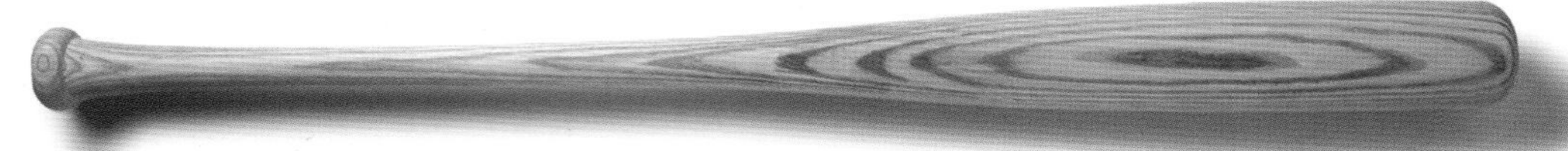

"Kenny can take over a game from the leadoff spot with his baserunning and with his glove. Kenny can distort the game with his speed." **Baltimore Orioles manager, Mike Hargrove**

Career milestones

1993 Won American League Gold Glove and led league in stolen bases

1994 Won American League Gold Glove and led league in stolen bases

1995 Won American League Gold Glove and led league in stolen bases

1996 Won American League Gold Glove and led league in stolen bases

1998 Recorded 400th career steal August 31 vs. Oakland

Kenny Lofton has proven over the years there are a lot of ways to win a baseball game. He can beat you with his bat. He can beat you by stealing a base and with his defense.

One of the top leadoff hitters in the game, Lofton has been showing his multiple skills since being traded from the Houston Astros to the Cleveland Indians following the 1991 season. He has helped the Indians become one of the top teams in baseball with his offense, which saw him win five straight stolen bases titles from 1992–96 in the American League, and his defense, which saw him win four straight Gold Gloves from 1993–96.

"He's a special player," said Indians general manager John Hart. "He always has been a special player."

Lofton has another solid season in 1999, despite being hampered by injuries. He batted .301, but stole just 25 bases, the lowest total of his Indians career after missing six weeks because of a hamstring injury. Lofton has topped the 50 stolen base mark in six of the last eight seasons and holds the Indians' club record for career steals (404).

While Lofton's offensive game has earned him headlines, he takes more pride in his defense. He knows spectacular defensive plays can change a game just as easily as a home run.

"A play like that can do something to take the air out of other teams," he said. "Any play that stops the team from getting a rally or a run is big."

While offense gets most of the time on the highlight shows, Lofton thinks defense is overlooked. He says: "Defense is part of the game," he says. "It just depends on how people look at it. I look at defense as being part of the game."

Lofton came to the Indians in one of the best trades in franchise history. He was acquired from the Houston Astros with infielder Dave Rohde for catcher Eddie Taubensee and pitcher Willie Blair on December 10, 1991.

Lofton's teams have been in the postseason every year, starting with 1995. The Indians were in the World Series that season and won the American League Central Division title in 1996. Lofton was traded to Atlanta before the 1997 season and the Braves advanced to the National League Championship Series. He re-signed with the Indians and they have won the division the last two seasons.

"I feel fortunate to be on a winning team each year," he said. "It's very important to be on a winning team. I've been to the playoffs and I've been to the World Series."

The last achievement would be winning the World Series.

"Everyone's ultimate goal once you get in the playoffs is to win it all," says Lofton. "I haven't done that yet. You have to win it all to you feel you've accomplished the ultimate feat."

Lofton will not be able to help Cleveland in the early part of the 2000 season. The shoulder he injured in the 1999 playoffs required major surgery.

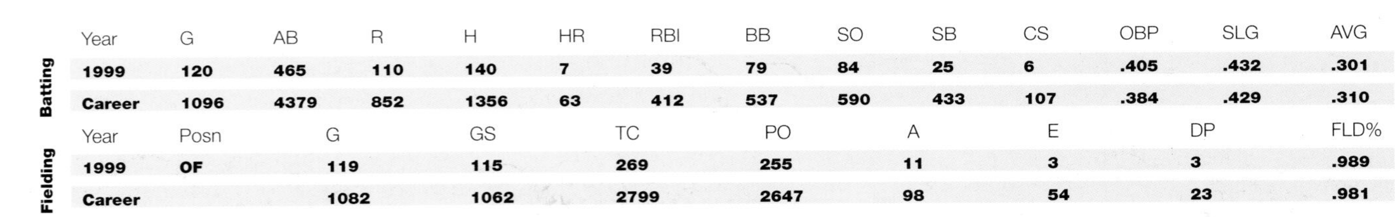

Batting

Year	G	AB	R	H	HR	RBI	BB	SO	SB	CS	OBP	SLG	AVG
1999	**120**	**465**	**110**	**140**	**7**	**39**	**79**	**84**	**25**	**6**	**.405**	**.432**	**.301**
Career	**1096**	**4379**	**852**	**1356**	**63**	**412**	**537**	**590**	**433**	**107**	**.384**	**.429**	**.310**

Fielding

Year	Posn	G	GS	TC	PO	A	E	DP	FLD%
1999	**OF**	**119**	**115**	**269**	**255**	**11**	**3**	**3**	**.989**
Career		**1082**	**1062**	**2799**	**2647**	**98**	**54**	**23**	**.981**

Profile

Name: Maurice Samuel Vaughn **Height:** 6–1 **Weight:** 245 **Throws:** Right **Bats:** Left **Position:** First Base, Designated Hitter **Born:** December 15, 1967, Norwalk, Connecticut **Drafted:** Selected by the Boston Red Sox in the first round (23rd overall) of the 1989 free-agent draft **Acquired:** Signed by the Anaheim Angels as a free agent, December 11, 1998 **Pre-Majors Highlights:** Hit .295 with 22 homers for Class AAA Pawtucket in 1990 **Personal Information:** Was All-America three seasons at Seton Hall University

Mo Vaughn

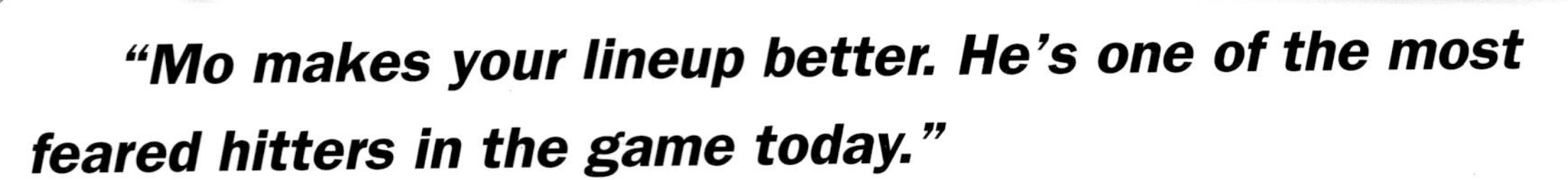

"Mo makes your lineup better. He's one of the most feared hitters in the game today."

Anaheim Angels general manager, Bill Stoneman

Career milestones

1994 Hit .310 with 26 homers and 82 runs batted in

1995 Named American League Most Valuable Player and led league in runs batted in

1996 First Major League player since Jim Rice in 1978 to hit 40 homers and have 200 hits in the same season

1998 Batted a career-high .337

Mo Vaughn and the Anaheim Angels went into the 1999 season with high hopes.

Vaughn was one of the most sought-after free agents on the market following the 1998 season. When the slugging first baseman/designated hitter finally signed with the Angels in December, big things were expected for both player and team.

It took all of one inning for those hopes to be shattered. In the first inning of the opening game of the season against Cleveland, Vaughn hustled toward the Indians dugout to catch a foul ball. As he reached the dugout, he lost his balance and fell down the steps. The result was a severely sprained ankle and Vaughn had to leave the game.

The injury limited Vaughn to 139 games, the lowest number of games he has played in a non-strike year since becoming a regular in the Major Leagues with Boston in 1993. The Angels ended up finishing last in the American League West with a 70–92 record.

Even though Vaughn was back in the lineup a few weeks later, he played hurt all season and was limited to being the designated hitter instead of playing his customary position of first base.

Despite the problems, Vaughn finished the season with good numbers. He batted .281 with 33 home runs and 108 runs batted in. As the season went on, Vaughn showed the Angels what he's capable of doing when he's close to full strength by hitting .327 with 10 homers and 27 RBIs in September.

"I felt a bit better late in the season," said Vaughn. "I was taking good swings at the ball. The situation is that you miss six weeks and then you're playing on the ankle. It never really gets better because you're playing on it."

Vaughn used a big season with the Boston Red Sox in 1998 to cash in on a big contract from the Angels. He did just about everything in leading the Sox to the wild-card playoff berth in the American League by hitting a career-high .337 with 205 hits, 31 doubles, 40 home runs and 115 RBIs. Vaughn, who became the third Red Sox player with at least two 40-home run seasons, led the team with 39 game-tying or go-ahead RBIs.

The 1999 season was the first time Vaughn has hit under .300 since 1994. In those five seasons, he hit .319 while averaging 37 home runs and 112 RBIs.

The Angels signed Vaughn to be a cornerstone of their franchise well into the next century. Considering his track record and his ability to put up big numbers, there's no reason to think he won't do that if he stays healthy.

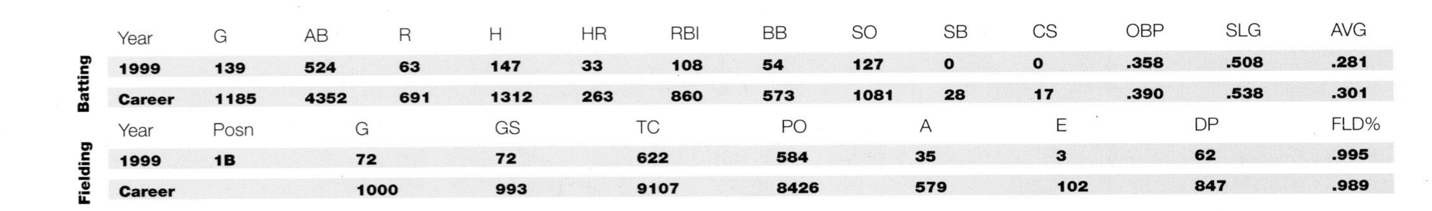

Batting

Year	G	AB	R	H	HR	RBI	BB	SO	SB	CS	OBP	SLG	AVG
1999	**139**	**524**	**63**	**147**	**33**	**108**	**54**	**127**	**0**	**0**	**.358**	**.508**	**.281**
Career	**1185**	**4352**	**691**	**1312**	**263**	**860**	**573**	**1081**	**28**	**17**	**.390**	**.538**	**.301**

Fielding

Year	Posn	G	GS	TC	PO	A	E	DP	FLD%
1999	**1B**	**72**	**72**	**622**	**584**	**35**	**3**	**62**	**.995**
Career		**1000**	**993**	**9107**	**8426**	**579**	**102**	**847**	**.989**

Mike Piazza

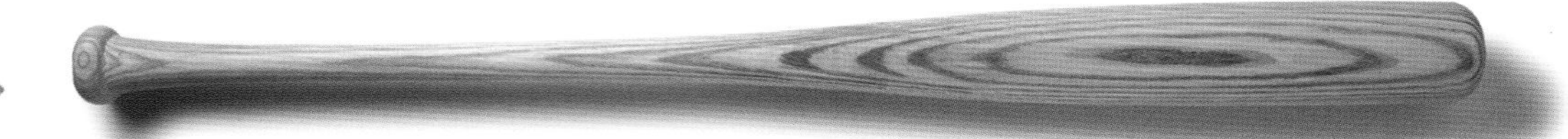

Profile

Name: Michael Joseph Piazza **Height:** 6-3 **Weight:** 215 **Throws:** Right **Bats:** Right **Position:** Catcher **Born:** September 4, 1968, Norristown, Pennsylvania **Drafted:** Selected by the Los Angeles Dodgers in the 62nd round of the 1988 free-agent draft **Acquired:** Traded from the Florida Marlins to the New York Mets, May 22, 1998 **Pre-Majors Highlight:** Hit 29 home runs at Class A Bakersfield in 1991 **Personal Information:** Is the godson of former Los Angeles Dodgers manager Tommy Lasorda

"Mike plays hurt and he played all the time. He's a leader in the clubhouse."

New York Mets manager, Bobby Valentine

Career milestones

1992 Made Major League debut, September 1

1993 Named National League Rookie of the Year

1996 Named Most Valuable player in the All-Star Game

1997 Finished second in the National League Most Valuable Player voting behind Colorado's Larry Walker

1999 Had his sixth season with 30 or more home runs and his fourth straight year with 100 or more RBIs

After what he experienced in 1998, the 1999 season must have seemed peaceful to Mike Piazza.

Not only did he have another big season with the bat while helping the New York Mets win the wild-card playoff berth in the National League, Piazza actually got to stay with one team the whole season.

Piazza was in the news the entire 1998 season. He started the year with the Los Angeles Dodgers, the team he began his Major League career with in 1992. On May 15, he was involved in one of the biggest trades in baseball history when the Dodgers dealt him to the Florida Marlins. Stars, such as Gary Sheffield, Bobby Bonilla and Charles Johnson, were sent to Los Angeles in the deal. Since the Marlins were unloading high salaries, it was obvious they were only renting Piazza and would deal him as soon as possible. That happened a week later when he was traded to the Mets.

Rarely is a player of Piazza's stature traded twice in the same season, but it didn't affect what he did on the field. He hit .328 with 32 homers and 111 RBIs.

"Getting traded is part of the game," said Piazza. "You deal with it and keep playing hard."

While moving around the country obviously didn't bother Piazza, he doesn't do too badly when he stays in one place. He had another top season in 1999, hitting .303 with 40 home runs and 124 RBIs, which tied a career high.

Piazza's story should be a lesson that players who aren't high draft picks can go on to be stars in the Majors. Piazza was the Dodgers' 62nd round draft pick in 1988. Most players drafted in that position never make it out of the low minors, but Piazza was an exception. He made it to Los Angeles in 1992 and was the Dodgers' every-day catcher by the next season.

Piazza has played more like a No. 1 draft pick throughout his career. He won the National League Rookie of the Year Award in 1993 by hitting .318 with 35 homers and 112 RBIs.

Piazza, who has made the All-Star team seven times, had one of the best offensive seasons of any catcher in Major League history in 1997. He hit a career-high .362 average, with a .638 slugging average, 40 homers, 124 RBIs, 201 hits, 32 doubles, 355 total bases and 104 runs scored in 152 games.

Piazza showed his toughness during the 1999 season when he played with his numerous injuries throughout the Mets' playoff run. A sore thumb was especially painful, but he kept playing and his home run in the eighth inning tied Game 6 of the National League Championship Series against Atlanta.

"There was no other option," said Piazza. "In the playoffs, you keep going. Injuries don't matter."

Batting

Year	G	AB	R	H	HR	RBI	BB	SO	SB	CS	OBP	SLG	AVG
1999	**141**	**534**	**100**	**162**	**40**	**124**	**51**	**70**	**2**	**2**	**.361**	**.575**	**.303**
Career	**981**	**3653**	**611**	**1200**	**240**	**768**	**381**	**563**	**13**	**13**	**.391**	**.575**	**.328**

Fielding

Year	Posn	G	GS	TC	PO	A	E	DP	FLD%
1999	**C**	**137**	**135**	**1011**	**953**	**47**	**11**	**5**	**.989**
Career		**940**	**921**	**7026**	**6477**	**471**	**78**	**55**	**.989**

YORK
31

Dante Bichette

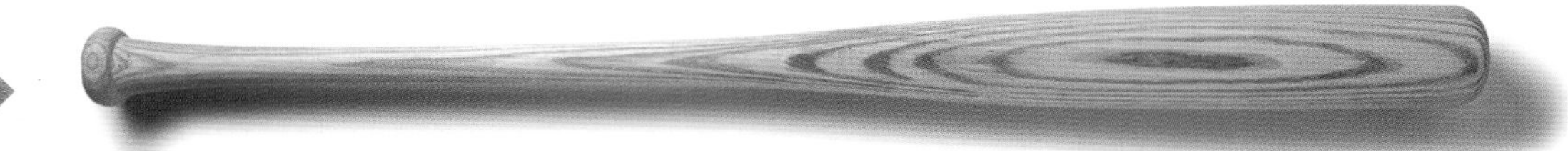

Profile

Name: Alphonse Dante Bichette **Height:** 6–3 **Weight:** 238 **Throws:** Right **Bats:** Right **Position:** Left Field **Born:** November 18, 1963, West Palm Beach, Florida **Drafted:** Selected by the California Angels in the 17th round of the 1984 free-agent draft **Acquired:** Traded by the Colorado Rockies to the Cincinnati Reds, October 30, 1999 **Pre-Majors Highlights:** Played baseball at Palm Beach Junior College, leading his club to the state tournament **Personal Information:** Wrote a column for the Denver Post while playing for the Colorado Rockies

"Dante Bichette's going to hit. As long as he keeps himself in top condition, he should be able to hit for three or four more years." **Cincinnati Reds general manager, Jim Bowden**

Career milestones

1992 Traded from the Milwaukee Brewers to the Colorado Rockies, November 17

1995 Led National League with 40 home runs and finished second to Barry Larkin in Most Valuable Player voting

1998 Led the Major Leagues with 219 hits

1999 Batted .298 with 34 homers and 133 runs batted in

Quick quiz: Who leads the Major Leagues in hits since 1993? It will probably surprise a lot of people to know the answer is Dante Bichette. The left fielder, who was traded from the Colorado Rockies to the Cincinnati Reds on October 30, 1999, has been one of the most consistent hitters in baseball, but has put up good numbers with little publicity. Bichette has 1,111 hits over the last seven years while batting .304 or higher every season.

"Dante Bichette is a pure hitter," said Cincinnati Reds general manager Jim Bowden. "He'll be a great addition to our ballclub."

The Reds pulled off the big trade with the Rockies to get a big bat to replace Greg Vaughn in the middle of their lineup.

"This is exciting for me," said Bichette, who made the National League All-Star team in 1994, 1995, 1996, 1998. "This is a challenge."

As has been the case with most hitters, Bichette took advantage of Denver's high altitude to put up good numbers at Mile High Stadium, then Coors Field. From 1994–98 he hit .369 at home with 105 homers and 404 RBIs, compared with .267 with 41 homers and 200 RBIs on the road in that span. Bichette's numbers were more balanced in 1999. He batted 308 with 20 homers and 82 RBIs at Coors; .287 with 14 homers and 51 RBI away from it.

However, Bichette has also hit well over the years at Cinergy Field, his new home. He compiled a .345 average there as a visiting player (39-for-113) with nine homers and 35 RBI.

"Leaving Coors might knock down some of the numbers, but I'm going to put up the No. 4 numbers," he said

Bowden doesn't care where Bichette hits. He thinks the slugger can put up the numbers in any ballpark.

"This was an opportunity for us to get a 100-RBI bat in the middle of the lineup," Bowden said. "The Reds had four good teams in the '90s: '90, '94, '95 and '99. All four of those teams had a big bat: Eric Davis in 1990, Kevin Mitchell in 1994, Ron Gant in 1995 and Greg Vaughn. It's very important to have that bat; that's how you build the lineup."

Bichette played a big role in building the Colorado franchise. He was the only player to be on the Rockies' Major League roster every day of the franchise's existence. His best season came in 1995 when the Rockies won the National League wild card spot as Bichette hit 40 homers with 128 RBIs, both league highs.

Even Vaughn, who was a teammate of Bichette's in Milwaukee from 1991–92, thinks the Reds have made a good acquisition.

"He's a good guy," said Vaughn. "The city of Cincinnati will love him. It should be a good fit."

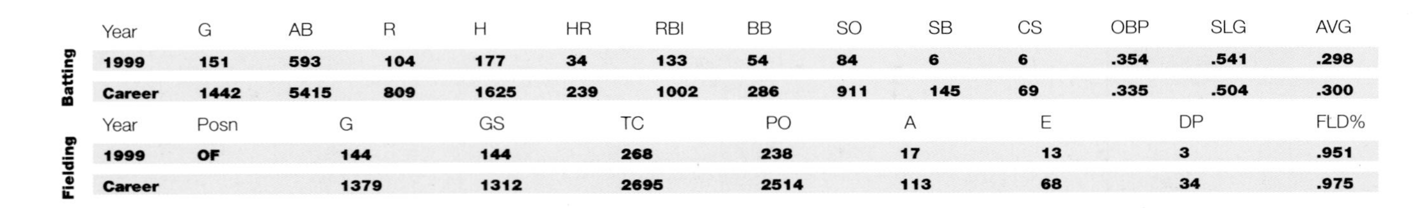

Batting

Year	G	AB	R	H	HR	RBI	BB	SO	SB	CS	OBP	SLG	AVG
1999	**151**	**593**	**104**	**177**	**34**	**133**	**54**	**84**	**6**	**6**	**.354**	**.541**	**.298**
Career	**1442**	**5415**	**809**	**1625**	**239**	**1002**	**286**	**911**	**145**	**69**	**.335**	**.504**	**.300**

Fielding

Year	Posn	G	GS	TC	PO	A	E	DP	FLD%
1999	**OF**	**144**	**144**	**268**	**238**	**17**	**13**	**3**	**.951**
Career		**1379**	**1312**	**2695**	**2514**	**113**	**68**	**34**	**.975**

Alex Fernandez

Profile

Name: Alexander Fernandez **Height:** 6–1 **Weight:** 225 **Throws:** Right **Bats:** Right **Position:** Pitcher **Born:** August 13, 1969, Miami Beach, Florida **Drafted:** Selected by the White Sox in the first round (fourth pick overall) of the 1990 free-agent draft **Acquired:** Signed by the Marlins as a free agent on December 9, 1996 **Pre-Majors Highlights:** Named the National Junior College Player of the Year at Miami-Dade South Community College for the 1990 season **Personal Information:** Named Baseball America's Freshman of the Year while at the University of Miami

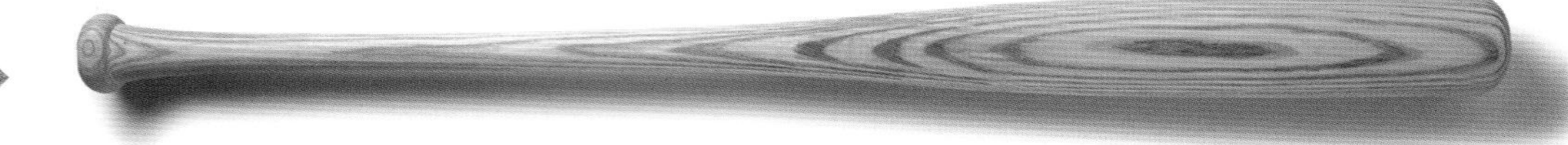

"I'm proud of my season and of the organization for supporting me in my comeback. This will help me come back stronger for next year." **Florida Marlins pitcher, Alex Fernandez**

Career milestones

1993 Had his best season when he went 18–9 with a 3.13 ERA in 34 starts with the Chicago White Sox

1994 Named American League Player of the Month in July after going 5–0 in six starts

1997 Collected a Florida club-record 17 wins. Pitched a one-hitter April 10 against the Chicago Cubs, losing the no-hitter with one out in the bottom of the ninth.

The highlight of Alex Fernandez's career came when he signed with the Florida Marlins on December 9, 1996.

The contract, which pays $7 million a season, made Fernandez one of the highest-paid players in the game. It also gave the Marlins one of the best pitchers in the game and it appeared Fernandez would be a key figure for Florida for several years.

Fernandez, who complied a 79–63 record while pitching for the Chicago White Sox fom 1990–96, helped the Marlins win the wild-card playoff berth in the National League. The right-hander was 17–12 with a 3.59 earned run average while pitching five complete games and one shutout.

Fernandez also won a game in the Division Series against San Francisco by holding the Giants to two runs in seven innings. Little did Fernandez or the Marlins know that would be his last highlight for almost two years. After lasting only 2.2 innings against the Atlanta Braves in Game 2 of the Championship Series, doctors discovered Fernandez had torn the rotator cuff in his right shoulder, an injury that would require surgery. While the Marlins celebrated their World Series win over the Cleveland Indians, Fernandez had surgery on October 29.

The prognosis wasn't good. Fernandez was told he'd miss the entire 1998 season and there was a chance his career was over.

"I knew the situation," said Fernandez. "I knew I would have to work hard to get back to where I was."

That's exactly what Fernandez did. He went through a rigorous rehabilitation program during the 1998 season and finally made it back to the mound in 1999. For someone whose career was in jeopardy, Fernandez had a solid season. He finished with a 7–8 record and a 3.38 ERA in 24 starts, which included one complete game.

The Marlins were cautious with Fernandez, who was on a 100-pitch limit all season. He spent two separate stints on the disabled list, once with soreness in the shoulder and the other time because of a pulled groin. The Marlins decided not to pitch him in the last month of the season as a precaution.

"There was no need to hurt myself," Fernandez said. "I could pitch but it's better for me to rehab and get ready for next season. It was frustrating not having my best stuff day in and day out and having to put three hours of work in just to go out there and pitch."

Fernandez and the Marlins expect him to come back stronger in the 2000 season. If that happens, he could draw some interest from contending teams looking for an ace pitcher. Fernandez thinks he has learned a lesson from his injury.

"I think it made me a better pitcher," he said.

Pitching

Year	W	L	ERA	G	GS	CG	SHO	SV	SVO	INN	H	R	ER	HR	HBP	BB	SO
1999	**7**	**8**	**3.38**	**24**	**24**	**1**	**0**	**0**	**0**	**141.0**	**135**	**60**	**53**	**10**	**4**	**41**	**91**
Career	**103**	**83**	**3.73**	**255**	**253**	**33**	**10**	**0**	**0**	**1708.0**	**1634**	**779**	**707**	**183**	**35**	**536**	**1225**

Batting

Year	G	AB	R	H	HR	RBI	BB	SO	SB	CS	OBP	SLG	AVG
Career	**257**	**109**	**6**	**20**	**3**	**11**	**6**	**25**	**0**	**0**	**.224**	**.330**	**.183**

Fielding

Year	Posn	G	GS	TC	PO	A	E	DP	FLD%
1999	**P**	**24**	**24**	**35**	**7**	**27**	**1**	**3**	**.971**
Career		**255**	**253**	**423**	**119**	**289**	**15**	**31**	**.965**

Profile

Name: Thomas Michael Glavine
Height: 6–0 **Weight:** 185
Throws: Left **Bats:** Left **Position:** Pitcher
Born: March 25, 1966, Concord, Massachusetts
Drafted: Selected by the Atlanta Braves in the second round of the 1984 free-agent draft **Pre-Majors Highlight:** Was drafted by two professional sports teams, in the second round by the Atlanta Braves and in the fourth round by the Los Angeles Kings of the NHL **Personal Information:** Brother, Mike, is a first baseman in the Atlanta Braves farm system

Tom Glavine

"Tommy's numbers say it all. There isn't much he hasn't done in this game."

Atlanta Braves manager, Bobby Cox

Career milestones

1991 Was named National League Cy Young Award winner
1995 Was named Most Valuable Player of the World Series
1997 Ranked fifth in the National League with 240 innings pitched, and seventh in earned run average at 2.96
1998 Was named National League Cy Young Award winner

When it came to the National League standings, the Atlanta Braves owned the 1990s. When it came to pitching, Tom Glavine owned the 1990s.

The Braves won the National League championship six times and won the World Series in 1995. During that time, Glavine was one of the dominant pitchers in the '90s by compiling a 164–87 record with a 3.21 earned run average. He's also been the winningest left-handed pitcher in baseball over the last 10 years.

"For a pitcher, consistency is the big thing," said Glavine. "That's all a pitcher can ask for, to stay healthy and pitch a lot of innings."

Along with Greg Maddux and John Smoltz, Glavine has helped the Braves form the best rotation in baseball in this era.

Glavine recovered from a rocky rookie season in 1988, in which he finished with a 7–17 record and a 4.56 ERA. Even though he led the league in losses, the Braves never had any intention of giving up on him.

"The numbers didn't show it, but we knew Tommy had what it took to be a good pitcher," said Cox. "We knew back then he had a real chance to be something special."

After a 14–8 record and a 3.68 ERA the following season, Glavine's numbers fell off in 1990 when he went 10–12 with a 4.28 ERA. That's the last time hitters got the best of Glavine, whose career took off the same time the Braves began dominating the National League.

In 1991, the year the Braves went from finishing last in the National League East to reaching the World Series, Glavine finished 20–11 with a 2.55 ERA, led the league with nine complete games and won the Cy Young Award. That started a three-year run in which he led the league in wins for three straight seasons. Glavine was 20–8 with a 2.76 ERA and a league-leading five shutouts in 1992 before going 22–6 with a 3.20 ERA and a league-high 36 starts the following year.

While winning 58 games the next four years, Glavine's next dominant season came in 1998 when he won his second Cy Young Award and led the league in victories again, finishing 20–6 with a 2.47 ERA.

Glavine has been especially effective in the World Series. He was the Most Valuable player of the 1995 Series when he pitched two classic games against the hard-hitting Cleveland Indians. In two starts, Glavine was 2–0 with a 1.29 ERA, allowing two runs and four hits in 14 innings. He held the Indians to one hit in eight innings in Game 6 as the Braves clinched the Series with a 1–0 win.

"That's something I'll always remember," said Glavine. "It's a big thrill to pitch that well with so much at stake."

Since he's turns 34 years old during spring training 2000, there should be plenty of thrills ahead for Glavine.

Pitching

Year	W	L	ERA	G	GS	CG	SHO	SV	SVO	INN	H	R	ER	HR	HBP	BB	SO
1999	**14**	**11**	**4.12**	**35**	**35**	**2**	**0**	**0**	**0**	**234.0**	**259**	**115**	**107**	**18**	**4**	**83**	**138**
Career	**187**	**116**	**3.38**	**399**	**399**	**45**	**18**	**0**	**0**	**2659.2**	**2529**	**1110**	**1000**	**178**	**36**	**900**	**1659**

Batting

Year	G	AB	R	H	HR	RBI	BB	SO	SB	CS	OBP	SLG	AVG
Career	**418**	**831**	**62**	**166**	**1**	**62**	**55**	**211**	**1**	**0**	**.251**	**.227**	**.200**

Fielding

Year	Posn	G	GS	TC	PO	A	E	DP	FLD%
1999	**P**	**35**	**35**	**72**	**12**	**59**	**1**	**6**	**.986**
Career		**399**	**399**	**693**	**168**	**507**	**18**	**39**	**.974**

Profile

Name: David Christopher Justice **Height:** 6-3 **Weight:** 200 **Throws:** Left **Bats:** Left **Positions:** Left Field, Designated Hitter **Born:** April 14, 1966, Cincinnati, Ohio **Drafted:** Selected by the Atlanta Braves in the fourth round of the 1985 free-agent draft **Acquired:** Traded by the Atlanta Braves to the Cleveland Indians, March 25, 1997 **Pre-Majors Highlight:** Hit 10 home runs to lead Appalachian League in 1985 **Personal Information:** Attended Thomas More College in Crestview Hills, Kentucky

David Justice

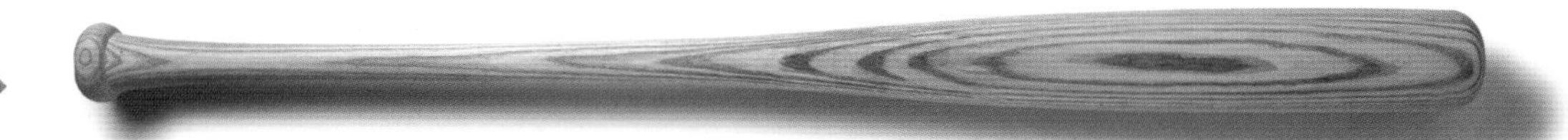

"At this point in my career, it's all about winning. That's what we play for and that's all that really matters."

Cleveland Indians outfielder, David Justice

Career milestones

1990 Was named National League Rookie of the Year in 1990

1993 Finished third in National League Most Valuable Player voting

1997 Was named Comeback Player of the Year by The Sporting News

1998 Hit 200th career homer May 3 vs. Tampa Bay and collected 1000th career hit May 24 vs. Toronto

David Justice knows he's been a lucky man. In his 10-year Major League career, Justice's name has become synonymous with postseason play. With the exception of 1994 when the players' strike canceled the World Series, the two teams Justice has played for—the Atlanta Braves and the Cleveland Indians—have qualified for the playoffs.

"There have been some great players who have gone their whole careers and never been in the postseason," he said. "I've been in the World Series five times. That's awesome."

Justice made it to the Series with the Braves in 1991, 1992, 1995 and 1996 before getting there with the Indians in 1997. The Braves also won the National League East Division title in 1993 while the Indians were American League Central Division champs the last two seasons.

"I feel very fortunate," said Justice. "I feel very blessed to be a part of so many winning teams."

Justice has been a big part of his teams' success. Ironically, his greatest moment came in the 1995 World Series when the Braves defeated the Indians. His home run in Game 6 was the decisive hit that gave the Braves the 1–0 win to clinch the championship.

Justice was named the National League Rookie of the Year in 1990 after hitting .282 with 28 homers and 78 runs batted in. He made a serious run at the league's Most Valuable Player Award in 1993 when he finished third in the voting after hitting 40 homers with 120 RBI.

Justice was involved in one of the biggest trades of the decade when the Braves sent him to the Indians on March 27, 1997. Justice and outfielder Marquis Grissom were traded to the Indians for outfielder Kenny Lofton and pitcher Alan Embree. Justice, Grissom and Lofton were all star players at the time. It's rare players of that caliber are traded for each other.

Justice, who played in only 40 games in 1996 because of a separated shoulder. flourished in his first year in the American League. He hit .329 with 33 homers and 101 RBIs. The numbers earned him the league's Comeback Player of the Year Award.

As the injuries have piled up during his career, Justice has seen more action at designated hitter. It's a role he has mixed emotions about.

"In my first seven years in the big leagues I played both sides of the game," he said. "Coming up I knew nothing but playing both sides. I was used to playing the outfield. When you're not hitting, you feel like you're not helping the team at all. If you're in the outfield, you at least feel like you're contributing something defensively if you aren't hitting."

Justice's contributions likely will continue. And look for them to continue well into October each season.

Batting

Year	G	AB	R	H	HR	RBI	BB	SO	SB	CS	OBP	SLG	AVG
1999	**151**	**593**	**104**	**177**	**34**	**133**	**54**	**84**	**6**	**6**	**.354**	**.541**	**.298**
Career	**1442**	**5415**	**809**	**1625**	**239**	**1002**	**286**	**911**	**145**	**69**	**.335**	**.504**	**.300**

Fielding

Year	Posn	G	GS	TC	PO	A	E	DP	FLD%
1999	**OF**	**144**	**144**	**268**	**238**	**17**	**13**	**3**	**.951**
Career		**1379**	**1312**	**2695**	**2514**	**113**	**68**	**34**	**.975**

EASTON

Frank Thomas

Profile

Name: Frank Edward Thomas **Height:** 6–5 **Weight:** 270 **Throws:** Right **Bats:** Right **Positions:** Designated Hitter, First Base **Born:** May 27, 1968, Columbus, Georgia **Drafted:** Selected by the Chicago White Sox in the first round (seventh pick overall) of the 1989 free-agent draft **Pre-Majors Highlights:** Batted .323 at Class AA Birmingham in 1990 **Personal Information:** Originally signed a football scholarship with Auburn in 1986 and played in only one game as a freshman, catching three passes for a total of 45 yards as a tight end. Quit football after one year to concentrate on baseball

"Frank makes your lineup better just by being in it. Teams always know he's there."

Chicago White Sox manager, Jerry Manuel

Career milestones

1990 Batted .330 in 60 games in rookie season with the Chicago White Sox

1991 Named designated hitter on The Sporting News All-Star team

1993 Named American League Most Valuable Player and Player of the Year by The Sporting News

1994 Named American League Most Valuable Player.

1997 Led American League in hitting

It doesn't take long to figure out why Frank Thomas is called "The Big Hurt".

First, just take a look at him. The man is 6-foot-5 and 270 pounds. Put him in the batter's box and he's an intimidating force for any pitcher. Thomas looks more like a tight end in the National Football League than he does a baseball player. In fact, he almost took another career path. Thomas was recruited by Auburn University to play tight end, but quit after his freshman year to play baseball.

Second, take a look at the numbers Thomas has posted in his career with the Chicago White Sox. He batted .308 or higher in his first eight years in the big leagues from 1990–97. That included seasons in which he won the American League Most Valuable Player Award in 1993 and 1994 and led the league in hitting in 1997.

Thomas' MVP years were two of the best back-to-back seasons by a right-handed hitter in Major League history. In 1993, he batted .317 with 41 home runs and 128 runs batted in. Thomas followed that with a .353 average, 38 homers and 101 RBIs in 1994. His batting title came in 1997 with a .341 average.

Thomas was named to the American League All-Star team five straight seasons from 1993–97.

Even though Thomas' production has slipped the last two seasons, most players would still be envious of his numbers. He hit .265 with 29 homers and 109 RBIs in 1998 while batting .305 with 15 homers and 77 RBIs in 1999. Thomas' production was cut short because of season-ending surgery on September 13 to remove a bone spur from his right ankle. The injury bothered Thomas throughout the second half of 1999 and obviously affected his numbers. He was limited to 135 games.

"He's a very dangerous hitter," said White Sox manager Jerry Manuel. "Frank can carry a team for a long time."

Thomas also shows a talent most power hitters don't have. He is one of the most patient hitters in baseball. He has drawn 109 or more walks in each year in which he has played a full season. Thomas has led the league five times and drew a career-high 138 walks in 1991.

"He doesn't swing at bad pitches," said Manuel. "That's what makes him so tough to pitch to."

"I think being patient is a big key for me," said Thomas. "If I swing at bad pitches, I get out of my game. If I stay patient I think it makes me a better hitter."

After being a first baseman for most of his career, Thomas has primarily been the White Sox designated hitter the last two seasons. The team would like for him to return to first base and hopes the ankle surgery will allow him to do that.

Opposing pitches can be sure Thomas will continue to live up to his nickname.

Batting

Year	G	AB	R	H	HR	RBI	BB	SO	SB	CS	OBP	SLG	AVG
1999	**135**	**486**	**74**	**148**	**15**	**77**	**87**	**66**	**3**	**3**	**.414**	**.471**	**.305**
Career	**1371**	**4892**	**968**	**1564**	**301**	**1040**	**1076**	**741**	**28**	**18**	**.440**	**.573**	**.320**

Fielding

Year	Posn	G	GS	TC	PO	A	E	DP	FLD%
1999	**1B**	**49**	**49**	**407**	**385**	**18**	**4**	**40**	**.990**
Career		**903**	**900**	**7888**	**7348**	**465**	**75**	**710**	**.990**

franklin

Robin Ventura

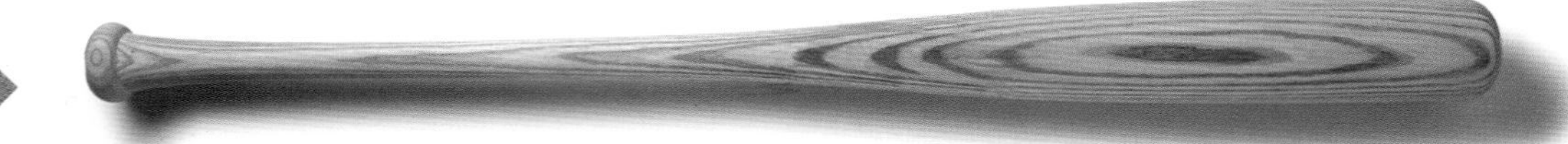

Profile

Name: Robin Mark Ventura **Height:** 6–1 **Weight:** 198 **Throws:** Right **Bats:** Left **Position:** Third Base **Born:** July 14, 1967, Santa Maria, California **Drafted:** Selected by the Chicago White Sox in the first round (10th pick overall) of the 1988 free-agent draft **Acquired:** Signed as a free agent by the New York Mets, December 1, 1998 **Pre-Majors Highlights:** Attended Oklahoma State University, where he had a 58-game hitting streak in 1987 **Personal Information:** Helped lead the U.S. Olympic Team to a gold medal, batting .409 in Seoul in 1988

"Robin is one of the best third basemen I've ever seen. He makes all the plays and stabilizes our infield."

New York Mets manager, Bobby Valentine

Career milestones

1991 Won American League Gold Glove
1992 Won American League Gold Glove
1993 Won American League Gold Glove
1996 Drove in a career-high 105 runs. Won American League Gold Glove
1998 Hit his 10th career grand slam on August 24 at Seattle. Won American League Gold Glove
1999 Won National League Gold Glove

The American League and National League hand out Comeback Player of the Year Awards after each season. Robin Ventura qualifies for the Comeback Player of the Decade Award.

While playing for the Chicago White Sox, Ventura suffered a horrifying leg injury in a spring-training game against the Boston Red Sox. The injury, which occurred while Ventura was sliding into home plate, resulted in a compound fracture in his right leg and a dislocated ankle. The injury was so gruesome many players on the field looked away and a woman in the stands fainted.

Many believed Ventura's career was over and there was serious doubt how effective he would be if he did come back.

Ventura proved all the doubters wrong. Not only was he back before the 1997 season ended, he is still one of the top third basemen in the game.

"I know a lot of people didn't think I could come back, but I never had any doubts," Ventura said. "I always believed I'd be back and that I'd be back at 100 percent."

Ventura was back in the White Sox lineup by July 24. He batted .262 with six homers and 26 RBIs in 54 games and followed that up with a solid season in 1998. Ventura batted .263 with 21 homers and 91 RBIs. He also won his fifth American League Gold Glove. Brooks Robinson (16) and Buddy Bell (six) are the only American League third basemen to win more Gold Gloves.

Ventura, who signed with the New York Mets on December 8, 1998, had the best year of his career in 1999. He batted .301 with 32 home runs and 120 RBIs. The batting average and RBI totals were career highs while the home-run mark was two of the career best of 34, which he hit in 1996 with the White Sox.

Ventura also won his sixth career Gold Glove and his first in the National League after committing only nine errors all season. He played a major role in the Mets' first playoff appearance since 1988, which resulted in New York winning the wild-card playoff berth in the National League. The Mets defeated the Arizona Diamondbacks in the Division Series and took the Atlanta Braves to six games in the National League Championship Series before being eliminated.

Ventura has driven in 100 or more runs three times in his career and has hit 20 or more homers six times.

Ventura came to the big leagues as one of the top players in the history of college baseball. Baseball America named him College Player of the Decade and the third baseman on college's All-Time Team. He also ranks first in College Baseball World Series history with a .459 batting average.

Batting

Year	G	AB	R	H	HR	RBI	BB	SO	SB	CS	OBP	SLG	AVG
1999	**161**	**588**	**88**	**177**	**32**	**120**	**74**	**109**	**1**	**1**	**.379**	**.529**	**.301**
Career	**1415**	**5130**	**746**	**1421**	**203**	**861**	**742**	**768**	**16**	**27**	**.366**	**.450**	**.277**

Fielding

Year	Posn	G	GS	TC	PO	A	E	DP	FLD%
1999	**3B**	**160**	**157**	**452**	**123**	**320**	**9**	**33**	**.980**
Career		**1401**	**1366**	**4175**	**1376**	**2636**	**163**	**300**	**.961**

Ray Lankford

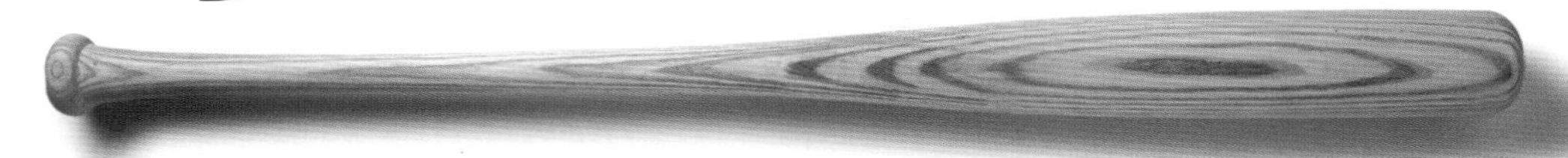

Profile

Name: Raymond Lewis Lankford **Height:** 5-11 **Weight:** 200 **Throws:** Left **Bats:** Left **Position:** Left Field **Born:** June 5, 1967, Modesto, California **Drafted:** Selected by the St. Louis Cardinals in the third round of the 1987 free-agent draft **Pre-Majors Highlights:** Became first running back to rush for 1,000 yards in a season for the Modesto Junior College football team **Personal Information:** Nephew of Carl Nichols, catcher with Baltimore Orioles (1986–88) and Houston Astros (1989–91)

"Ray has done a solid job for us. He has driven in some big runs and given us some protection behind Mark (McGwire)." **St. Louis manager, Tony LaRussa**

Career milestones

1991 Finished third in the National League Rookie of the Year voting
1996 Played 108 games before committing an error
1997 Named to National League All-Star Team. Hit 31 home runs
1998 Equaled his career best with 31 homers and set a personal high with 105 runs batted in

Thanks to a teammate who has achieved a high level of fame the last few years, St. Louis Cardinals outfielder Ray Lankford is one of the best-kept secrets in Major League Baseball.

Mark McGwire's quest of home run records the last two years has captivated baseball fans everywhere. It has made headlines not only in St. Louis, but around the world, making his Cardinals teammates seem like bit players at times to people who don't follow the game.

Make no mistake about this. Lankford is no bit player. The left-handed hitter puts up solid numbers every year and has a combination of skills any team would want to have in its lineup. Lankford hits for high average, he hits for power, he drives in runs, he steals bases and is a good defensive player.

With McGwire belting pitches out of the park, Lankford's numbers in 1997 and 1998 almost went unnoticed. He hit .295 with 31 homers and 98 runs batted in while stealing 21 bases in 1997. Lankford followed that by hitting .293 with 31 homers, 105 RBIs and 26 steals. The 31 homers and105 RBIs are both career highs.

Lankford's production fell off a bit in 1999 only playing in 122 games because of sore knees and a pulled abdominal muscle. He hit 15 homers and drove in 63 runs, but still batted a career-high .306 and stole 14 bases. It was the first time he hit .300 in his career after coming close the previous years.

Consistency has been one of Lankford's strengths. He has topped the .290 mark five times, has hit 20 or more home runs five times and has driven in 82 or more runs five times. He also has topped the 20 stolen base mark six times and has hit 32 or more doubles six times. Lankford also has scored 81 or more runs seven times, including a career-high 100 in 1996.

It didn't take long for Lankford to make it to the big leagues after being drafted by the Cardinals in 1987. He was in the Majors by 1990 and has been an every-day outfielder in the St. Louis lineup since. In 1991—his first full season in the big leagues—Lankford led the National League with 15 triples and stole a career-high 44 bases.

Lankford's versatility makes him a valuable player in the lineup. He can hit high in the order to take advantage of his speed and base-stealing ability. His run production makes him a good middle-of-the-order hitter.

Lankford's knee problems forced him to move from center field, the position he played most of his career, to left field. He made the adjustment well and had an excellent season defensively committing just three errors. The Cardinals think the knee problems cut down on his power and they are confident his numbers will go up in 2000.

Batting

Year	G	AB	R	H	HR	RBI	BB	SO	SB	CS	OBP	SLG	AVG
1999	**122**	**422**	**77**	**129**	**15**	**63**	**49**	**110**	**14**	**4**	**.380**	**.493**	**.306**
Career	**1269**	**4561**	**781**	**1267**	**181**	**703**	**637**	**1141**	**239**	**105**	**.367**	**.480**	**.278**

Fielding

Year	Posn	G	GS	TC	PO	A	E	DP	FLD%
1999	**OF**	**106**	**103**	**223**	**214**	**6**	**3**	**0**	**.987**
Career		**1217**	**1170**	**3070**	**2970**	**57**	**43**	**9**	**.986**

Roberto Alomar

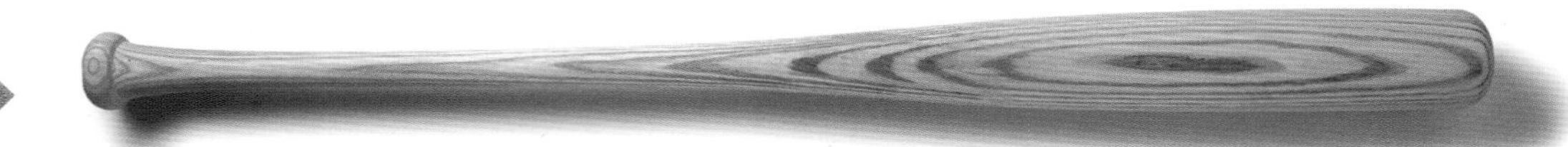

Profile

Name: Roberto Velazquez Alomar
Height: 6–0 **Weight:** 185 **Throws:** Right **Bats:** Both **Position:** Second Base
Born: February 5, 1968, Ponce, Puerto Rico
Drafted: Signed as an undrafted free agent by the San Diego Padres, February 16, 1985 **Acquired:** Signed as a free agent by the Cleveland Indians, November 24, 1998
Pre-Majors Highlight: Led California League with .346 average at Class A Reno, 1986
Personal Information: Father, Sandy Sr., played in the Major Leagues from 1964-78. Brother, Sandy Jr., plays for the Cleveland Indians

"Robbie is truly an artist. He's a potential future Hall of Famer."

Cleveland Indians general manager, John Hart

Career milestones

1991 Won first of eight American League Gold Glove Awards
1992 Was named Most Valuable Player of American League Championship Series
1996 Had 22-game hitting streak, the second-longest in Baltimore Orioles history
1998 Was named Most Valuable Player of All-Star Game MVP
1999 Drove in 129 runs, topping the 100-RBI mark for the first time in his career

When the Cleveland Indians signed Roberto Alomar on November 24, 1998, they knew they had acquired one of the best all-around players in Major League baseball today.

Alomar proved that assumption correct, and more by having one of the most complete seasons in team history. At the plate, the switch-hitter batted .323 with 138 runs scored, 40 doubles, 24 home runs, 120 runs batted in, 99 walks and 37 stolen bases. In the field, he won his eighth Gold Glove Award and made spectacular plays throughout the season.

Alomar provided whatever the Indians needed at a particular time, whether it was hitting a homer, driving in a run, advancing a runner, bunting, stealing a base or making a great play in the field.

"Robbie has the ability to take a walk to get on base, to steal a base, to score a big run," said Indians general manager John Hart. "He has the ability defensively to make the big play."

Even Hart, who had been trying to acquire Alomar since 1996, had to admit he was a little surprised about how good Alomar really is.

"Until you see Robbie play every day and see what he brings to your team you don't appreciate how good he is," said Hart.

Alomar, who appeared in his 10th All-Star Game in 1999 reached his previous career high in RBIs in late August. He cracked 100 soon after that.

"That's real special," he said of hitting the 100 RBI mark. "I never thought I would get there."

Alomar's biggest contribution has been his play at second base. The Indians searched to fill that hole for three years.

"I always take great pride in my defense," he said. "You can win a lot of games hitting, but you can win more with defense. Sometimes defense gets overlooked, but it's so important. Defense is the most important part of the game to me."

Alomar is no stranger to winning. He was a member of the Toronto Blue Jays teams that won the World Series in 1992 and 1993. Alomar is at his best when it counts the most. He's a career .347 hitter with six home runs in two World Series. In five League Championship Series, he has three homers and 15 RBIs with a .316 average. In three Division Series, he's a .327 hitter with a home run and nine RBIs.

Signing with the Indians was important to Alomar because he is now teammates with his brother, Sandy, the team's catcher.

"It's always been our dream to play together," he said. "We want to win a World Series together. That's always been our ultimate dream."

For Indians fans, watching Alomar has been like the ultimate dream.

Batting

Year	G	AB	R	H	HR	RBI	BB	SO	SB	CS	OBP	SLG	AVG
1999	**159**	**563**	**138**	**182**	**24**	**120**	**99**	**96**	**37**	**6**	**.422**	**.533**	**.323**
Career	**1722**	**6611**	**1117**	**2007**	**151**	**829**	**758**	**796**	**377**	**96**	**.375**	**.446**	**.304**

Fielding

Year	Posn	G	GS	TC	PO	A	E	DP	FLD%
1999	**2B**	**156**	**154**	**742**	**270**	**466**	**6**	**102**	**.992**
Career		**1686**	**1660**	**8341**	**3301**	**4901**	**139**	**1009**	**.983**

Profile

Name: Michael Cole Mussina **Height:** 6–2 **Weight:** 185 **Throws:** Right **Bats:** Both **Position:** Pitcher **Born:** December 8, 1968, Williamsport, Pennslyvania **Drafted:** Selected by the Baltimore Orioles in the first round (20th pick overall) of the 1990 free-agent draft **Pre-Majors Highlights:** Was a star pitcher at Stanford University. Finished his career with a 25–12 record, tied for sixth most wins in school history **Personal Information:** Was offered a football scholarship to Penn State after kicking a 60-yard field goal in a Penn State football camp

Mike Mussina

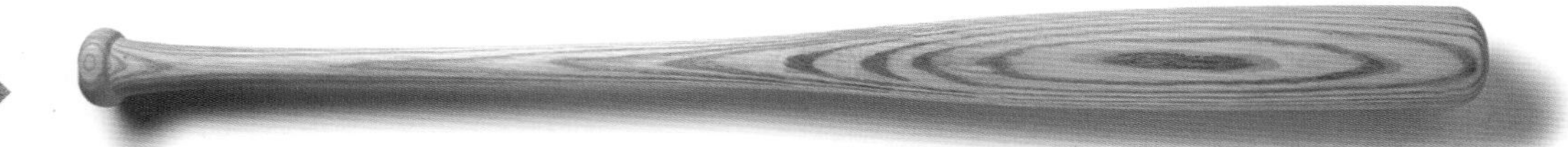

"Mike Mussina is a winner. I'm looking forward to being on his side."

Baltimore Orioles manager, Mike Hargrove

Career milestones

1992 Named to first American League All-Star team

1996 Won American League Gold Glove

1997 Recorded 100th career win vs. Philadelphia, June 30. Won American League Gold Glove

1998 Won American League Gold Glove

1999 Named to fifth American League All-Star team. Also made team in 1993, 1994 and 1997

While the Baltimore Orioles have been a disappointment the last two seasons, the same can't be said for ace starter Mike Mussina.

The right-hander is one of the top starting pitchers in Major League Baseball today. If wins and innings pitched are the barometer for a successful pitcher, Mussina ranks high in both categories. He has averaged 17 wins and 211 innings pitched since his first full season in the big leagues in 1992.

Mussina has no bigger fans than his managers. They know every fifth day they can count on him to pitch well and their team has a good chance to win.

"You give Mike the ball and you know he'll go deep into the game," said former Orioles manager Ray Miller, who was fired at the end of the 1999 season. "You know Mike will keep you in the game."

Consistency has been Mussina's trademark. He has won at least 13 games in each of the last seven seasons and has threatened the 20-win mark on three occasions. His best season came in 1992 when he finished with an 18–5 record, had the highest winning percentage in the league (.783) and posted a 2.54 earned run average.

"It means a lot to be able to pitch innings and be consistent," said Mussina. "That's what a starting pitcher is supposed to do."

Mussina surely would have hit the 20-win plateau in 1995 if not for the players' strike that canceled the 1994 World Series and the first month of the '95 season. He went 19–9 with a league-high four shutouts and seven complete games. The strike cost him at least three or four starts and his chance at 20 wins.

Mussina followed that with another solid year in 1997, going 15–8 with a 3.20 ERA and starting a league-high 36 games.

Although the Orioles were one of the biggest disappointments in baseball in 1999, Mussina had another solid season. He finished the season with an 18–7 record, tying him for second in the league in wins, and a 3.50 ERA.

Mussina almost pitched himself into the record books when he came within two outs of a perfect game against the Cleveland Indians on May 30, 1997. The perfect game was broken up by a one-out single in the ninth by Sandy Alomar Jr.

In addition to pitching, Mussina helps himself win in another area. He has won the American League Gold Glove three times (1996–98).

It's easy to see why Mussina has made the American League All-Star team five times (1992, 1993, 1994, 1997 and 1999). Since he will be only 31 at the start of the 2000 season, it's also easy to see why he should continue to be one of the top pitchers in baseball well into the new century.

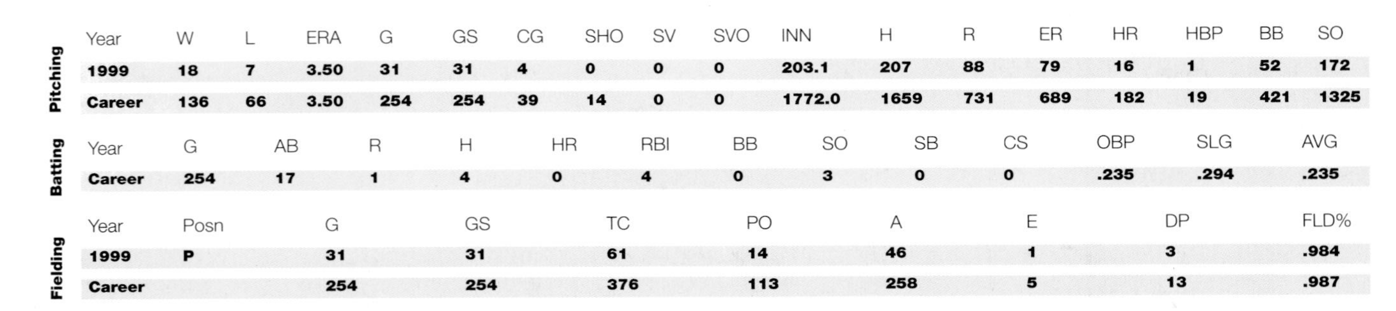

Pitching

Year	W	L	ERA	G	GS	CG	SHO	SV	SVO	INN	H	R	ER	HR	HBP	BB	SO
1999	**18**	**7**	**3.50**	**31**	**31**	**4**	**0**	**0**	**0**	**203.1**	**207**	**88**	**79**	**16**	**1**	**52**	**172**
Career	**136**	**66**	**3.50**	**254**	**254**	**39**	**14**	**0**	**0**	**1772.0**	**1659**	**731**	**689**	**182**	**19**	**421**	**1325**

Batting

Year	G	AB	R	H	HR	RBI	BB	SO	SB	CS	OBP	SLG	AVG
Career	**254**	**17**	**1**	**4**	**0**	**4**	**0**	**3**	**0**	**0**	**.235**	**.294**	**.235**

Fielding

Year	Posn	G	GS	TC	PO	A	E	DP	FLD%
1999	**P**	**31**	**31**	**61**	**14**	**46**	**1**	**3**	**.984**
Career		**254**	**254**	**376**	**113**	**258**	**5**	**13**	**.987**

Orioles
35

Profile

Name:
Jeffrey Robert Bagwell
Height: 6-0 **Weight:** 195 **Throws:** Right **Bats:** Right **Position:** First Base
Born: May 27, 1968, Boston, Massachusetts
Drafted: Selected by the Boston Red Sox in the fourth round of the 1989 free-agent draft **Acquired:** Traded by the Boston Red Sox to the Houston Astros on August 31, 1990 **Pre-Majors Highlights:** Led the Eastern League in hits (160) in 1990
Personal Information:
Attended Hartford University

Jeff Bagwell

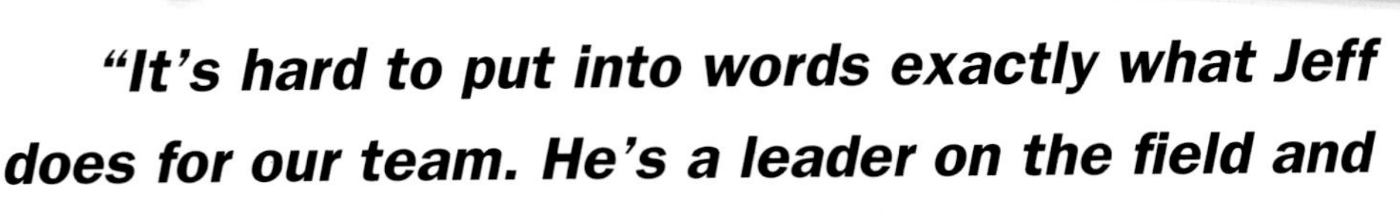

"It's hard to put into words exactly what Jeff does for our team. He's a leader on the field and in the clubhouse." **Houston Astros manager, Larry Dierker**

Career milestones

1991 Named National League Rookie of the Year
1994 Named National Most Valuable Player, led league in runs batted in and won Gold Glove
1998 Became the first player in Houston franchise history to hit 30 home runs and steal 30 bases in one season
1999 Became the first player in club history to have 100-or-more RBI in three consecutive seasons

Houston Astros fans will never forget the date August 31, 1990. It will go down as one of the most important days in the history of the franchise.

On that day, the Astros sent journeyman relief pitcher Larry Andersen to the Boston Red Sox for a young infield prospect named Jeff Bagwell. The Red Sox made the trade to bolster their bullpen for the playoff drive that season.

Little did anyone know Bagwell would bolster the Astros' playoff drive through the rest of the 1990s and become one of the top power hitters in Major League baseball.

The ultimate irony about the trade is Bagwell, who grew up in New England, had a life-long dream of playing for the Red Sox. It looked liked that would come true when Boston selected Bagwell in the fourth round of the 1989 free-agent draft. He was working his way up in the Red Sox minor-league farm system when fate intervened and sent him to Houston and future stardom.

"At first it was hard because I always wanted to play for the Sox and play in Fenway (Park), but it couldn't have worked out better," said Bagwell.

Boston fans finally got a chance to see Bagwell play in Fenway Park last season when the Red Sox hosted the All-Star Game. Of course, it came after Bagwell averaged 25 homers and 93 runs batted in over the nine years since he joined the Astros. The All-Star Game appearance was the fourth of Bagwell's career.

Bagwell is one of the few power hitters who is a threat to run once he gets on base. He has averaged 18 stolen bases over the last nine years, including a career-high 31 in 1997 and 30 in 1999.

"Jeff has the ability to do a lot of things," said Houston Astros manager Larry Dierker. "He can do a lot of things to help us win."

Bagwell had another big season in 1999 as the Astros won their third straight national League Central title. He batted .304 with 42 homers,126 RBIs and 30 stolen bases. His best season came in 1997 when he was named the winner of The Sporting News Silver Slugger Award as the best offensive player at his position. He established club single season records for home runs (43), RBIs (135), total bases (335) and extra base hits (85).

Bagwell, who led the National League with 116 RBIs in 1994, also is one of the game's iron men. He has appeared in all of Houston's 162 games four times (1992, 1996, 1997 and 1999).

While the trade from his beloved Red Sox shattered one dream for Bagwell, it catapulted him to stardom and will always be remembered in Houston.

Batting

Year	G	AB	R	H	HR	RBI	BB	SO	SB	CS	OBP	SLG	AVG
1999	**162**	**562**	**143**	**171**	**42**	**126**	**149**	**127**	**30**	**11**	**.454**	**.591**	**.304**
Career	**1317**	**4759**	**921**	**1447**	**263**	**961**	**885**	**906**	**158**	**58**	**.416**	**.545**	**.304**

Fielding

Year	Posn	G	GS	TC	PO	A	E	DP	FLD%
1999	**1B**	**161**	**158**	**1451**	**1336**	**107**	**8**	**141**	**.994**
Career		**1306**	**1289**	**12242**	**11046**	**1110**	**86**	**1001**	**.993**

John Valentin

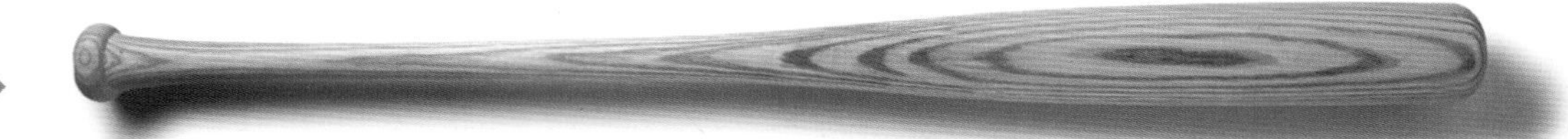

Profile

Name: John William Valentin **Height:** 6–0 **Weight:** 185 **Throws:** Right **Bats:** Right **Position:** Third Base **Born:** February 18, 1967, Mineola, New York **Drafted:** Selected by the Boston Red Sox in the fifth round of the 1988 free-agent draft **Pre-Majors Highlight:** Led New-York Penn League shortstops in fielding percentage in 1988 **Personal Information:** Attended Seton Hall University

"John is a real pro. I'm glad he's on our side."

Boston Red Sox manager, Jimy Williams

Career milestones

1995 Became just the fifth shortstop in Major League history to hit three home runs in one game, June 2, and went 5-for-5 in that game
1997 Led American League with 47 doubles
1998 Had eight game-winning runs batted in and 26 game-tying or go-ahead RBIs. Went 65 games without an error (July 5–Sept. 20)

John Valentin saved his best for last during the 1999 season. Valentin didn't have an outstanding season, but he made a solid contribution as the Boston Red Sox won the wild card playoff spot in the American League East. Valentin batted .253 with 12 home runs and 70 runs batted in while making 14 errors in 113 games at third base.

However, Valentin came through when his team needed him the most. Boston lost the first two games of the best-of-five Division Series against the heavily favored Cleveland Indians. Only one loss from elimination, it looked like the Red Sox were finished.

That's when Valentin took over. In a 9–3 win in Game 3, he had two hits, drove in three runs and scored twice. His bases-loaded double in the seventh inning broke a 3–3 tie and gave the Red Sox the momentum.

Valentin then put on one of the greatest hitting displays in postseason history in Game 4. He hit a two-run homer in the first inning to put the Red Sox on top, 2–1. Valentin hit another two-run homer in his next at-bat in the third that gave Boston a 10–2 lead. When it was all over, Valentin had four hits in five at-bats, drove in seven runs, tying a postseason record and scored twice in Boston's 23–7 win.

The Red Sox completed their historic comeback with a 12–8 win in Game 5. Valentin had a hit, drove in two runs and scored twice.

"To be a part of this is very special," said Valentin. "I've never had a hot streak like that. To do it with so much at stake is something I'll always remember."

The playoff series summed up Valentin's career. He's done whatever the Red Sox have asked him to. He came up as a shortstop in 1992, but moved to second base in 1997 to make room for Nomar Garciaparra. Valentin then moved to third base when Tim Naerhing was injured. Valentin is the Red Sox's longest serving player, but it seemed as if his days with them were numbered. He missed significant playing time as the 1999 season wound down—Boston went to a youth policy at third base—but came through when it most mattered.

Valentin was in the big leagues by 1992 when he hit .276 with five homers and 25 RBIs. He became the Red Sox everyday shortstop the following season, batting .278 with 11 homers and 66 RBIs.

Valentin hit a career-high .316 in 1994 with nine homers and 49 RBIs the following season, despite missing a month with a knee injury. His best overall season came in 1995 as the Red Sox won the American League East title. Valentin hit .298 with 27 homers and 102 RBIs while leading American League shortstops with 414 assists. The home run and RBI totals are career highs.

Boston fans have learned over the years they can always count on Valentin to do what's best for the team.

Batting

Year	G	AB	R	H	HR	RBI	BB	SO	SB	CS	OBP	SLG	AVG
1999	**113**	**450**	**58**	**114**	**12**	**70**	**40**	**68**	**0**	**1**	**.315**	**.398**	**.253**
Career	**961**	**3614**	**582**	**1022**	**118**	**521**	**430**	**474**	**47**	**30**	**.362**	**.463**	**.283**

Fielding

Year	Posn	G	GS	TC	PO	A	E	DP	FLD%
1999	**3B**	**111**	**110**	**306**	**84**	**208**	**14**	**16**	**.954**
Career		**956**	**942**	**3955**	**1324**	**2507**	**124**	**506**	**.969**

Cal Ripken Jr.

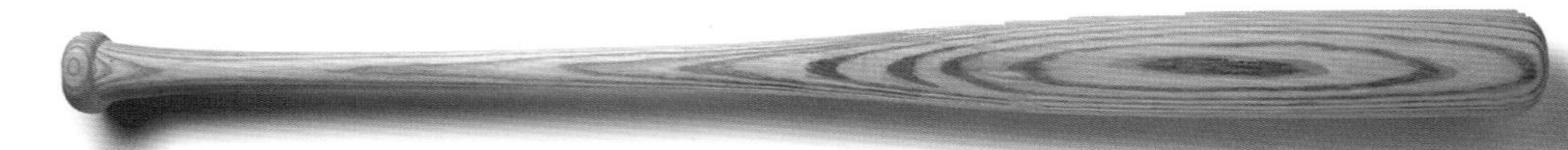

Profile

Name: Calvin Edward Ripken, Jr **Height:** 6—4 **Weight:** 220 **Throws:** Right **Bats:** Right **Position:** Third Base **Born:** August 24, 1960, Havre de Grace, Maryland **Drafted:** Selected by the Baltimore Orioles in the second round of the 1978 free-agent draft **Pre-Majors Highlight:** Tied for Appalachian League lead in double plays by shortstop in 1978 **Personal Information:** Cal played with his brother Bill for two seasons. He also played parts of 12 seasons with his father in an Orioles uniform as a coach and manager.

"Cal's got another year to play for sure. He might have another 1,000 hits in him."

Former Baltimore Orioles manager, Ray Miller

Career milestones

1982 Named American League Rookie of the Year

1983 Named American League Most Valuable Player.

1991 Named American League Most Valuable Player and Most Valuable Player of All-Star Game. Won Gold Glove Award

1992 Won Gold Glove Award

1995 Played 2,131st consecutive game, breaking Lou Gehrig's record, September 8

1998 Ended consecutive-games played streak at 2,632, September 20

A piece of advice for baseball fans for the 2000 season. Don't bet against the Iron Man.

It's true Cal Ripken Jr.'s streak for consecutive games played ended in 1998 at 2,632. It's also true he played in just 86 games last season and missed the last month after having back surgery. But to bet Ripken's career is over would be a big mistake.

Ripken batted .340 with 18 homers—reaching 402 in his career—and 57 runs batted in last season in the most trying year of his career. His father and mentor, Cal Sr., died of lung cancer in spring training. Ripken's sore back had him in and out of the lineup. He was on the disabled list twice—the first time he was on the DL in his career—before finally deciding to have surgery in late September.

"I think everybody around knew he was having a tough time," Baltimore pitcher Mike Mussina said. "I've seen him go through a lot in nine years. It must have been unbearable to make him stop."

There are several reasons for Ripken, who will be 40 during the 200 season to attempt a comeback. First, a man who played over 16 seasons without taking a day off will surely want to get back on the field as soon as possible. Second, he goes into the 2000 season just nine hits away from the 3,000 mark.

Despite all the problems, the 1999 season was one of the most successful of Ripken's career. His batting average was the highest since 1994 and he was in his hottest stretch of the season when he decided to have the surgery. His batting average and .581 slugging percentage were both team highs.

There's little doubt Ripken's record for consecutive games played will never be broken. The streak began on May 30, 1982, his second year in the Major Leagues. Many thought Lou Gehrig's record of 2,130 would never be broken, but the relentless Ripken never let up. In one of the biggest celebrations in baseball history, Ripken finally passed Gehrig on September 6, 1995 in a game against the Anaheim Angels.

However, the new streak was far from over. Ripken played in 501 straight games after breaking Gehrig's mark and played in his 2,500th game on April 25, 1998. The streak finally ended on September 20, 1998 when Ripken asked Miller to sit out a game against the New York Yankees.

Ripken holds the Major League record for home runs by a shortstop with 345 and has the most RBIs among active Major Leaguers (1,571).

Ripken was confident he would recover from the surgery and return to his certain Hall of Fame stature for the 2000 season. If that happens, it will be another chapter in his legacy.

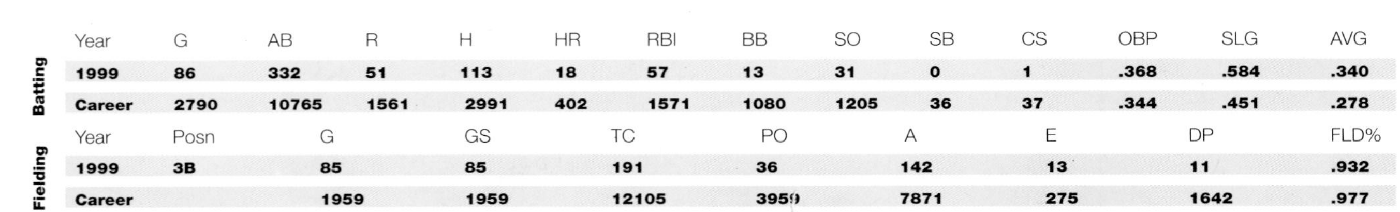

Batting

Year	G	AB	R	H	HR	RBI	BB	SO	SB	CS	OBP	SLG	AVG
1999	**86**	**332**	**51**	**113**	**18**	**57**	**13**	**31**	**0**	**1**	**.368**	**.584**	**.340**
Career	**2790**	**10765**	**1561**	**2991**	**402**	**1571**	**1080**	**1205**	**36**	**37**	**.344**	**.451**	**.278**

Fielding

Year	Posn	G	GS	TC	PO	A	E	DP	FLD%
1999	**3B**	**85**	**85**	**191**	**36**	**142**	**13**	**11**	**.932**
Career		**1959**	**1959**	**12105**	**3959**	**7871**	**275**	**1642**	**.977**

RIPKEN
8

Profile

Name: Paul Andrew O'Neill **Height:** 6–4 **Weight:** 215 **Throws:** Left **Bats:** Left **Position:** Right Field **Born:** February 25, 1963, Columbus, Ohio **Drafted:** Selected by the Cincinnati Reds in the fourth round of the 1981 free-agent draft **Acquired:** Traded by the Cincinnati Reds to the New York Yankees, November 3, 1992 **Pre-Majors Highlights:** Led American Association outfiielders with 19 assists, 1985 **Personal Information:** Is a direct descendant of author Mark Twain

Paul O'Neill

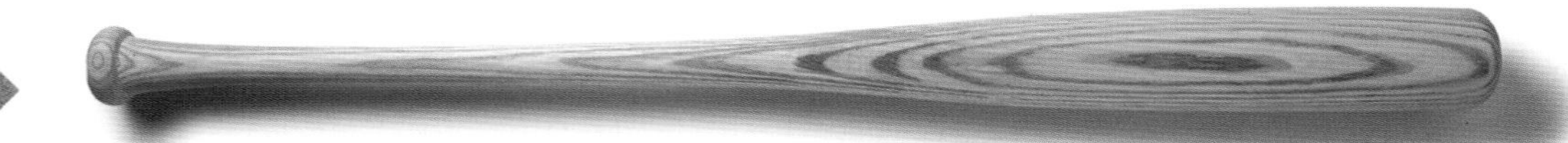

"Paul O'Neill plays the game the way it should be played. That's the best thing you can say about any player." **New York Yankees manager, Joe Torre**

Career milestones

1984 Made his Major League debut with the Cincinnati Reds, September 3

1987 Homered in three consecutive games and had a five-hit game

1990 Won first World Series with Cincinnati Reds

1994 Led American League in batting average (.359)

1997 Had 16-game hitting streak

1998 Hit 200th career home run, May 3 at Kansas City and named to fifth All-Star team

During the postseason, new baseball fans learned that nothing keeps Paul O'Neill out of the lineup.

O'Neill played the entire playoffs with a cracked rib, an injury he suffered late in the season. That would have put most players on the bench, but it didn't stop O'Neill, one of the hottest competitors in the game today.

That's no surprise to long-time baseball fans. In addition to his steady production every season, O'Neill is known for his intensity, which has seen him throw bats and helmets, argue with umpires and attack water coolers when he makes an out in a key situation.

"Paul brings the same intensity to the game every day," said Yankees manager Joe Torre. "It doesn't matter if it's a game in April or in the playoffs. Paul plays the same way every game. That's why he's such a good player."

O'Neill was a major contributor as the New York Yankees won their third World Series in the last four years of the 1990s. The right fielder batted .285 with 19 home runs and 110 RBIs in 1999.

O'Neill has been one of the most consistent hitters in Major League Baseball for the last several seasons. He hit .300 or better for six straight seasons from 1993–98. Since being traded from the Cincinnati Reds to the Yankees after the 1992 season, O'Neill has a .312 batting average while averaging 21 homers and 98 RBIs a season.

His best season with the Yankees came in 1994 when he led the American League with a .359 average, also a career high. He hit 21 home runs with 83 RBIs.

O'Neill has been especially productive in the Yankees' title years. In 1996, he hit .302 with 19 homers and 91 RBIs. In 1998, O'Neill hit .317 with 24 homers and 116 RBIs. He also was among the American League leaders in hits, multiple-hit games, RBI and sacrifice flies.

O'Neill also was a member of the Cincinnati team that won the National League title and upset the Oakland A's in the World Series with a four-game sweep in 1990. He batted .270 with 16 homers and 78 RBIs.

In addition to his good offensive numbers, O'Neill is one of the best right fielders in the game today. He has a strong arm and is fearless when it comes to diving for catches or leaping at the wall to try and take away home runs.

O'Neill is the type of player fans either love or hate. If he's playing on your team, you love him for his intensity. If he's on the other team, you boo him at every opportunity for his temper. Considering the way O'Neill plays the game, he'd probably take that as the ultimate compliment.

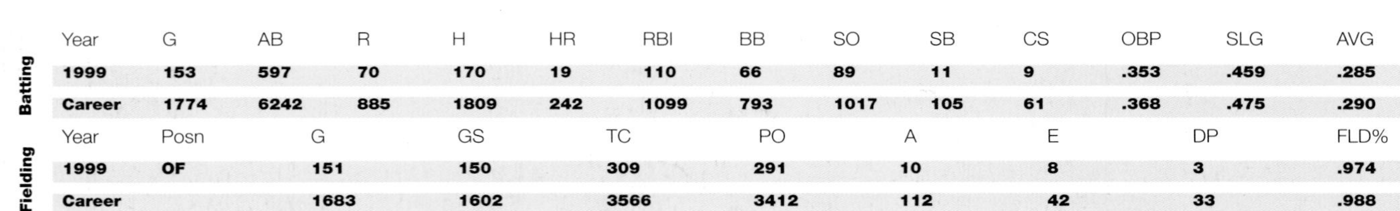

Batting

Year	G	AB	R	H	HR	RBI	BB	SO	SB	CS	OBP	SLG	AVG
1999	**153**	**597**	**70**	**170**	**19**	**110**	**66**	**89**	**11**	**9**	**.353**	**.459**	**.285**
Career	**1774**	**6242**	**885**	**1809**	**242**	**1099**	**793**	**1017**	**105**	**61**	**.368**	**.475**	**.290**

Fielding

Year	Posn	G	GS	TC	PO	A	E	DP	FLD%
1999	**OF**	**151**	**150**	**309**	**291**	**10**	**8**	**3**	**.974**
Career		**1683**	**1602**	**3566**	**3412**	**112**	**42**	**33**	**.988**

21
cosby

Profile

Name: John Karl Wetteland **Height:** 6–2 **Weight:** 215 **Throws:** Right **Bats:** Right **Position:** Pitcher **Born:** August 21, 1966, San Mateo, California **Drafted:** Selected by the Los Angeles Dodgers in the secondary phase of the 1985 free-agent draft **Pre-Majors Highlight:** Won 12 games for Class A Vero Beach in 1987 **Acquired:** Signed as a free agent with the Texas Rangers, December 16, 1998 **Personal Information:** His father Ed is a former minor league player in the Chicago Cubs organization

John Wetteland

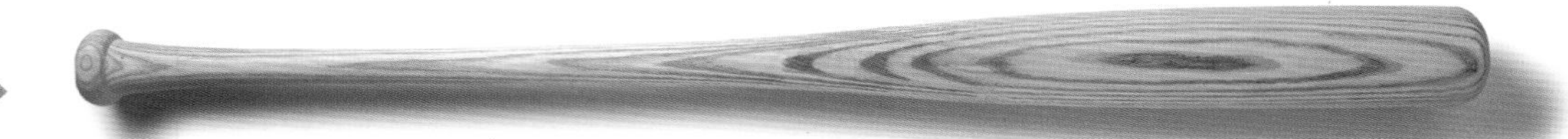

"You always feel good when you give the ball to John Wetteland in the ninth inning."

Texas Rangers manager, Johnny Oates

Career milestones

1995 Traded from Montreal Expos to New York Yankees, April 5

1996 Named Winner of Rolaids Relief Award in the American League. Named Most Valuable Player of the World Series

1997 Earned his 200th career save, July 25, at Chicago

1998 Held opposing hitters to .182 batting average

1999 Saved a Texas club-record 43 games

A funny thing happened to John Wetteland on his way to being one of the top closers in Major League Baseball.

His career as a closer almost ended up being a career as a starting pitcher.

The Los Angeles Dodgers took Wetteland in the secondary phase of the 1985 free-agent draft. The Dodgers have been known to produce some of the best starting pitchers in baseball, and that's what they tried to do with Wetteland.

The hard-throwing right-hander was used almost exclusively as a starter throughout his minor-league career. Even when he reached the big leagues in 1989, the Dodgers still toyed with the idea of using him as a starter over the next three seasons.

Wetteland's career took off, thanks to a series of trades after the 1991 season. On November 25, he was traded by the Dodgers along with pitcher Tim Belcher to the Cincinnati Reds for outfielder Eric Davis and pitcher Kip Gross. Wetteland never got a chance to put on a Cincinnati uniform because the Reds traded him, along with pitcher Bill Risley to the Montreal Expos for outfielder Dave Martinez, pitcher Scott Ruskin and shortstop Willie Greene on December 11.

The trades turned out to be the biggest moments of Wetteland's career. It didn't take long for the Expos to find the right place for him. Wetteland became a full-time closer in 1992 with the Montreal Expos and saved 37 games. From 1992–99, he saved 295 games while terrorizing hitters in both leagues.

Wetteland has saved 43 games three times in his career for three different teams—1993 with Montreal, 1996 with the New York Yankees and 1999 with the Texas Rangers. He also saved 42 games with the Rangers in 1998, giving him four seasons of 40 or more saves.

"You have to want the ball in those situations," said Wetteland. "There's always a rush when you're out there with the game on the line."

Although he saved 105 games for Montreal from 1992–94, the Expos traded him to the Yankees in a cost-cutting move before the 1995 season. Wetteland saved 31 games that season before enjoying his best moment in 1996. His 43 saves led the American League and he had a 2–3 record with a 2.83 ERA. Wetteland was at his best in the playoffs. He saved two games in the Division Series as the Yankees defeated Texas before recording one save in the American League Championship Series against Baltimore.

Wetteland was even better in the World Series as the Yankees defeated the Atlanta Braves in six games. He saved all four of the Yankees' wins and set a Major League record.

Wetteland signed with the Rangers after that season, and he's still going strong with 116 saves the last three years.

Judging from the results, it's a good thing for Wetteland his career as a starting pitcher didn't work out.

Pitching

Year	W	L	ERA	G	GS	CG	SHO	SV	SVO	INN	H	R	ER	HR	HBP	BB	SO
1999	**4**	**4**	**3.68**	**62**	**0**	**0**	**0**	**43**	**50**	**66.0**	**67**	**30**	**27**	**9**	**0**	**19**	**60**
Career	**42**	**40**	**2.82**	**556**	**17**	**0**	**0**	**296**	**348**	**705.0**	**549**	**252**	**221**	**63**	**14**	**228**	**751**

Batting

Year	G	AB	R	H	HR	RBI	BB	SO	SB	CS	OBP	SLG	AVG
Career	**556**	**42**	**4**	**7**	**1**	**8**	**0**	**19**	**0**	**0**	**.167**	**.286**	**.167**

Fielding

Year	Posn	G	GS	TC	PO	A	E	DP	FLD%
1999	**P**	**62**	**0**	**7**	**1**	**5**	**1**	**0**	**.857**
Career		**556**	**17**	**91**	**24**	**55**	**12**	**2**	**.868**

WETTELAND
35

Scott Erickson

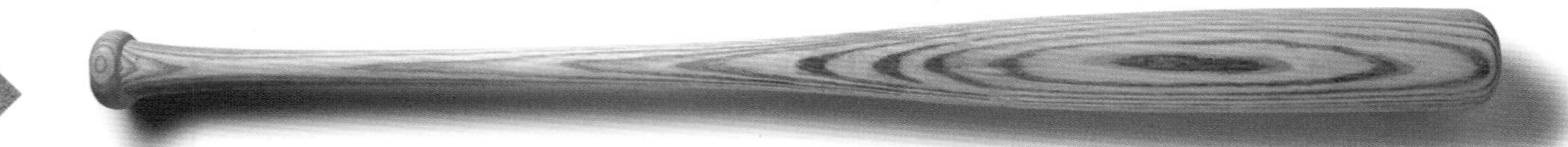

Profile

Name: Scott Gavin Erickson **Height:** 6–4 **Weight:** 230 **Throws:** Right **Bats:** Right **Position:** Pitcher **Born:** February 2, 1968, Long Beach, California **Drafted:** Selected by the Minnesota Twins in the fourth round of the 1989 free-agent draft **Acquired:** Traded by the Minnesota Twins to the Baltimore Orioles, July 7, 1995 **Pre-Majors Highlight:** While at the University of Arizona, he tied for the lead among NCAA pitchers with 173 innings pitched and 18 wins in 1989 **Personal Information:** Graduate of Homestead High School in Cupertino, California, where he played baseball, football and soccer

"My goal is to get the batter to hit the ball on the ground and take advantage of our defense. That's my game." **Baltimore Orioles pitcher, Scott Erickson**

Career milestones

1991 Finished second in the American League Cy Young voting

1994 Pitched no-hitter for Minnesota Twins against Milwaukee, April 27

1996 Tossed three straight complete games in June

1997 Struck out a career-best 131 in 221.2 innings

1998 Earned 100th career victory with April 1 complete-game win over Kansas City

Every time trade talk comes up when Major League teams are looking for pitching, Scott Erickson's name is mentioned.

It's easy to see why. It's also easy to see why the Baltimore Orioles have been reluctant to trade him.

Erickson has been one of the most dependable right-handed pitchers in baseball for most of his 10-year Major League career. Relying mostly on a hard-breaking split-finger fastball, Erickson has reached double figures in wins six times and has won at least 15 games in four seasons.

Erickson had another solid season with the Orioles in 1999. He finished with a 15–12 record and a 4.81 earned run average. Erickson was second in the league in innings pitched (230.1) and tied for second with six complete games. He also led the league with three shutouts.

The strong season came after Erickson got off to a 1–8 start. "I started out in a bad groove then busted my tail to get back," he said. "I didn't give up. I still get a little irritated for messing myself up early in the season. I wasted two months."

Durability has always been one of Erickson's strengths. Over the last four seasons, he has averaged 34 starts and 231 innings pitched a season. He led the league in 1998 in starts (36), innings pitched (251.1) and complete games (11). All are career highs.

Erickson's performance helped the Orioles in their last two playoff seasons, going 13–12 in 1996 and 16–7 in 1997.

Erickson holds the distinction of being drafted four times by Major League teams before finally signing with the Minnesota Twins in 1989. Erickson turned down offers from the New York Mets (1986), Houston Astros (1987) and Toronto Blue Jays (1988) to go to college. He finally signed with the Twins, who took him in the fourth round of the 1989 draft after he won 18 games at the University of Arizona.

It didn't take long for Erickson to reach Minnesota. He appeared in only 27 minor-league games before the Twins called him up in 1990. His Major League debut was a victory over the Texas Rangers on June 25, 1990 and he went 8–4 with a 2.87 ERA in the second half of the season.

Erickson and the Twins had big seasons in 1991. His 20–8 record helped the Twins win the American League West title. Erickson led the league in wins and pitched three shutouts. He made three postseasons start as the Twins defeated the Blue Jays in the League Championship Series and the Atlanta Braves in the World Series.

Another highlight for Erickson came in 1994 when he pitched a no-hitter against the Milwaukee Brewers. He was traded to the Orioles for pitcher Scott Klingenbeck and outfielder Kimera Bartee on July 7, 1995. The deal turned out right for Baltimore as Erickson has compiled a 69–48 record with the Orioles.

Pitching

Year	W	L	ERA	G	GS	CG	SHO	SV	SVO	INN	H	R	ER	HR	HBP	BB	SO
1999	**15**	**12**	**4.81**	**34**	**34**	**6**	**3**	**0**	**0**	**230.1**	**244**	**127**	**123**	**27**	**11**	**99**	**106**
Career	**130**	**108**	**4.27**	**310**	**306**	**47**	**16**	**0**	**0**	**2013.2**	**2154**	**1045**	**956**	**177**	**83**	**697**	**1111**

Batting

Year	G	AB	R	H	HR	RBI	BB	SO	SB	CS	OBP	SLG	AVG
Career	**310**	**10**	**2**	**0**	**0**	**0**	**4**	**6**	**0**	**0**	**.286**	**.000**	**.000**

Fielding

Year	Posn	G	GS	TC	PO	A	E	DP	FLD%
1999	**P**	**34**	**34**	**68**	**24**	**42**	**2**	**5**	**.971**
Career		**310**	**306**	**574**	**197**	**354**	**23**	**37**	**.960**

Ron Gant

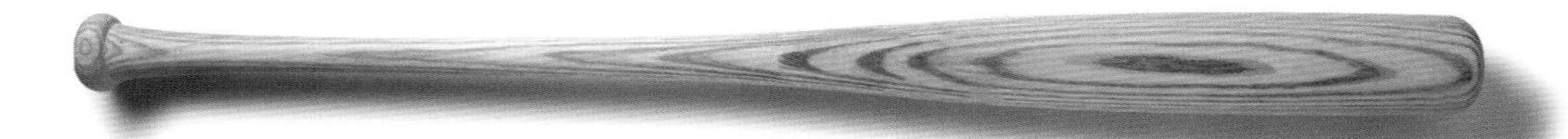

"If I'm healthy, I think I can put up good numbers. That's always been the key for me."

Philadelphia Phillies left fielder, Ron Gant

Profile

Name: Ronald Edwin Gant **Height:** 6–0 **Weight:** 200 **Throws:** Right **Bats:** Right **Position:** Left Field **Born:** March 2, 1965, Victoria, Texas **Drafted:** Selected by the Atlanta Braves in the fourth round of the 1983 free-agent draft. **Acquired:** Traded by the St. Louis Cardinals to the Philadelphia Phillies, November 19, 1998 **Pre-Majors Highlight:** Led Carolina League with 26 home runs in 1986 while playing for Durham **Personal Information:** He was drafted by the Atlanta Braves when he was 18 years old

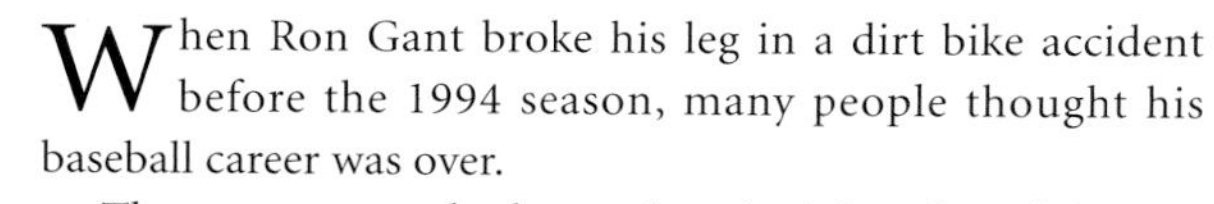

When Ron Gant broke his leg in a dirt bike accident before the 1994 season, many people thought his baseball career was over.

There were more doubters when the injury forced Gant to miss the entire '94 season. He was released by the Atlanta Braves, the team he had developed into a star with, and signed with the Cincinnati Reds. Cincinnati general manager Jim Bowden was willing to take a chance on Gant, who hit 147 homers for the Braves between 1988–93.

Gant and Bowden proved the doubters wrong. In a season that earned him The Sporting News' Comeback Player of the Year Award, Gant hit 29 homers, drove in 88 runs, batted .276 and stole 23 bases while making the National League All-Star team for the second time. Gant's efforts helped the Reds win the National League Central title and advance to the League Championship Series.

Gant has shown he's still a productive hitter since the injury. He has averaged 24 homers and 75 RBIs the last five seasons, which also has seen him play with the St. Louis Cardinals and Philadelphia Phillies.

Gant signed with the Cardinals following the 1995 season and had three solid power years, hitting 30 homers in 1996, 17 in 1997 and 26 in 1998. The 30 homers were most by a Cardinal left fielder since Stan Musial hit 32 in 1951.

The Cardinals traded Gant, along with pitchers Jeff Brantley and Cliff Politte, to the Phillies for pitchers Ricky Bottalico and Garrett Stephenson on November 19, 1998. Gant hit .260 with 17 homers and 77 RBIs with the Phillies last season. Until pitching woes surfaced at midseason, it looked as if Gant would help his new team to break the .500 mark for the first time since Philadelphia went to the 1993 World Series.

While Gant has been productive the last five seasons, he was one of the best all-around hitters in baseball before the dirt bike accident. He gave the Braves one of the best power and speed combinations in the Majors from 1990-1993. The numbers were impressive: 32 homers with 33 stolen bases in 1990, 32 homers with 34 steals in 1991, 17 homers with 32 steals in 1992 and 36 homers with 26 steals in 1993. His best batting average was .303 in 1990 and he hit .259 with 19 homers and 19 steals in 1988 rookie season.

The dirt bike accident wasn't the first setback in Gant's career. After his solid rookie season, he struggled in 1989 and was sent back to the minors. Not only that, he was asked to move from third base to center field. Gant made the transition, was back in the big leagues to stay in 1990 and helped the Braves reach the World Series in 1991 and 1992.

While Gant's numbers were down a bit last season, he's made a habit of beating the odds. No one would be surprised if he did it again.

Career milestones

1992 Made National League All-Star team while playing for Atlanta Braves. Also made the team in 1995

1995 Signed as a free agent by the St. Louis Cardinals, December 23

1997 Hit 12 of his 17 homers before the All-Star Break.

1998 Hit 26 home runs, his sixth career 20-homer season

Batting

Year	G	AB	R	H	HR	RBI	BB	SO	SB	CS	OBP	SLG	AVG
1999	**138**	**516**	**107**	**134**	**17**	**77**	**85**	**112**	**13**	**3**	**.364**	**.430**	**.260**
Career	**1497**	**5422**	**903**	**1393**	**266**	**856**	**641**	**1172**	**228**	**89**	**.336**	**.467**	**.257**

Fielding

Year	Posn	G	GS	TC	PO	A	E	DP	FLD%
1999	**OF**	**133**	**131**	**269**	**260**	**7**	**2**	**2**	**.993**
Career		**1425**	**1391**	**3480**	**2750**	**629**	**101**	**123**	**.971**

Craig Biggio

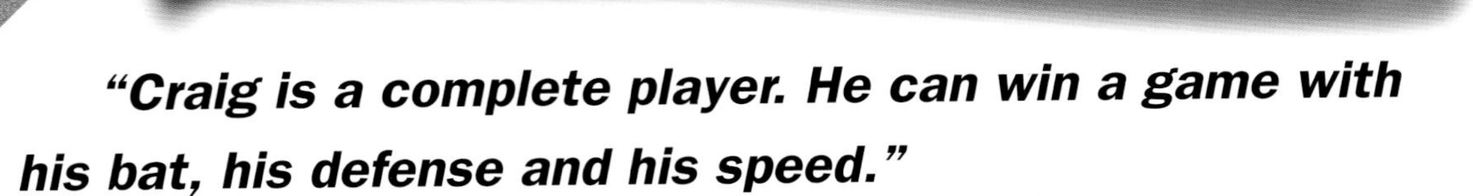

Profile

Name: Craig Alan Biggio **Height:** 5–11 **Weight:** 180 **Throws:** Right **Bats:** Right **Position:** Second Base **Born:** December 14, 1965, Smithtown, New York **Drafted:** Selected by the Houston Astros in the first round (22nd pick overall) of the 1987 free-agent draft **Pre-Majors Highlights:** Named first team All-American after hitting .407 with 14 home runs and 68 runs batted in as a junior at Seton Hall University **Personal Information:** Married (Patty) with two sons (Connor and Cavan)

"Craig is a complete player. He can win a game with his bat, his defense and his speed."

Houston Astros manager, Larry Dierker

Career milestones

1988 Got first Major League hit off Orel Hershiser, June 28

1991 Led National League catchers in putouts (889) and total chances (963). Made National League All-Star team

1992 Moved from catcher to second base

1994 Won first National League Gold Glove Award. Also won the award in 1995, 1996, 1997 and 1999

1998 Joined Hall of Famer Tris Speaker as the only players in this century to collect 50-plus doubles and 50-plus stolen bases in the same season

Craig Biggio's Major League career started as a catcher. He then played the outfield. For the last seven years he's been a second baseman.

Throughout all the position switches, Biggio has maintained one constant. The Houston Astros' veteran is one of the top stars in the game today.

Biggio has compiled an impressive resume since becoming a full-time player with the Astros in 1989. He has made the National League All-Star team eight times, won five Gold Gloves at second base, topped the .300 mark in batting average four times, played in all 162 games three times, led the league in runs scored twice and stole 50 bases once.

Drafted in the first round by the Astros in 1987, Biggio didn't spend much time in the minors. He played 64 games at Class A Asheville in '87 and appeared in 77 games at Class AAA Tucson in 1988 before the Astros called him up late in the season.

Biggio never went back to the minors and quickly became a fixture in the Astros' lineup behind the plate. He led National League catchers with 889 putouts and 963 total chances in 1991. Biggio showed unusually good speed for a catcher, stealing 65 bases from 1989–91.

His speed led the Astros to make the decision to move Biggio, who made the All-Star team in 1991, out of the catcher's spot in an attempt to save his legs. Biggio became Houston's regular second baseman in 1992 and has become one of the top players at that position in baseball. He has made the All-Star team seven times as a second baseman and won his fifth Gold Glove in 1999.

Biggio's power numbers have increased throughout his career. After hitting 14 home runs from 1990–92, he hit 21 in 1993, 22 in 1995, 15 in 1996, 22 in 1997, 20 in 1998 and 16 in 1999.

A solid all-around season in 1995, which also saw him hit .302 and steal 39 bases, earned Biggio the National League Silver Slugger Award. He became the first Astros player to hit over 20 homers and steal over 20 bases since 1986.

Biggio led the Major Leagues with 146 runs scored in 1997 while hitting .309 with 22 homers, 84 walks, and 47 stolen bases.

Biggio's best season came in 1998 when he reached career highs in batting average (.325) and RBIs (88) while hitting 20 home runs. His 210 hits were an Astros' club record.

As the Astros won the National League Central title for the third straight season, Biggio hit .294 with 56 doubles, 16 homers, 73 RBIs and 123 runs scored.

These offensive and defensive accomplishments have made Biggio a complete player, no matter the position he plays.

Batting

Year	G	AB	R	H	HR	RBI	BB	SO	SB	CS	OBP	SLG	AVG
1999	**160**	**639**	**123**	**188**	**16**	**73**	**88**	**107**	**28**	**14**	**.386**	**.457**	**.294**
Career	**1699**	**6389**	**1120**	**1868**	**152**	**706**	**786**	**973**	**346**	**104**	**.380**	**.437**	**.292**

Fielding

Year	Posn	G	GS	TC	PO	A	E	DP	FLD%
1999	**OF/2B**	**161**	**156**	**811**	**368**	**431**	**12**	**117**	**.985**
Career		**1680**	**1632**	**8918**	**5144**	**3640**	**134**	**726**	**.985**

Roberto Hernandez

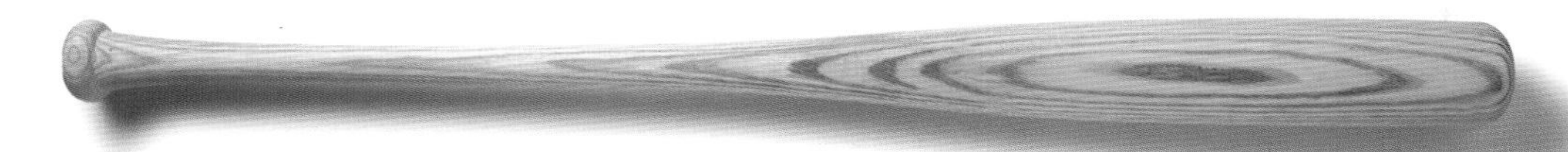

"I take the ball whenever they want me to and try to put up the numbers."

Tampa Bay pitcher, Roberto Hernandez

Profile

Name: Roberto Manuel Hernandez **Height:** 6–4 **Weight:** 250 **Throws:** Right **Bats:** Right **Position:** Pitcher **Born:** November 11, 1964, Santurce, Puerto Rico **Drafted:** Selected by the California Angels in the first round (16th pick overall) of the 1986 free-agent draft **Acquired:** Signed by the Tampa Bay Devil Rays as a free agent, November 18, 1997 **Pre-Majors Highlights:** His alma mater, University of South Carolina at Aikens, named their refurbished stadium after Hernandez in 1993. **Personal Information:** Married with two children

Being a closer on a Major League team is one of the toughest jobs in baseball. Being a closer on an expansion team might be the toughest job of all. Most expansion teams struggle in their early years, which means the opportunities to save games don't come along that often.

This situation hasn't bothered Tampa Bay Devil Rays closer Roberto Hernandez one bit. In two seasons with the Devil Rays, Hernandez has recorded 69 saves, even though his team has finished last in the American League East both years.

Hernandez, who has been one of the top closers in baseball since 1993, was especially effective in 1999. He saved 43 of the Devil Rays' 69 wins while recording a 2–3 record and a 3.07 earned run average. The save total was a career high.

Hernandez has been one of the few things Tampa Bay manager Larry Rothschild has been able to count on the last two seasons. If it had not been for Hernandez, the Devil Rays would have been buried even deeper in the standings in the first two seasons.

"Roberto has done the job for us," said Rothschild. "We know if we can get him the ball with the lead we have a chance."

The teams Hernandez has played for in his career have discovered that very thing. He has saved 218 games the last seven seasons, an average of 31 a year. Hernandez has saved 38 games in two seasons (in 1993 and 1996, both times with the Chicago White Sox). He saved 32 with the White Sox in 1995 and a combined 30 with the White Sox and San Francisco Giants in 1997.

Hernandez was involved in one of the biggest trades in recent memory during the '97 season. Despite the fact he was third in the American League with 26 saves, the White Sox—who were only three-and-a-half games behind Central Division leaders Cleveland—traded him to San Francisco on July 31. Chicago wanted to slash its payroll and traded Hernandez and fellow pitchers Wilson Alvarez and Danny Darwin for a package of young players. The deal helped the Giants win the National League West title. Hernandez, pitching mostly out of the setup role because the Giants had Robb Nen as their closer, was 5–2 with four saves and a 2.48 ERA in 28 games.

Good closers must be durable and Hernandez has averaged 66 appearances in the last seven seasons. His 1.91 ERA in 1996 also led American League relievers.

After being drafted in the first round of the 1986 free-agent draft by the California Angels, it took Hernandez six years to make it to the big leagues. He was in the Majors to stay by the next season and has been one of the best relief pitchers in baseball since.

Career milestones

1996 Finished second in the Rolaids Relief Man standings and held hitters to a .208 average with men on base

1997 Began season with Chicago White Sox. Was traded to the San Francisco Giants on July 31 as part of a nine-player trade

1998 Opposing batters hit only .212 against him

1999 Recorded a career-high 43 saves

Pitching

Year	W	L	ERA	G	GS	CG	SHO	SV	SVO	INN	H	R	ER	HR	HBP	BB	SO
1999	**2**	**3**	**3.07**	**72**	**0**	**0**	**0**	**43**	**47**	**73.1**	**68**	**27**	**25**	**1**	**4**	**33**	**69**
Career	**38**	**35**	**3.02**	**512**	**3**	**0**	**0**	**234**	**289**	**582.0**	**491**	**215**	**195**	**40**	**18**	**244**	**570**

Batting

Year	G	AB	R	H	HR	RBI	BB	SO	SB	CS	OBP	SLG	AVG
Career	**512**	**2**	**0**	**1**	**0**	**0**	**0**	**1**	**0**	**0**	**.500**	**.500**	**.500**

Fielding

Year	Posn	G	GS	TC	PO	A	E	DP	FLD%
1999	**P**	**72**	**0**	**15**	**4**	**10**	**1**	**1**	**.933**
Career		**512**	**3**	**93**	**26**	**59**	**8**	**4**	**.914**

Jay Bell

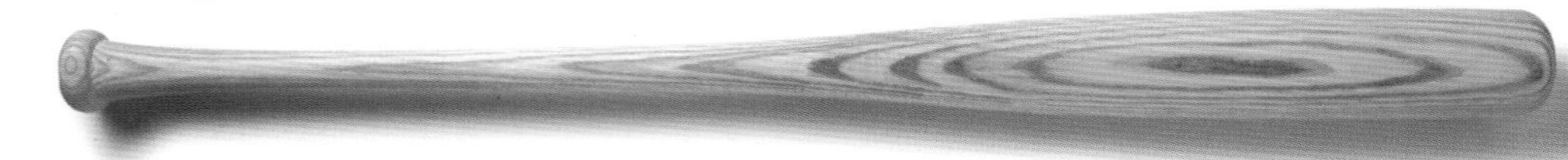

Profile

Name: Jay Stuart Bell
Height: 6–0 **Weight:** 184
Throws: Right **Bats:** Right **Positions:** Second Base **Born:** December 11, 1965, Eglin AFB, Florida **Drafted:** Selected by the Minnesota Twins in the first round (eighth pick overall) of the 1984 free-agent draft **Acquired:** Signed by the Arizona Diamondbacks as a free agent, November 17, 1997 **Pre-Majors Highlight:** Traded by the Minnesota Twins to the Cleveland Indians, September 17, 1985 **Personal Information:** Was 18 years old when drafted by the Twins

"Jay has done everything we thought he would do for us. He's done the job for us offensively and defensively."

Arizona Diamondbacks manager, Buck Showalter

Career milestones

1986 Hit a home run in his first Major League at-bat, against Minnesota's Bert Blyleven, September 9, a player he was traded for

1993 Won National League Gold Glove at shortstop

1996 Led Major League shortstops with a .986 fielding percentage, committing 10 errors in 703 chances

1998 Collected his 1,500th big league hit with a run-scoring single off Atlanta's Greg Maddux, September 18

1999 Set career highs in home runs, runs batted in and runs scored in helping Arizona to the biggest single-season improvement in Major League history

Jay Bell picked the perfect time to have the best season of his career.

In the 14th year of his Major League career, Bell helped lead the Arizona Diamondbacks to the National League West title in the franchise's second season of existence.

While the Diamondbacks have several solid players who had big years in 1999, there's no doubt they couldn't have accomplished what they did without Bell. A solid player throughout his career, which began in 1986, Bell raised his game to a new level last season.

Bell's biggest contributions came with the bat. He batted .289, but his power and production numbers were especially significant. Bell hit 38 homers and drove in 112 runs, both career highs. He also set a career-high in runs scored with 132. His 170 hits were his most since 1993 (when he had 187) and he had his highest batting average since he hit .310 in '93. His .557 slugging percentage make him look like a power-hitting outfielder than a second baseman.

Until last season, Bell's best overall year came in 1993 when he was playing for the Pittsburgh Pirates. He hit .310 with nine home runs and won the National League Gold Glove Award at shortstop. Winning the Gold Glove, he snapped Ozzie Smith's 13-year reign as the National League's top shortstop.

Bell has been a versatile hitter throughout his career. His 1993 numbers earned him a place on the National League Silver Slugger team named by The Sporting News. In 1991, he hit 16 homers and led the Majors in sacrifice bunts (30) for the second straight year.

Bell was drafted by the Minnesota Twins in the first round of the 1984 free-agent draft and was traded to the Cleveland Indians on September 17, 1985 in a deal that sent pitcher Bert Blyleven to Minnesota. Bell was in the big leagues the following season. In an ironic twist, he homered off Blyleven in his first Major League at-bat.

The biggest break of Bell's career came when he was traded to the Pittsburgh Pirates for Felix Fermin in an even-up trade of shortstops on March 25, 1989. Bell was the Pirates' regular shortstop from 1990–1996. He played 1,106 games for Pittsburgh, hitting .269 with 78 homers and 58 steals.

Bell was traded to the Kansas City Royals on December 13, 1996. He had a big year for the Royals, hitting .291 with 89 runs, 21 homers, 92 RBIs and 10 stolen bases while being named the team's Player of the Year. Bell also tied for second in the American League in fielding percentage at shortstop.

Bell played shortstop from 1986–97. He was moved to second base in 1998 and played there full-time last season.

Batting

Year	G	AB	R	H	HR	RBI	BB	SO	SB	CS	OBP	SLG	AVG
1999	**151**	**589**	**132**	**170**	**38**	**112**	**82**	**132**	**7**	**4**	**.374**	**.557**	**.289**
Career	**1681**	**6240**	**963**	**1677**	**162**	**732**	**691**	**1229**	**84**	**56**	**.344**	**.420**	**.269**

Fielding

Year	Posn	G	GS	TC	PO	A	E	DP	FLD%
1999	**SS/2B**	**149**	**145**	**682**	**320**	**340**	**22**	**86**	**.968**
Career		**1668**	**1613**	**7818**	**2649**	**4969**	**200**	**969**	**.974**

Andy Benes

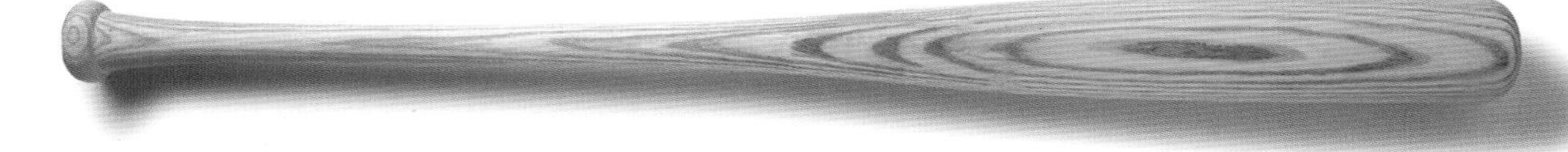

"Andy gives you a lot of starts and a lot of innings. He gives you what a rotation needs."

Arizona Diamondbacks manager, Buck Showalter

Profile

Name: Andrew Charles Benes **Height:** 6–6 **Weight:** 245 **Throws:** Right **Bats:** Right **Position:** Pitcher **Born:** August 20, 1967, Evansville, Indiana **Drafted:** Selected by the San Diego Padres in the first round (first pick overall) of the 1988 free-agent draft **Acquired:** Signed by the Arizona Diamondbacks as a free agent, February 3, 1998 **Pre-Majors Highlights:** Made NCAA All-American team during junior season at Evansville University, posting a 16-3 record and 1.42 earned run average **Personal Information:** His brother, Alan, is a pitcher in the St. Louis Cardinals organization

Andy Benes will go down as a big part of the Arizona Diamondbacks' history.

Benes was on the mound for the inaugural Diamondbacks' game against the Colorado Rockies on March 31, 1998. The right-hander has played a big role in Arizona's progression in the franchise's two-year existence.

Benes has compiled a 27–25 record and started 66 games in the last two seasons. He posted a 14–13 record with a 3.97 earned run average in the Diamondbacks' first season—1998. Benes won seven of his last nine decisions to finish the year with a 14–13 record and recorded a season-high 10 strikeouts on September 2 at Pittsburgh. He started 34 games and pitched 231.1 innings.

As the Diamondbacks won the National League West title last season—the fastest an expansion team has ever qualified for the playoffs—Benes was 13–12 with a 4.81 ERA. He worked 198.1 innings in 33 appearances (32 starts).

Benes has been making news throughout his pitching career. He was rated as one of the country's top prospects during his standout career at the University of Evansville and made the United States Olympic team in 1988. The San Diego Padres made Benes the first pick in the country in the 1988 draft.

Benes started the 1989 season in the minors, but it was only a temporary stay.

After just 21 minor-league appearances, the 21-year-old was called up to the Major Leagues and went 6–3 with a 3.51 ERA in 10 starts for the Padres in 1989. He was a mainstay in San Diego's rotation for the next six years, winning 59 games and pitching over 220 innings three times before being traded to the Seattle Mariners on July 31, 1995.

The Mariners were in the middle of the race for the American League West title and wanted Benes to bolster their rotation. That's exactly what he did, going 7–2 in 12 starts as Seattle made a late-season charge to steal the West crown from the California Angels with one of the biggest comebacks in Major League history.

Seeing what Benes had done down the stretch for the Mariners, the St. Louis Cardinals signed him as a free agent on December 23, 1995. The move paid off as Benes helped the Cardinals win the National League Central title. He recorded some impressive numbers, finishing the season with an 18–10 record and a 3.83 ERA. In 36 games (34 starts), Benes had three complete games, one shutout and pitched 230.1 innings.

An administrative mix-up meant that Benes left the Cardinals after the 1997 season to sign with Arizona as a free agent. It's no surprise he and winning teams keep finding each other.

Career milestones

1988 Member of the United States Olympic baseball team

1994 Led National League in strikeouts

1995 Signed with the St. Louis Cardinals as a free agent, December 23

1996 Won career-high 18 games wins with 3.83 ERA in 34 starts

1998 Pitched 8.1 hitless innings before yielding a single at Cincinnati, September 13

Pitching

Year	W	L	ERA	G	GS	CG	SHO	SV	SVO	INN	H	R	ER	HR	HBP	BB	SO
1999	**13**	**12**	**4.81**	**33**	**32**	**0**	**0**	**0**	**0**	**198.1**	**216**	**117**	**106**	**34**	**4**	**82**	**141**
Career	**131**	**119**	**3.79**	**328**	**324**	**19**	**9**	**1**	**1**	**2135.0**	**2001**	**980**	**898**	**219**	**43**	**729**	**1721**

Batting

Year	G	AB	R	H	HR	RBI	BB	SO	SB	CS	OBP	SLG	AVG
Career	**329**	**625**	**43**	**90**	**6**	**43**	**28**	**264**	**0**	**0**	**.187**	**.200**	**.144**

Fielding

Year	Posn	G	GS	TC	PO	A	E	DP	FLD%
1999	**P**	**33**	**32**	**30**	**13**	**15**	**2**	**1**	**.933**
Career		**328**	**324**	**354**	**140**	**205**	**9**	**14**	**.975**

Chuck Knoblauch

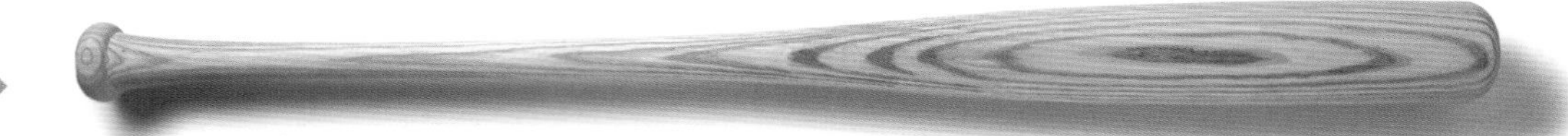

Profile

Name: Edward Charles Knoblauch **Height:** 5–9 **Weight:** 170 **Throws:** Right **Bats:** Right **Position:** Second Base **Born:** July 7, 1968, Houston, Texas **Drafted:** Selected by the Minnesota Twins in the first round (25th pick overall) of the 1989 free-agent draft **Acquired:** Traded by the Minnesota Twins to the New York Yankees, February 6, 1998 **Pre-Majors Highlights:** Named to Baseball America All-American team in junior year, hitting .364 witheight home runs, 64 RBI and 36 stolen bases **Personal Information:** Father Ray and Uncle Ed played minor league baseball

"Chuck has done a great job for us. He's fit in very well with our club."

New York Yankees manager Joe Torre

Career milestones

1991 Named American League Rookie of the Year as Minnesota won the World Series

1997 Won American League Gold Glove. Reached base in 36 straight games, September 15, 1996–April 26, 1997

1998 Homered in three consecutive games (July 14–16), becoming the first Yankee second baseman to do so since Gil McDougal in 1954.

When the New York Yankees acquired Chuck Knoblauch from the Minnesota Twins on February 6, 1998, the idea was clear.

The Yankees wanted Knobluach to help them regain the World Series title they won in 1996. Two years, and two World Series championships later, one could say the arrangement has worked out perfectly.

"This has been like a dream come true for me," Knoblauch said. "Just to be part of a special team like this has been a thrill."

The Yankees gave up a package of top prospects to get Knoblauch, sending left-hander Eric Milton, shortstop Christian Guzman, outfielder Brian Buchanan and right-hander Daniel Mota to Minnesota, but the deal has been well worth it.

Putting together two of the best back-to-back seasons in Major League Baseball history, the Yankees rolled to the World Series title in 1998 and '99, giving Knoblauch three championships in his nine years in the big leagues. In winning the American League Rookie of the Year Award in 1991, Knoblauch helped lead the Minnesota Twins to the World Series title.

Hitting in the leadoff spot for the Yankees, Knoblauch had a solid season with the bat in 1999. He batted .292, scored 120 runs, hit 18 homers, drove in 68 runs and stole 28 bases. Knoblauch showed good extra-base punch for a leadoff hitter. His home-run total was a career high and he added 36 doubles for .459 slugging percentage. And as the leadoff hitter he set the table for the Yankees' big hitters behind him with 176 hits and 83 walks.

After batting .375 in 1998's World Series when the Yankees swept San Diego, Knoblauch came through again in the 1999 sweep of the Atlanta Braves. His two-run homer in the eighth inning of Game 3 off the Braves' Tom Glavine tied the game. The Yankees went on to win the game in 10 innings and completed the sweep the following night.

The postseason has produced some of the biggest moments in Knoblauch's career. In the Twins' championship season in 1991, he hit .326 in the playoffs and set a rookie record with 15 hits. During the regular season, he batted 281 and was named the league's top rookie.

Knoblauch was named to the American League All-Star team in 1992, 1994, 1996, and 1997. His best overall season came in 1996 when he batted .341 with 140 runs scored, 35 doubles, 14 triples, 13 homers, 45 stolen bases and only eight errors.

Even though Knoblauch has been in the big leagues since the '91 season, he ended 1999 aged only 31. It would be no surprise if there are more titles and awards in his future.

Batting

Year	G	AB	R	H	HR	RBI	BB	SO	SB	CS	OBP	SLG	AVG
1999	**150**	**603**	**120**	**176**	**18**	**68**	**83**	**57**	**28**	**9**	**.393**	**.454**	**.292**
Career	**1313**	**5145**	**950**	**1533**	**78**	**523**	**672**	**580**	**335**	**98**	**.388**	**.419**	**.298**

Fielding

Year	Posn	G	GS	TC	PO	A	E	DP	FLD%
1999	**2B**	**150**	**150**	**705**	**254**	**425**	**26**	**67**	**.963**
Career		**1302**	**1286**	**6133**	**2387**	**3641**	**105**	**794**	**.983**

Moises Alou

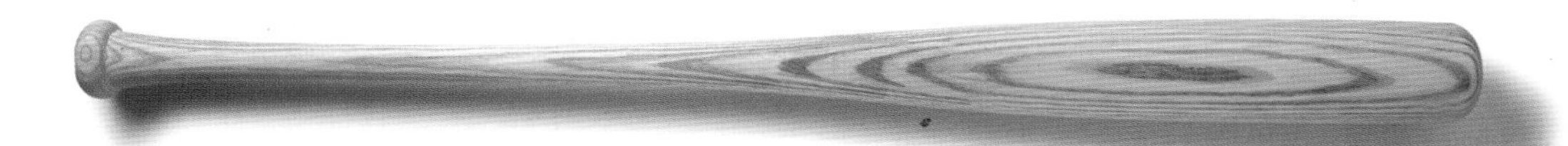

"It's difficult to put a timetable on a severe injury. We hope to have Moises back for the 2000 season."

Houston Astros general manager, Gerry Hunsicker

Profile

Name: Moises Rojas Alou **Height:** 6–3 **Weight:** 195 **Throws:** Right **Bats:** Right **Position:** Left Field **Born:** July 3, 1966, Atlanta, Georgia **Drafted:** Selected by the Pittsburgh Pirates in the first round (second pick overall) of the 1986 free-agent draft **Acquired:** Traded from the Florida Marlins to the Houston Astros, November 11, 1997 **Pre-Majors Highlight:** Batted .302 with 14 home runs for Class A Salem in 1989 **Personal Information:** Son of Montreal Expos manager Felipe Alou and nephew of former Major Leaguers Matty and Jeses Alou

When Moises Alou suffered a devastating ankle injury while playing for the Montreal Expos, many wondered if his career was over.

The injury occurred late in the 1993 season while Alou, one of the bright young stars in the game at the time, was trying to stretch a single into a double. He suffered torn ligaments in the ankle and there was doubt if he would ever play again.

Alou proved the doubters wrong. Not only did he return the following season, his numbers actually got better. He batted .339 with 22 homers and 78 runs batted in while playing in only 107 games in the strike-shortened 1994 season. That started a string of five solid seasons in a row, which included appearances in the All-Star Game in 1994 and 1997. Alou also was one of the stars of the Florida Marlins team that won the World Series in the '97 season.

Going into the 2000 season season, Alou finds himself overcoming another career-threatening injury. The outfielder, who now plays for the Houston Astros, missed the entire 1999 season after tearing knee ligaments after he fell off a treadmill in an offseason workout. Judging by the way he bounced back from his first injury, it's a good bet Alou will return to stardom again.

The highlight of Alou's career came in 1997, his only year with the Marlins, whom he signed with as a free agent after the 1996 season. He hit .292 with 23 homers and 115 RBIs as the Marlins became the first wild-card team to win the World Series. While Florida pitcher Livan Hernandez was voted the Series' Most Valuable Player, Alou was the real star of the Marlins' dramatic seven-game win over the Cleveland Indians. He hit .321 with three homers and nine RBIs. That included a pair of three-run homers off the Indians' Orel Hershiser that turned Games 1 and 5 in Florida's favor.

Soon after the Series, the Marlins, in an attempt to cut their payroll, traded Alou to Houston, where he put up his best numbers of his career. He batted .312—the second-highest average of his career—with 38 homers and 124 RBIs, both career highs. He also scored 104 runs, the first time he had 100 runs in his career, while 14 of his 38 home runs either tied games or gave the Astros the lead. Alou also matched his career-best with five RBIs in one game, drove in four runs in a game five times and had three games with two home runs.

Alou, a three-time All-Star, comes from solid baseball bloodlines. His father, Felipe, manages the Montreal Expos and is a former Major League player. His uncles, Matty and Jesus, also played in the big leagues.

Career milestones

1990 Traded by the Pittsburgh Pirates to the Montreal Expos, September 1

1996 Signed by the Florida Marlins as a free agent, December 12

1997 Hit a home run in his first at-bat with the Florida Marlins. Hit 100th career homer, Aug. 17. Won World Series title with Florida

1998 Established career-bests in nearly every offensive category

Batting

Year	G	AB	R	H	HR	RBI	BB	SO	SB	CS	OBP	SLG	AVG
Career	**919**	**3271**	**535**	**966**	**145**	**612**	**337**	**476**	**73**	**29**	**.362**	**.506**	**.295**

Fielding

Year	Posn	G	GS	TC	PO	A	E	DP	FLD%
Career	**OF**	**887**	**842**	**1595**	**1520**	**50**	**25**	**10**	**.984**

Profile

Name: Charles Harrison Nagy **Height:** 6–3 **Weight:** 200 **Throws:** Right **Bats:** Left **Position:** Pitcher **Born:** May 5, 1967, Fairfield, Connecticut **Drafted:** Selected by the Cleveland Indians in the first round (17th pick overall) of the 1988 free-agent draft **Pre-Majors Highlights:** Member of the United States Olympic team that won the gold medal in 1988 Olympics at Seoul, Korea **Personal Information:** Active in the Cleveland community with Cystic Fibrosis "65 Roses Sports Club."

Charles Nagy

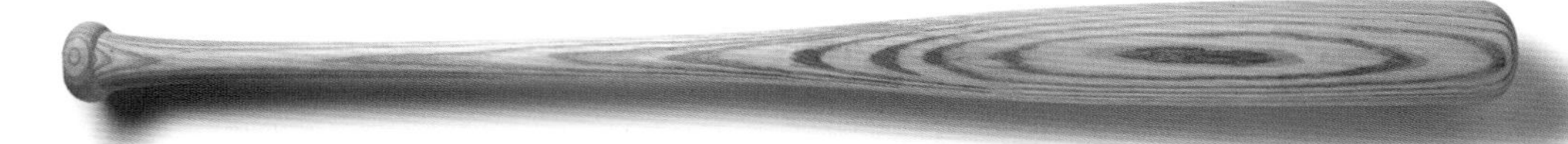

"Charlie Nagy is a winner. He doesn't get a lot of fanfare, but he wins and that's all that matters."

Cleveland Indians general manager, John Hart

Career milestones

1990 Made Major League debut, June 29

1992 Threw one-hitter, August 8 against Baltimore

1996 Second in American League with .773 winning percentage, going 17–5. Began season 11–1

1997 Pitched into seventh inning in 28 of 34 starts

1998 Collected his 100th career win on Aug. 25 against Seattle

1999 Recorded fifth straight 15-win season

If the ultimate judge of a starting pitcher is wins, then Charles Nagy is at the top of the game.

The 1999 season was vintage Nagy, who helped the Cleveland Indians win their fifth straight American League Central title. The right-hander was 17–11 with a 4.95 earned run average while pitching 202 innings.

Nagy has won 15 or more games in each of the last five seasons. He was 16–6 in 1995, 17–5 in 1996, 15–11 in 1997 and 15–10 in 1998. Those totals are more impressive when this fact is considered: Atlanta Braves' ace Greg Maddux is the only other pitcher in Major League Baseball to win 15 or more games in each of the last five years.

Durability is another Nagy strength. He has pitched 200 or more innings in each of the last four seasons and has topped that mark six times in his nine-year career. Nagy also has gone 184 straight starts without missing his turn in the rotation. That streak started on October 3, 1993 and continued through the 1999 season. Nagy missed most of the '93 season after having surgery on his right shoulder. He started the final game of the season and hasn't been out of the rotation since. Over the last five years, Nagy has averaged 16 wins and 208 innings pitched since.

Nagy was the Indians' No. 1 pick in 1989 and quickly made it to Cleveland the following season. After going 10–15 as a rookie, he turned in a strong 17–10 year with a 2.96 ERA in 1992.

Nagy started on opening day in 1993, but experienced shoulder problems and was 2–6 with a 6.29 ERA before undergoing surgery in June. He bounced back more quickly than anticipated and started the final ever game at Cleveland Stadium on October 3.

There's nothing spectacular about Nagy's style. He doesn't have an overpowering fastball and doesn't dominate hitters, but he keeps his team in games and pitches a lot of innings.

Nagy is always quick to downplay his accomplishments.

"I just try to make them hit the ball and take advantage of my defense," he said. "I try to hit my spots and get my team back in the dugout as fast as possible."

"You always know what you're going to get from Charlie," said Baltimore Orioles manager Mike Hargrove, who managed Nagy in Cleveland from 1991–99. "Charlie just goes about his business and gives his team a chance to win. Charlie's quiet, but he's a great competitor."

Nagy, who will be 33 in May 2000, has shown few signs of slowing up. There's every reason to believe his knack for winning will continue.

Pitching

Year	W	L	ERA	G	GS	CG	SHO	SV	SVO	INN	H	R	ER	HR	HBP	BB	SO
1999	**17**	**11**	**4.95**	**33**	**32**	**1**	**0**	**0**	**0**	**202.0**	**238**	**120**	**111**	**26**	**6**	**59**	**126**
Career	**121**	**86**	**4.20**	**268**	**266**	**31**	**6**	**0**	**0**	**1766.1**	**1924**	**897**	**824**	**182**	**47**	**529**	**1143**

Batting

Year	G	AB	R	H	HR	RBI	BB	SO	SB	CS	OBP	SLG	AVG
Career	**269**	**16**	**1**	**1**	**0**	**0**	**0**	**10**	**0**	**0**	**.063**	**.063**	**.063**

Fielding

Year	Posn	G	GS	TC	PO	A	E	DP	FLD%
1999	**P**	**33**	**32**	**55**	**21**	**33**	**1**	**3**	**.982**
Career		**268**	**266**	**476**	**161**	**304**	**11**	**27**	**.977**

Bobby Bonilla

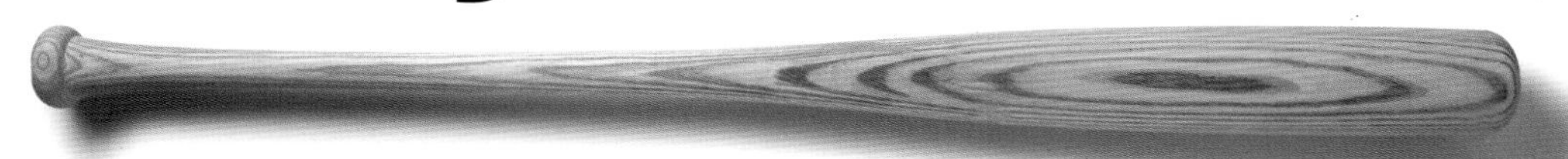

"Bobby Bonilla is a productive hitter. He's a dangerous hitter from both sides of the plate."

Former Major League manager, Jim Leyland

Profile

Name: Robert Martin Antonio Bonilla **Height:** 6–3 **Weight:** 240 **Throws:** Right **Bats:** Both **Position:** Right Field, Left Field **Born:** February 23, 1963, New York, New York **Drafted:** Not drafted. Signed by the Pittsburgh Pirates as a free agent, July 11, 1981 **Acquired:** Traded by the Los Angeles Dodgers to the New York Mets, November 11, 1998 **Pre-Majors Highlight:** Hit 11 homers with 71 runs batted in for Class AA Nashua, 1984 **Personal Information:** Attended New York Tech.

Since coming to the Major Leagues in 1986, Bobby Bonilla has been one of the top switch-hitters in baseball.

Bonilla holds the National League record for home runs by a switch-hitter with 237. He has 277 career homers.

Most of Bonilla's success came with the Pittsburgh Pirates, who signed him as an undrafted free agent in 1981. After spending four seasons in the Pirates' farm system, Bonilla was taken in the Rule 5 draft by the Chicago White Sox following the 1985 season.

The Pirates' organization, seeing the error of its ways, wanted Bonilla back and traded pitcher Jose DeLeon to the White Sox on July 23, 1986. Bonilla returned to Pittsburgh and became a star for the Pirates over the next six seasons.

From 1986–91, Bonilla batted .300 or better twice (1987 and 1991), topped the 20-home run mark three times (1988–90) and reached 100 or more RBIs three times (1989–91).

Bonilla's best seasons came when the Pirates won back-to-back National League East titles in 1990 and 1991. Playing in 160 games in 1990, Bonilla hit .280 with 32 homers and 120 RBIs, a career high. In 157 games the following season, Bonilla had one of the best years of his career, batting .302 with a league-leading 44 doubles, 18 homers and 100 RBIs.

Bonilla showed his versatility in the field in those two seasons as he played third base, first base and the outfield.

A free agent after the 1991 season, Bonilla signed with the New York Mets on December 2. He put in 3.1 solid seasons with the Mets. The best came in 1993 when he hit a career-high 34 homers while hitting .265 with 87 RBIs.

Bonilla was traded to the Baltimore Orioles on July 28, 1995 and had 1.1 productive years in the American League. He hit .33 with 10 homers and 46 RBIs in 61 games in '95 before hitting 28 homers with 116 RBIs and a .287 average in 1996.

A free agent again after the 1996 season, Bonilla signed with Florida on November 22 and was a central figure on the Marlins' World Series championship team. In a solid overall season, he hit .297 with 17 homers and 96 RBIs. He hit two homers with eight RBIs in the playoffs, which culminated with the Marlins defeating the Cleveland Indians in a thrilling seven-game World Series.

Because the Marlins decided to cut their payroll after winning the title, Bonilla's time in Florida didn't last very long. He was traded to the Los Angeles Dodgers on May 15, 1998 in one of the biggest deals in baseball history.

Going into the 2000 season, Bonilla's career includes six playoff appearances, a World Series title and six All-Star Games.

Career milestones

1988 Named third baseman on The Sporting News National League All-Star team and The Sporting News Silver Slugger team

1996 Led American League with 17 sacrifice flies

1997 Tied for National League lead with three grand slams while helping the Florida Marlins to win the World Series

1998 Split season between the Florida Marlins and the Los Angeles Dodgers

Batting

Year	G	AB	R	H	HR	RBI	BB	SO	SB	CS	OBP	SLG	AVG
1999	**60**	**119**	**12**	**19**	**4**	**18**	**19**	**16**	**0**	**1**	**.277**	**.303**	**.160**
Career	**1906**	**6800**	**1044**	**1912**	**277**	**1124**	**852**	**1100**	**44**	**56**	**.359**	**.478**	**.281**

Fielding

Year	Posn	G	GS	TC	PO	A	E	DP	FLD%
1999	**OF**	**25**	**23**	**39**	**36**	**2**	**1**	**0**	**.974**
Career		**1720**	**1680**	**4837**	**2756**	**1857**	**224**	**224**	**.954**

Profile

Name: Pedro Julio Astacio
Height: 6–2 **Weight:** 210
Throws: Right **Bats:** Right **Position:** Pitcher **Born:** November 28, 1969, Hato Mayor, Dominican Republic **Drafted:** Signed by the Los Angeles Dodgers as an undrafted free agent, November 21, 1987 **Acquired:** Traded by the Los Angeles Dodgers to the Colorado Rockies, August 19, 1997 **Pre-Majors Highlight:** Named to Gulf Coast League All-Star, 1989 **Personal Information:** Was only 17 years old when he was signed by the Los Angeles Dodgers

Pedro Astacio

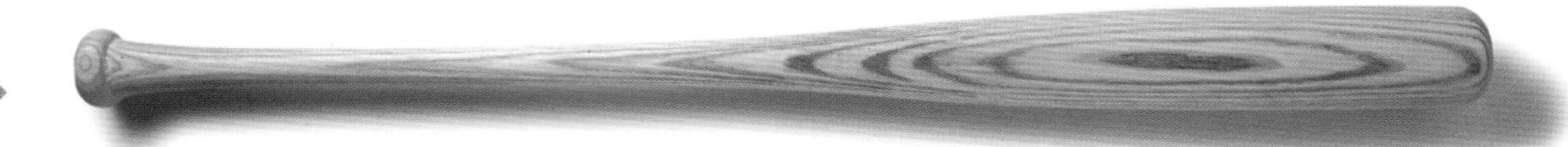

"It was a great season. I got my 1,000th strikeout and a career high in wins."

Colorado Rockies pitcher, Pedro Astacio

Career milestones

1992 Pitched a three-hit shutout against Philadelphia in his Major League debut, July 3
1993 Won 14 games for the Dodgers in his first full Major League season
1996 Pitched one scoreless appearance for the Dodgers in the Division Series
1998 Led the National League with 17 hit batsmen and 39 home runs allowed
1999 Enjoyed career highs in wins, innings pitched and complete games. Also recorded his 1,000th career strikeout

It's easy to see why a lot of Major League teams wouldn't mind having Pedro Astacio in their rotation.

There are plenty of plusses on Astacio's side. He ended 1999 aged 30 years old, despite being in the big leagues since 1992. He has a live arm and a variety of pitches. He's also coming off the best season of his career and pitches a lot of innings.

Astacio, a right-hander for the Colorado Rockies, had a solid year in 1999. He finished with a 17–11 record, threw seven complete games and pitched 232 innings, hitting career highs in all categories.

There's a lot to like about Astacio, who was originally signed by the Los Angeles Dodgers. His fastball hits 92 to 93 miles-per-hour and all of his pitches have good movement.

Astacio's record was a bit deceptive. After losing his first three decisions, he went 9–3 after the All-Star break. In one stretch after the break, Astacio pitched at least seven innings in eight straight starts and was 6–1 in those games. In one four-start stretch, he was 3–0 with a 1.40 ERA and has allowed seven earned runs and 23 hits in 35 innings with five walks and 38 strikeouts.

Astacio also has turned into a workhorse. His innings pitched broke the team record of 230.1 for a single season set by Darryl Kile in 1998. Astacio has pitched over 200 innings for four straight years, has averaged 214 innings pitched a season in that stretch and hasn't missed a start since joining the Rockies in August 1997. He also recorded his 1,000th career strikeout in 1999.

Astacio took several steps forward in 1999. Not only did he become the Rockies' ace, he turned into one of the top starters in the league. Astacio tied the single-season Rockies record for victories set by Kevin Ritz, who won 17 games in 1996. Astacio had 14 victories for Los Angeles in 1993, his first full season in the majors.

The Dodgers signed Astacio in 1989 and he made it to Los Angeles in 1992. He made an instant splash, going 5–5 with four shutouts and a 1.98 ERA in 11 starts.

Astacio's 1999 earned run average was high at 5.04, but a lot of that can be attributed to pitching in the high altitude of Denver's Coors Field, where every pitcher's ERA is inflated. Astacio was 12–6 on the road. He led the league in road victories.

Astacio's acquisition was one of the best in the Rockies' seven-year history. Colorado traded second baseman Eric Young to the Dodgers for Astacio on August 18, 1997. Astacio paid immediate dividends, going 5–1 in seven starts through the rest of the '97 season. He has gone 35–26 as a Rockie.

Pitching

Year	W	L	ERA	G	GS	CG	SHO	SV	SVO	INN	H	R	ER	HR	HBP	BB	SO
1999	17	11	5.04	34	34	7	0	0	0	232.0	258	140	130	38	11	75	210
Career	83	73	4.32	250	207	20	9	0	2	1376.2	1400	717	661	164	61	441	1029

Batting

Year	G	AB	R	H	HR	RBI	BB	SO	SB	CS	OBP	SLG	AVG
Career	253	427	20	60	0	17	3	168	0	1	.150	.159	.141

Fielding

Year	Posn	G	GS	TC	PO	A	E	DP	FLD%
1999	P	34	34	45	16	25	4	3	.911
Career		250	207	330	138	180	12	13	.964

Chuck Finley

Profile

Name:
Charles Edward Finley
Height: 6–6 **Weight:** 226
Throws: Left **Bats:** Left **Position:** Pitcher
Born: November 26, 1962, Monroe, Louisiana
Drafted: Selected by the California Angels in the secondary phase of the 1985 free-agent draft
Pre-Majors Highlight: Appeared in only 43 minor league games before being called up by the Angels in 1987
Personal Information: Attended Northeast Louisiana University

"Chuck is 37, but he's a young 37. He keeps himself in great shape and he's a great competitor."

Cleveland Indians pitching coach, Dick Pole

Chuck Finley hasn't played on a lot of winning teams in his career, but that doesn't detract from his record.

Take one look at Finley's numbers and it's easy to see why he's been one of the most consistent starting pitchers in the Major Leagues over the last 14 years.

Finley goes into the 2000 season with a lifetime mark of 165–140. The left-hander has been a stalwart for the Anaheim Angels, with club records for wins, innings pitched (2,674.2) and games pitched (436). Finley finished 1999 with a 3.72 career earned run average.

Taking the ball when his team has needed him has been another Finley trademark. He has averaged 27 starts and 191 innings pitched per season in his career. Finley has started over 30 games nine times and has pitched over 200 innings in nine different seasons.

The Angels knew they were getting something special when they took Finley in the secondary phase of the free-agent draft in 1985. After appearing in only 43 minor-league games, he was in Anaheim the following year at the age of 23, going 3–1 with a 3.30 ERA in 25 relief appearances. Finley pitched well enough down the stretch to make the Angels' postseason roster after they won the American League West title. He pitched three scoreless appearances in the League Championship Series against Boston, which the Angels lost in seven games. Unfortunately for Finley, the Angels have not come close to reaching the World Series since then.

The Angels brought Finley along slowly. He pitched out of the bullpen for most of the 1987 season before joining the rotation in 1988. The first season as a starter was a struggle as he went 9–15 with a 4.17 ERA, but he was in the rotation to stay and reeled off 52 wins from 1989–91, which included a 2.57 ERA in 1989 and a 2.40 ERA in 1990. Finley turned in back-to-back records of 18–9 in 1990 and 1991.

Finley led the American League in complete games with 13 in 1993 while going 16–14 with a 3.15 ERA. In the strike-shortened year of 1995, he led the league in innings pitched (183.1) and was tied for the league lead in starts (25).

Finley was a member of the American League All-Star team in 1989, 1990, 1995 and 1996. Even though the Angels had a disastrous season in 1999, he turned in his usual consistent performance, going 12–11 with a 4.43 ERA. He has won 66 games the last four seasons while pitching 238 innings in 1996, 223.1 innings in 1998 and 213.1 in 1999.

Age doesn't seem to be catching up with Finley, who turned 37 in November 1999. In fact, he shows few signs of letting up any time soon.

Career milestones

1986 Made Major League debut, May 29, against the Detroit Tigers
1989 Threw one-hitter against the Boston Red Sox, May 26
1997 Set career Angels records with 312 starts and 142 wins, surpassing marks held by Nolan Ryan
1998 Registered 400th career appearance on September 6 against the Kansas City Royals
1999 Signed for Cleveland Indians on December 16 as a free agent

Pitching

Year	W	L	ERA	G	GS	CG	SHO	SV	SVO	INN	H	R	ER	HR	HBP	BB	SO
1999	**12**	**11**	**4.43**	**33**	**33**	**1**	**0**	**0**	**0**	**213.1**	**197**	**117**	**105**	**23**	**8**	**94**	**200**
Career	**165**	**140**	**3.72**	**436**	**379**	**57**	**14**	**0**	**0**	**2675.0**	**2544**	**1234**	**1107**	**254**	**71**	**1118**	**2151**

Batting

Year	G	AB	R	H	HR	RBI	BB	SO	SB	CS	OBP	SLG	AVG
Career	**436**	**14**	**1**	**0**	**0**	**0**	**0**	**8**	**0**	**0**	**.000**	**.000**	**.000**

Fielding

Year	Posn	G	GS	TC	PO	A	E	DP	FLD%
1999	**P**	**33**	**33**	**38**	**7**	**28**	**3**	**1**	**.921**
Career		**411**	**379**	**412**	**105**	**271**	**36**	**22**	**.913**

Profile

Name: Vinicio Soria Castilla **Height:** 6–1 **Weight:** 205 **Throws:** Right **Bats:** Right **Positions:** Third Base **Born:** July 4, 1967, Oaxaca, Mexico **Drafted:** Not drafted. Sold by Saltillo of the Mexican League to the Atlanta Braves, March 19, 1990 **Acquired:** Selected by the Colorado Rockies in the second round (40th pick overall) of the 1992 Expansion Draft **Pre-Majors Highlight:** Started playing in the Mexican League when he was 19 years old **Personal Information:** He is a 1985 graduate of Carlos Gracida Institute, earning baseball Most Valuable Player honors

Vinny Castilla

"You have to give Vinny a lot of credit. He's worked hard to become a good hitter."

Colorado Rockies hitting coach, Clint Hurdle

Career milestones

1995 Hit three home runs in four Division Series games against Atlanta

1997 Posted a 22-game hitting streak, August 9–September 1

1998 Hit his 150th career home run, July 10. Became the seventh National League player ever to collect 40 or more home runs in three consecutive seasons

1999 Collected 1,000th career hit. Acquired by Tampa Devil Rays on December 12 for pitcher Rolando Arrojo

Vinny Castilla is a perfect example of what a player can do once he gets an opportunity.

When the 1990s began, Castilla found himself buried in the Atlanta Braves organization. The Braves purchased his contract from Saltillo of the Mexican League on March 19, 1990. On one hand, the transaction was a break because it got Castilla, a native of Mexico, into a Major League organization. On the other, it came at a time when the Braves were becoming one of the top teams in baseball.

The Braves' rise was bad news for Castilla. As Atlanta made it to the World Series in the 1991 and 1992 seasons, Castilla spent most of each year in the minors. He got five at-bats with the Braves in 1991 and 16 in 1992. It was obvious Castilla would never get a legitimate chance to play with Atlanta.

That's when the second break of Castilla's career came along. Major League Baseball held its expansion draft following the 1992 season to stock its new teams in Colorado and Florida that would begin play the following year. The Rockies took Castilla in the second round with the 40th pick overall.

Castilla appeared in 105 games at shortstop with the Rockies in their first season, hitting .255 with nine homers and 30 runs batted in. Playing all four infield positions in 1994, Castilla batted .331 with three homers and 18 RBIs.

Castilla's career began to blossom in 1995 when he turned into a legitimate offensive force. In 139 games, he hit .309 with 32 homers and 90 RBIs as the Rockies qualified for the National League playoffs as the wild-card team. Castilla even got a bit of revenge against the Braves in the Division Series by hitting three homers and driving in six runs in Atlanta's three-game sweep.

That was just the beginning for Castilla, who became one of the most dangerous hitters in the National League over the next four seasons. The streak started with almost identical back-to-back seasons the next two years. Castilla batted .304, hit 40 homers and drove in 113 runs in both the 1996 and 1997 seasons.

As it turned out, he was just getting warmed up. Castilla batted .319 with 46 homers and 144 RBIs in 1998 while playing all 162 games. He followed that up by hitting .275 with 33 homers and 102 RBIs in 1999.

Castilla, who has played primarily at third base since 1996, also has turned into a solid defensive player. He led National League third basemen in assists in 1996 and 1997 and also led N.L. third basemen in double plays in 1997.

Castilla, who made the National League All-Star team in 1995 and 1998, turned the opportunity of an expansion draft into a chance to make himself a solid all-around player. There's no reason to think he'll stop now.

Batting

Year	G	AB	R	H	HR	RBI	BB	SO	SB	CS	OBP	SLG	AVG
1999	**158**	**615**	**83**	**169**	**33**	**102**	**53**	**75**	**2**	**3**	**.331**	**.478**	**.275**
Career	**956**	**3516**	**518**	**1049**	**203**	**611**	**223**	**521**	**22**	**32**	**.342**	**.528**	**.298**

Fielding

Year	Posn	G	GS	TC	PO	A	E	DP	FLD%
1999	**3B**	**157**	**155**	**414**	**96**	**299**	**19**	**32**	**.954**
Career		**938**	**895**	**2788**	**717**	**1969**	**102**	**268**	**.963**

Jeff Kent

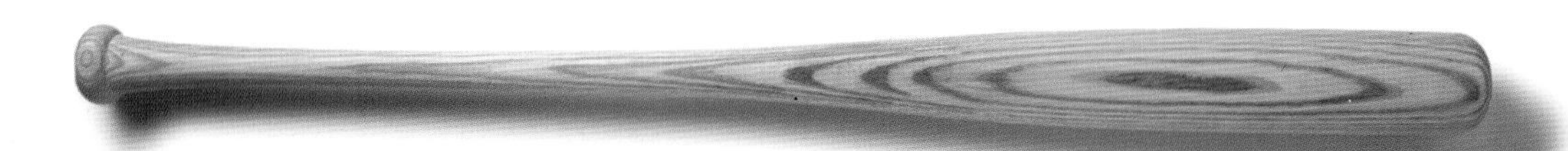

"You can't argue with Jeff's numbers. He has put together three very good years for us."

San Francisco Giants manager, Dusty Baker

Profile

Name: Jeffrey Franklin Kent **Height:** 6–1 **Weight:** 205 **Throws:** Right **Bats:** Right **Position:** Second Base **Born:** March 7, 1968, Bellflower, California **Drafted:** Selected by the Toronto Blue Jays in the 20th round of the 1989 free-agent draft **Acquired:** Traded by the Cleveland Indians to the San Francisco Giants, November 13, 1996 **Pre-Majors Highlight:** Led New York-Penn League with 13 homers in 1989 **Personal Information:** Attended the University of California

So much for first impressions. When San Francisco traded third baseman Matt Williams to the Cleveland Indians for infielders Jeff Kent and Jose Vizcaino and pitcher Julian Tavarez on November 13, 1996, Giants fans howled their disapproval.

Williams, a perennial All-Star, home-run hitter and Gold Glove winner, was wildly popular in San Francisco and fans were stunned over the trade. Giants fans thought their team was giving up and they were unimpressed with the package of players coming back in return.

Thanks to Kent, those negative thoughts have changed significantly. Kent has put together three of the best offensive seasons for a second baseman in Major League Baseball history. In three years with the Giants, he has averaged 28 homers and 117 runs batted in while playing a position traditionally not known for big offensive numbers.

Kent made an immediate impact in 1997 by hitting 29 homers, driving in 121 runs and hitting .250. He also stole 11 bases and scored 90 runs in helping the Giants win the National League West title.

If Giants fans thought that was a good season, they hadn't seen anything yet. Kent raised his batting average 47 points to .297 in 1998, hit 31 homers and drove in 128 runs. He also had 156 hits and scored 94 runs. All were career highs. Kent also finished fourth in the league in RBIs while leading the Giants with a .332 batting average with runners in scoring position. The numbers earned him his first All-Star Game appearance. That production came despite missing 24 games with a sprained right knee from June 10 to July 9.

Just how good was Kent's season? It put him in some very select company. He set a franchise record for most RBIs by a second baseman, surpassing Hall of Famer Rogers Hornsby's mark of 125 in 1927. He also became the second second baseman in Major League history to collect at least 120 RBIs in multiple seasons, a feat Hornsby accomplished five times.

While Mark McGwire and Sammy Sosa pursued Rogers Maris' home-run record, Kent chased the two sluggers in another category. He was third in the league for RBI Ratio (at bats per RBI) with a 4.2 mark, trailing only McGwire (3.5) and Sosa (4.1).

Kent had another strong season in 1999. He hit .290 with 23 homers and 101 RBIs with a career-high 40 doubles.

Kent has been involved in trades featuring big-name players. He was traded from Toronto to the Mets in a deal that sent pitcher David Cone to the Blue Jays in 1992. The Mets traded him to the Indians in 1996 for Carlos Baerga, an All-Star player at the time. Then came the deal involving Williams.

Considering his production the last three years, it's obvious Kent is a big-name player, too.

Career milestones

1996 Traded with Jose Vizcaino by the New York Mets to the Cleveland Indians for Carlos Baerga and Alvaro Espinoza

1997 Hit three grand slams during regular season and two homers in Division Series against Florida

1998 Had a career-high 13-game hitting streak from August 21–September 2

1999 Drove in more than 100 runs for the third straight season

Batting

Year	G	AB	R	H	HR	RBI	BB	SO	SB	CS	OBP	SLG	AVG
1999	**138**	**511**	**86**	**148**	**23**	**101**	**61**	**112**	**13**	**6**	**.366**	**.511**	**.290**
Career	**1032**	**3742**	**566**	**1032**	**161**	**668**	**297**	**770**	**49**	**31**	**.335**	**.477**	**.276**

Fielding

Year	Posn	G	GS	TC	PO	A	E	DP	FLD%
1999	**2B**	**133**	**132**	**614**	**279**	**325**	**10**	**90**	**.984**
Career		**1012**	**979**	**4776**	**2022**	**2626**	**128**	**565**	**.973**

Profile

Name:
Brady Kevin Anderson
Height: 6–1 **Weight:** 202 **Throws:** Left **Bats:** Left **Position:** Center Field
Born: January 18, 1964, Silver Spring, Maryland
Drafted: Selected by the Boston Red Sox in the 10th round of the 1985 free-agent draft **Acquired:** Traded by the Boston Red Sox to the Baltimore Orioles, July 30, 1988
Pre-Majors Highlight: Named to Florida State League All-Star team, 1986
Personal Information: Attended California-Irvine University

Brady Anderson

"You have to admire Brady's style. He plays hard and he plays when he's hurting."

Baltimore Orioles shortstop, Cal Ripken Jr.

Career milestones

1996 Finished second in the American League with 50 home runs
1997 Led the American League by being hit by 19 pitches.
1998 Collected a career-high five hits, August 7 vs. Minnesota. Had pair of two-homer games, May 13 vs. Cleveland and August 7 vs. Minnesota

It was a season for the ages. In 1996, Brady Anderson made headlines all over Major League Baseball with a year fans will never forget.

Anderson, the center fielder for the Baltimore Orioles, belted 50 homers, drove in 110 runs, batted 297, scored 117 runs and stole 21 bases.

Those numbers alone are amazing enough, but there was another aspect of the season that made Anderson's year even more incredible. The numbers came from the leadoff spot.

"That might have been the greatest year by a leadoff hitter in baseball history" said Davey Johnson, who managed the Orioles at the time and is now managing the Los Angeles Dodgers. "We might not ever see another year from a leadoff hitter like that again."

Anderson set the Major League record for home runs leading off games with 12. His power helped the Orioles qualify for the American League playoffs as the wild-card team, but it didn't stop with the regular season. He hit a leadoff homer in Game 1 of the Division Series against the Cleveland Indians and homered again in Game 4 in the Orioles' upset win. Anderson batted .294 for the series.

While the 1996 season was the best year of Anderson's career, he has been one of the best leadoff hitters in the game since becoming a regular with the Orioles in 1992. Baltimore acquired Anderson and pitcher Curt Schilling, who has gone on to stardom with the Philadelphia Phillies, for pitcher Mike Boddicker on July 29, 1988. While the Red Sox picked up the pitcher they needed for their playoff run, the long-range advantage went to the Orioles.

Anderson bounced between Baltimore and the minor leagues before finally sticking in 1992. His first full season in the Majors was a sign of things to come. He hit .271 with 21 homers, 80 RBIs and a career-high 53 stolen bases.

Anderson has been a fixture with the Orioles ever since. He has scored 100 or more runs four times, has hit at least 12 home runs each of the last eight years and has stolen 20 or more bases seven times. In Baltimore's American League East championship season in 1997, Anderson hit .288 with 18 homers and 73 RBIs.

Anderson had another solid season in 1999. He hit .282 with 24 homers, 81 RBIs and 36 stolen bases.

Anderson, who made the American League All-Star team in 1992, 1996 and 1997, also is one of the top defensive players in center field in baseball. His reckless style going after fly balls has seen him attempt diving catches and crash into walls. That style has led to several injuries, including broken ribs and leg problems, but Anderson's toughness keeps him in the lineup.

Batting

Year	G	AB	R	H	HR	RBI	BB	SO	SB	CS	OBP	SLG	AVG
1999	**150**	**564**	**109**	**159**	**24**	**81**	**96**	**105**	**36**	**7**	**.404**	**.477**	**.282**
Career	**1528**	**5483**	**919**	**1431**	**182**	**661**	**790**	**987**	**283**	**87**	**.365**	**.438**	**.261**

Fielding

Year	Posn	G	GS	TC	PO	A	E	DP	FLD%
1999	**OF**	**136**	**134**	**312**	**308**	**3**	**1**	**1**	**.997**
Career		**1415**	**1331**	**3209**	**3121**	**51**	**37**	**11**	**.988**

Travis Fryman

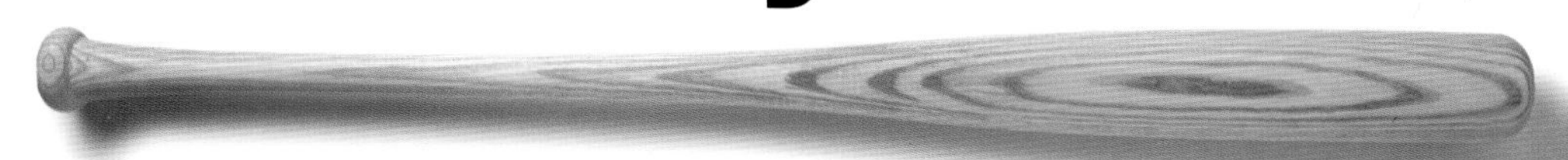

"Playing in Cleveland is a great situation. The team sells out every night and has a great chance to get to the World Series every year." **Cleveland Indians third baseman, Travis Fryman**

Profile

Name: David Travis Fryman **Height:** 6–1 **Weight:** 195 **Throws:** Right **Bats:** Right **Position:** Third Base **Born:** March 25, 1969, Lexington, Kentucky **Drafted:** Selected by the Detroit Tigers in the third round of the 1987 free-agent draft **Acquired:** Traded by the Arizona Diamondbacks to the Cleveland Indians, December 1, 1997 **Pre-Majors Highlight:** 1989 Led Double-A Eastern League in doubles and was named to the All-Star team, while playing for London, Ontario **Personal Information:** Younger brother, Troy, played in the Chicago White Sox and Chicago Cubs organizations

After being one of the most durable players in the Major Leagues, Travis Fryman had a year of firsts in 1999.

Unfortunately for Fryman and the Cleveland Indians, the firsts weren't very enjoyable.

After averaging 147 games played between 1991 and 1998, Fryman appeared in 85 games, his lowest total since becoming a regular in the big leagues. Thanks to back and knee injuries, Fryman landed on the disabled list for the first time in his career.

Fryman was able to play through chronic back pain throughout his career, but it finally put him on the disabled list from June 6–25. His return lasted less than two weeks when he tore a ligament in his right knee in a collision at first base. That injury kept him out until September 2. In all, Fryman spent 80 days on the disabled list.

The injuries cut into Fryman's production. He ended the season with the lowest offensive totals of his career, batting 255 with 10 homers and 48 runs batted in.

Fryman's game doesn't have a lot of flair, but his durability and numbers can't be disputed. He averaged 21 home runs and 94 RBIs between the 1991 and 1998 seasons.

Fryman's most productive years came with the Detroit Tigers, who drafted him in 1987. Primarily playing shortstop, Fryman advanced through the farm system and was in Detroit midway through the 1990 season. He hit .297 with nine homers and 27 RBIs in his rookie season.

Fryman became a mainstay in the Tigers' lineup for the next seven years. He played 144 or more games six times and led the American League in at-bats in 1992 and 1994. Fryman hit 20 or more homers in six seasons (1991, 1992, 1993, 1996, 1997 and 1998), drove in 100 or more runs twice (1996 and 1997) and hit .300 once (1993). Fryman, who made the All-Star team in 1992, 1993, 1994 and 1996, drove in a career-high 102 runs in 1997.

After all that success in Detroit, Fryman thought he would finish is career with the Tigers, but all that changed after the 1997 season. Following the expansion draft, Fryman was traded to the Arizona Diamondbacks on November 18.

The trade was the first of Fryman's career. He would experience the second trade of his career two weeks later when the Diamondbacks traded him and pitcher Tom Martin for third baseman Matt Williams.

After a slow start with the Indians, Fryman adjusted well to his new team. After batting .188 in April, he hit .308 for the rest of the year to go along with a career-high 28 homers, a .287 average and 96 RBIs in 557 at-bats.

Career milestones

1990 Voted Detroit Tiger Rookie of the Year. Hit .297 in 66 games after starting season in the minor leagues

1997 Drove in a career-high 102 runs. Led American League third basemen in fielding percentage

1998 Tied a career-best by homering in three straight games from July 10–12

Batting

Year	G	AB	R	H	HR	RBI	BB	SO	SB	CS	OBP	SLG	AVG
1999	**85**	**322**	**45**	**82**	**10**	**48**	**25**	**57**	**2**	**1**	**.309**	**.410**	**.255**
Career	**1327**	**5176**	**726**	**1418**	**187**	**823**	**459**	**1113**	**70**	**35**	**.333**	**.449**	**.274**

Fielding

Year	Posn	G	GS	TC	PO	A	E	DP	FLD%
1999	**3B**	**85**	**84**	**193**	**41**	**146**	**6**	**12**	**.969**
Career		**1320**	**1312**	**4322**	**1191**	**2982**	**149**	**397**	**.966**

Profile

Name: Gregory Lamont Vaughn **Height:** 6–0 **Weight:** 202 **Throws:** Right **Bats:** Right **Position:** Left Field **Born:** July 3, 1965, Sacramento, California **Drafted:** Selected by the Milwaukee Brewers in the first round (secondary phase) of the 1986 free-agent draft **Acquired:** Traded from the San Diego Padres to the Cincinnati Reds, February 2, 1999 **Pre-Majors Highlight:** Never stole fewer than 20 bases or hit fewer than 26 home runs in a full minor league season **Personal Information:** Cousin, Mo Vaughn, plays with the Anaheim Angels

Greg Vaughn

"Greg made everyone around him better. He had an outstanding season for us."

Cincinnati Reds manager, Jack McKeon

Career milestones

1990 Hit 17 homers while driving in 61 runs in first full season in Major Leagues

1996 Hit a combined 41 home runs for the Milwaukee Brewers and the San Diego Padres

1997 Drove in season-high five RBIs, September 20

1998 Hit at least one home run against every National League club except the Los Angeles Dodgers. Smashed a career high 50 homers as San Diego won the National League championship

1999 Hit 45 home runs and helped Cincinnati to a surprising National League Wild Card playoff game

Wherever Greg Vaughn goes, it's a pretty good bet that home runs are sure to follow.

The slugging outfielder, who played for the Cincinnati Reds in 1999, has cracked the 40-home-run mark three times in the last four seasons and has hit 292 home runs in his 11-year Major League career.

Vaughn played a key role in helping the surprising Reds challenge for a playoff spot in the National League last season. He crashed 45 home runs with 118 runs batted in while hitting .245. Vaughn also showed good speed with 15 stolen bases.

"Having Greg on our team changed our whole lineup," said Reds general manager Jim Bowden. "He made our entire lineup better."

Vaughn's numbers were even more impressive in 1998 when he was playing for the San Diego Padres. He established a club record with 50 home runs while helping the Padres reach the World Series for only the second time in franchise history.

The power display also put Vaughn in the company of some of the greatest sluggers to ever play the game. He became the 27th player in Major League history and the 10th ever in National League history to hit 50 or more home runs in one season. He also collected 119 RBIs, tied for second-most by a Padre in club history and finished 10th in the league in 1998. No 50 homer has had less publicity.

Vaughn also ranked fourth in the league in extra-base hits (82) and was fifth in slugging percentage (.597). He also hit two homers in a game seven times. Vaughn, who batted . 272, also had two 11-game hitting streaks.

The effort earned Vaughn a spot on the National League All-Star team. He was named to the American League All-Star team in 1993 and 1996 while playing for the Milwaukee Brewers.

Vaughn batted .237 with three home runs and five RBIs in the 1998 postseason. He homered and batted .333 as the Padres beat the Houston Astros in the Division Series before hitting .250 in the League Championship Series win over the Atlanta Braves. The Padres were swept by the New York Yankees in the World Series, but Vaughn hit two homers and drove in four runs.

Vaughn also helped the Padres win the National League West after being acquired from the Brewers on July 31, 1996 by hitting 10 home runs in the final 43 games.

Because Vaughn was headed for free agency after the 1999 season, the Padres traded him to the Reds for outfielder Reggie Sanders, infielder Damian Jackson and pitcher Josh Harris on February 2. The trade turned out well for the Reds as Vaughn was a consistent run producer the entire season.

Batting

Year	G	AB	R	H	HR	RBI	BB	SO	SB	CS	OBP	SLG	AVG
1999	**153**	**550**	**104**	**135**	**45**	**118**	**85**	**137**	**15**	**2**	**.347**	**.535**	**.245**
Career	**1377**	**4869**	**824**	**1197**	**292**	**882**	**665**	**1160**	**99**	**51**	**.337**	**.479**	**.246**

Fielding

Year	Posn	G	GS	TC	PO	A	E	DP	FLD%
1999	**OF**	**144**	**144**	**276**	**264**	**8**	**4**	**2**	**.986**
Career		**1099**	**1079**	**2245**	**2159**	**53**	**33**	**7**	**.985**

Aaron Sele

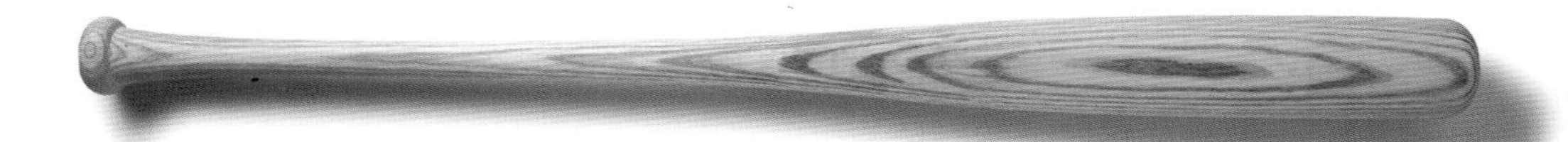

"Aaron is a stabilizing force in our rotation. He'll pitch a lot of innings and keep you in games."

Texas Rangers general manager, Doug Melvin

Profile

Name: Aaron Helmer Sele
Height: 6–5 **Weight:** 220
Throws: Right **Bats:** Right
Position: Pitcher **Born:** June 25, 1970, Golden Valley, New Mexico **Drafted:** Selected by the Boston Red Sox in the first round (23rd pick overall) of the 1991 free-agent draft **Acquired:** Traded by the Boston Red Sox to the Texas Rangers, November 6, 1997
Pre-Majors Highlight: Played for Team USA in 1990 and hurled a three-hit shutout vs. Cuba
Personal Information: Attended Washington State University

Following the 1997 season, the Texas Rangers went out to look for some pitching help.

Thanks to Aaron Sele, they found it. And thanks in part to Sele, the Rangers have become the dominant team in the American League West.

Texas found its pitching help on November 6, 1997 when it traded catcher Jim Leyritz and outfielder Damon Buford to the Boston Red Sox for Sele, pitcher Mark Bradenburg and catcher Bill Haselman.

Sele's production the last two seasons gives the Rangers the big edge in the trade. Since putting on a Texas uniform, the right-hander has won 37 games while averaging 33 starts and 209 innings pitched a season. The Rangers have won the division both seasons.

"Aaron has done an excellent job for us," said Texas manager Johnny Oates. "We always feel good about our chances when he's on the mound."

Sele, who throws in the low to mid 90s and relies on a sweeping curveball, made an immediate impact after the trade. He finished the 1998 season with a 19–11 record and a 4.23 earned run average. Sele achieved career highs in wins, starts (33), innings pitched (212.2), complete games (three) and shutouts (two). The numbers earned him his first selection to the American League All-Star team.

Sele had another strong showing in 1999, compiling an 18–9 record with a 4.79 ERA while striking out a career-high 186. He pitched 205 innings while again making 33 starts, completing three games and throwing two shutouts.

"This is a good situation for me," said Sele. "We have a good offense that scores a lot of runs and there's a good defense behind me. That makes a pitcher's job a lot easier."

Sele has recovered from the injury problems he had with the Red Sox, who took him in the first round of the 1991 draft. Sele quickly shot through the Red Sox's farm system and was in Boston midway through the 1993 season. He was impressive immediately, going 7–2 with a 2.74 ERA in 18 starts and was named The American League Rookie of the Year by The Sporting News.

Sele followed up his rookie year with an 8–7 record and a 3.83 ERA in 22 starts, but injuries cut into his production the next two seasons. Sele came down with a sore arm in 1995 and made only six starts, going 3–1 with a 3.06 ERA. A rib-cage injury limited him to 29 starts in 1996 when he was 7–11 with a 5.32 ERA. In his final season with Boston, Sele was 13–12 with a 5.38 ERA in 33 starts.

Sele has already compiled 75 wins, even though he will not turn 30 years old until midway through the 2000 season. Judging by the results of the last two seasons, there should be plenty of wins ahead for the pitcher and the Rangers.

Career milestones

1993 Finished third in the American League Rookie of the Year voting, and was named Rookie Pitcher of the Year by The Sporting News

1997 Threw 14 consecutive scoreless innings, July 3–12

1998 Won 19 games and was selected to the American League All-Star team for the first time

1999 Won 18 games and recorded a .667 winning percentage as the Rangers won the American League West Division again

Pitching

Year	W	L	ERA	G	GS	CG	SHO	SV	SVO	INN	H	R	ER	HR	HBP	BB	SO
1999	**18**	**9**	**4.79**	**33**	**33**	**2**	**2**	**0**	**0**	**205.0**	**244**	**115**	**109**	**21**	**12**	**70**	**186**
Career	**75**	**53**	**4.45**	**174**	**174**	**9**	**4**	**0**	**0**	**1039.2**	**1143**	**580**	**514**	**95**	**67**	**423**	**831**

Batting

Year	G	AB	R	H	HR	RBI	BB	SO	SB	CS	OBP	SLG	AVG
Career	**174**	**10**	**0**	**1**	**0**	**0**	**1**	**3**	**0**	**0**	**.182**	**.200**	**.100**

Fielding

Year	Posn	G	GS	TC	PO	A	E	DP	FLD%
1999	**P**	**33**	**33**	**40**	**8**	**30**	**2**	**2**	**.950**
Career		**174**	**174**	**189**	**54**	**121**	**14**	**9**	**.926**

Rod Beck

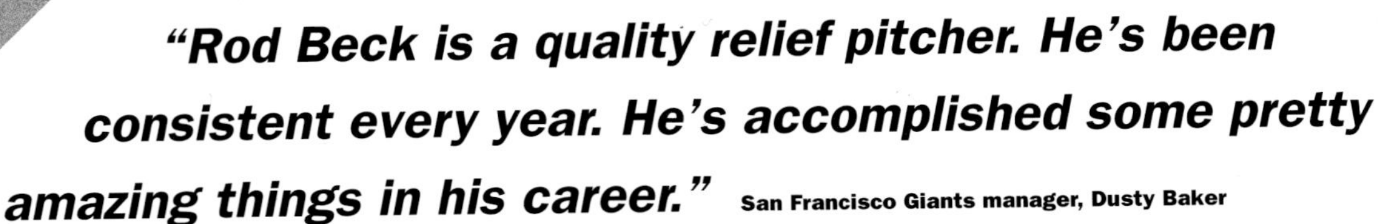

Profile

Name: Rodney Roy Beck
Height: 6–1 **Weight:** 235
Throws: Right **Bats:** Right **Position:** Pitcher **Born:** August 3, 1968, Burbank, California **Drafted:** Selected by the Oakland Athletics in the 13th round of the 1986 free-agent draft **Acquired:** Traded by the Chicago Cubs to the Boston Red Sox, August 31, 1999 **Pre-Majors Highlight:** Had 11-2 record for Class A San Jose in 1989 **Personal Information:** His Babe Ruth team advanced to the World Series in Michigan in 1984

"Rod Beck is a quality relief pitcher. He's been consistent every year. He's accomplished some pretty amazing things in his career." **San Francisco Giants manager, Dusty Baker**

Career milestones

1994 Named winner of National League Rolaids Relief Award. Went 28-for-28 in save situations

1996 Finished season with an 0–9 record, but saved 35 games

1997 Posted 37 saves for the National League Western Division champion San Francisco Giants

1998 Recorded 250th big league save, September 28 vs. San Francisco

After being a starting pitcher throughout his time in the minor leagues, Rod Beck was moved into the bullpen during the 1991 season.

One might say that turned out to be a good career move.

Beck was one of the most effective relief pitchers in the Major Leagues from 1993 through 1998. The burly right-hander recorded 232 saves in that six-year span while pitching for the San Francisco Giants and the Chicago Cubs.

Beck's best moment came in 1998 with the Cubs. He had one of the top seasons for a relief pitcher in Major League history, recording 51 saves to go along with a 3–4 record and a 3.02 ERA in a National League-high 81 games. He became just the fifth reliever ever to reach the 50-save mark, converting 51 of 58 save opportunities. Beck also led the league in games finished (70) and was second to San Diego's Trevor Hoffman in the National League Rolaids Relief Man standings.

Beck signed with the Cubs before the 1998 season after spending the previous seven years with the Giants. Ironically, he capped his historic season with his 250th big league save in the Cubs' wild card playoff 5–3 triumph over the Giants. The teams finished the regular season tied and had a one-game playoff to determine who would advance to the postseason.

"It's a year I'll always remember," said Beck. "To save that many games you need everything to fall the right way. That's what happened."

While 1998 was certainly Beck's best season, it wasn't his only dominant one. In 1992, his first full season as a closer in the big leagues, Beck saved 17 games and had a 1.76 ERA. In 1993, Beck recorded 48 saves and had a 2.16 ERA. He was a perfect 28-for-28 in save situations in 1994 and won the Rolaids Relief Man Award.

Beck, who holds the Giants' record in saves with 199, was a member of the National League All-Star team in 1993, 1994 and 1997.

Since Beck isn't an overpowering pitcher, control has always been the key to his success. He walked only eight men in 70 innings during the 1997 season.

After pitching so well for most of the decade, the 1999 season was a tough one for Beck, who started the season with a sore arm and had surgery in May. He had a 2–4 record with seven saves and a 7.80 ERA when the Cubs traded him to the Boston Red Sox on August 31. Beck looked like the Beck of old in helping Boston win the wild card playoff berth in the American League. In 12 games he was 0–1 with three saves and a 1.93 ERA.

Pitching

Year	W	L	ERA	G	GS	CG	SHO	SV	SVO	INN	H	R	ER	HR	HBP	BB	SO
1999	**2**	**5**	**5.93**	**43**	**0**	**0**	**0**	**10**	**15**	**44.0**	**50**	**29**	**29**	**5**	**1**	**18**	**25**
Career	**26**	**37**	**3.20**	**540**	**0**	**0**	**0**	**260**	**311**	**587.1**	**540**	**226**	**209**	**68**	**14**	**131**	**499**

Batting

Year	G	AB	R	H	HR	RBI	BB	SO	SB	CS	OBP	SLG	AVG
Career	**540**	**18**	**0**	**4**	**0**	**1**	**0**	**9**	**0**	**0**	**.222**	**.222**	**.222**

Fielding

Year	Posn	G	GS	TC	PO	A	E	DP	FLD%
1999	**P**	**43**	**0**	**11**	**5**	**6**	**0**	**0**	**1.000**
Career		**540**	**0**	**107**	**35**	**69**	**3**	**5**	**.972**

Eric Karros

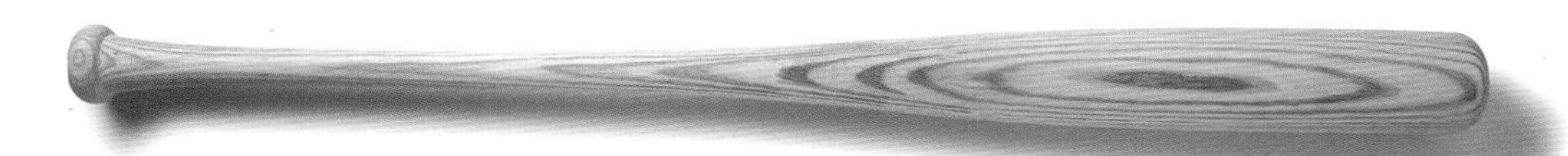

"He's Mr. Consistency. Thirty-plus homers and 100-plus RBIs. You can pencil Eric in for that."

Los Angeles Dodgers general manager, Kevin Malone

Profile

Name: Eric Peter Karros **Height:** 6-4 **Weight:** 226 **Throws:** Right **Bats:** Right **Position:** First Base **Born:** November 4, 1967, Hackensack, New Jersey **Drafted:** Selected by the Los Angeles Dodgers in the sixth round of the 1988 free-agent draft **Pre-Majors Highlights:** Batted over .300 in all four of his minor league seasons **Personal Information:** Attended college at UCLA

When it comes to consistent production, few players do it better than Eric Karros.

With little fanfare or notoriety, the Los Angeles Dodgers first baseman puts up big numbers every season.

Over the last five years, Karros' numbers can stand up to anyone's. Since 1995, Karros has averaged 31 homers and 104 runs batted in a season. He has cracked the 30-homer mark and the 100-RBI mark four times in the last five seasons.

"Eric is all about production," said Los Angeles general manager Kevin Malone. "Eric keeps putting up the numbers and he does it every year."

Karros had his most productive year in 1999, tying or setting career highs in every offensive category while being one of the few bright spots in another disappointing season for the Dodgers.

In 153 games, Karros batted .304 with 40 doubles, 34 homers and 112 RBIs. He set career highs in batting average, doubles and RBIs while tying his career best in home runs. Karros also hit 34 home runs in 1996.

Karros has been a consistent hitter for the Dodgers since reaching the Major Leagues in 1991. He was drafted by Los Angeles in 1988 and was called up for the final part of the '91 season after four outstanding years in the minors, which included a .352 batting average at Class AA San Antonio in 1990 and a 22-homer, 101-RBI season at Class AAA Albuquerque in 1991.

Karros was named National League Rookie of the Year in 1992, after hitting .257 with 30 doubles, 20 home runs and 88 RBIs.

Karros hit 20 homers with 80 RBIs in 1993, 14 homers with 46 RBIs in the strike-shortened season in 1994, 32 homers and 105 RBIs in 1995, 34 homers and 111 RBIs in 1996, 31 homers and 104 RBIs in 1997 and 23 homers and 87 RBIs in 1998.

His '98 numbers were down a bit because he missed the first 21 games of the season due to cartilage damage in his left knee. Karros didn't hit his first home run until May 19, his 72nd at-bat of the season, but had a strong finish.

Karros was named the first baseman on The Sporting News National League All-Star team and The Sporting News National League Silver Slugger team in 1995.

With more flamboyant teammates over the years such as Mike Piazza, who now plays for the New York Mets, and left fielder Gary Sheffield, Karros doesn't get the national publicity worthy of his numbers.

"Eric isn't flashy," said Dodgers manager Davey Johnson. "He just goes about his business and swings the bat. That's what you have to like about him. He just goes and puts up big numbers."

Career milestones

1992 Named National League Rookie of the Year

1993 Tied for the National League lead in assists for first basemen (147)

1997 Saw action in all 162 games. Hit .303 in 16 interleague games and led the Majors with 10 interleague home runs

1999 Batted a career-high .304

Batting

Year	G	AB	R	H	HR	RBI	BB	SO	SB	CS	OBP	SLG	AVG
1999	**153**	**578**	**74**	**176**	**34**	**112**	**53**	**119**	**8**	**5**	**.362**	**.550**	**.304**
Career	**1183**	**4456**	**574**	**1217**	**211**	**734**	**376**	**808**	**46**	**23**	**.329**	**.470**	**.273**

Fielding

Year	Posn	G	GS	TC	PO	A	E	DP	FLD%
1999	**1B**	**151**	**147**	**1430**	**1291**	**126**	**13**	**108**	**.991**
Career		**1165**	**1151**	**10850**	**9782**	**980**	**88**	**857**	**.992**

Profile

Name: Timothy James Salmon **Height:** 6–3 **Weight:** 241 **Throws:** Right **Bats:** Right **Positions:** Right Field, Designated Hitter **Born:** August 24, 1968, Long Beach, California **Drafted:** Selected by the California Angels in the third round of the 1989 free-agent draft **Pre-Majors Highlight:** Established school records with 225 runs, 51 home runs and 192 RBI in three seasons at Grand Canyon (Ariz.) College **Personal Information:** Married (Marci) with two children (Callie and Jacob)

Tim Salmon

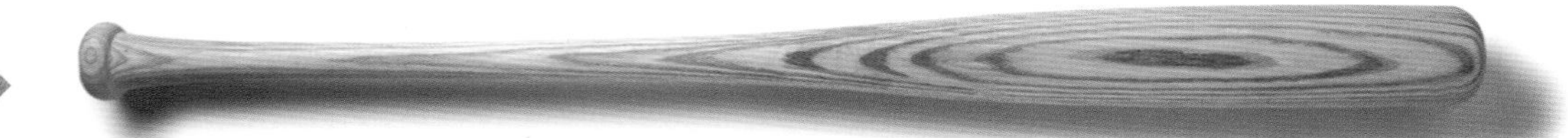

"Tim is a solid player. He's a productive hitter and a good outfielder."

Anaheim Angels manager, Mike Scioscia

Career milestones

1993 Named American League Rookie of the Year

1996 Set club record for most homers in one month with 13 in June. Hit 100th career home run, June 5

1997 Voted Angels Most Valuable Player by his teammates

1998 Became first Angel in club history to score five runs in one game, April 12 vs. Cleveland

There has been one constant about Tim Salmon's career: When he's been injury-free, he has been able to put up big offensive numbers.

Unfortunately for the Anaheim Angels outfielder, staying healthy hasn't been easy. Salmon has missed 90 games the last two seasons because of injuries, which have cut into both his playing time and production. Salmon also missed a month of the 1994 season.

Salmon admits to frustration trying to deal with the many injuries.

"It doesn't do us any good for me to come back hurt and be battling it all year," he said. "I need to take the time, get healthy and come back and play a full season."

Even in the tough times, a lot of players would love to have Salmon's numbers. In 90 games last season, when he sprained his left wrist in May and went on the disabled list for the third time in his career, he hit .266 with 17 homers and 69 runs batted in. The wrist still bothered Salmon after he returned and affected his swing all season as he had a career-low 353 at-bats.

In 1998, Salmon suffered an injured left foot in May and went on the DL. The injury bothered him throughout the rest of the year and he had surgery in September. Despite all those problems, he hit .300 with 26 home runs, 88 RBIs and 83 runs scored in 463 at-bats and 136 games. Salmon led the team in home runs, sacrifice flies (10), walks (90), slugging percentage (.533) and on-base percentage (.410).

Thanks to a strained hamstring that kept him sidelined for a month and the players' strike in 1994, Salmon appeared in 100 games and was limited to 373 at-bats. He still put together a good season, batting .287 with 23 homers and 87 RBIs.

Salmon, the Angels' third-round draft pick in 1989, made an immediate impact in his first full season in the Major Leagues during the 1992 season. He hit .283 with 31 homers and 95 runs batted in. The effort earned him the American League Rookie of the Year honors and he became the 19th rookie in Major League history to hit 30-or-more homers in a season.

When he's been able to play a full season, Salmon can match his power numbers with any other outfielder in baseball. In 1995, he hit .330 with 34 homers (both career highs) and 105 RBIs. He followed that up by batting .286 with 30 homers and 98 RBIs. Salmon's best season came in 1997 when he drove in a career-high 129 runs and a .296 average.

As the Angels hope to bounce back from a very disappointing year in 1999, they will be counting on Salmon to lead the way.

Batting

Year	AB	R	H	HR	RBI	BB	SO	SB	CS	OBP	SLG	AVG	
1999	**98**	**353**	**60**	**94**	**17**	**69**	**63**	**82**	**4**	**1**	**.372**	**.490**	**.266**
Career	**955**	**3483**	**608**	**1015**	**196**	**660**	**579**	**820**	**29**	**31**	**.393**	**.524**	**.291**

Fielding

Year	Posn	G	GS	TC	PO	A	E	DP	FLD%
1999	**OF**	**89**	**89**	**215**	**204**	**7**	**4**	**1**	**.981**
Career		**816**	**813**	**1926**	**1815**	**65**	**46**	**13**	**.976**

Steve Finley

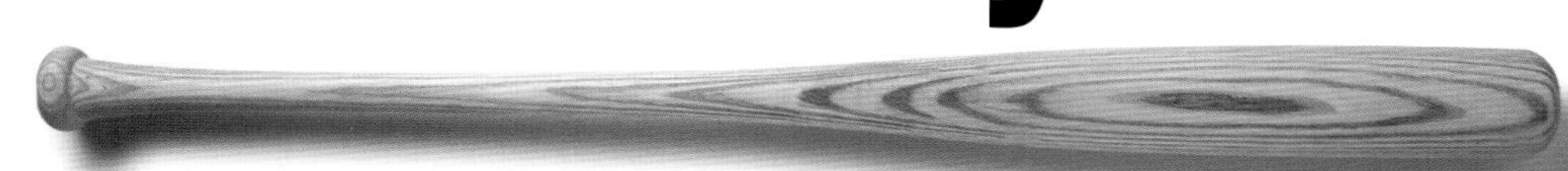

"I look over my shoulder and I see all of these young guys coming up ... I try to keep an advantage over them ... that's one of the reasons I'm able to play out there every day."

Arizona Diamondbacks outfielder, Steve Finley

Profile

Name: Steve Allen Finley **Height:** 6–2 **Weight:** 180 **Throws:** Left **Bats:** Left **Position:** Center Field **Born:** March 12, 1965, Union City, Tennessee **Drafted:** Selected by the Baltimore Orioles in the 13th round of the 1987 free-agent draft **Acquired:** Signed as a free agent with the Arizona Diamondbacks, December 7, 1998 **Pre-Majors Highlights:** Led International League with a .314 batting average and 143 hits, 1988 **Personal Information:** Attended Southern Illinois University

Steve Finley and playoff teams are making a habit of finding each other.

That's probably not a coincidence.

"Steve Finley is a winner," said Arizona Diamondbacks manager Buck Showalter. "He brings a lot to your team. He gets on base, he scores runs, he has power and he plays great defense."

Finley has been doing that for most of his 11-year career in the Majors Leagues. And he's been doing it for playoffs teams in three of the last four years.

After helping the San Diego Padres win the National League West title and a World Series appearance in 1998, Finley signed with the Diamondbacks. The move turned out to be a coup for Arizona. Not only was Finley a key member of another N.L. West championship team, he also had the best season of his career.

Finley reached career highs in home runs (34) and runs batted in (103) while winning his third National League Gold Glove Award. An outstanding center fielder, he made two errors in 156 games. Baseball fans have become accustomed to seeing Finley crashing into walls to make spectacular catches on nightly highlight shows.

"I've always taken a lot of pride in my defense," said Finley, who also won Gold Gloves in 1995 and 1996.

"Steve Finley is probably the most fundamentally sound outfielder I've ever seen," said Showalter.

Finley was a part of the San Diego teams that won the N.L. West in 1996 and 1998. He batted .298 with 30 homers, 95 RBIs, 126 runs scored, 22 stolen bases and seven errors in 143 games in 1996. Finley hit .249 with 14 homers, 67 RBIs, 92 runs scored, 12 stolen bases and seven errors in 159 games as the Padres made it to the World Series two years later.

Most center fielders can't match Finley's power numbers. Following his big year in 1996, Finley belted 28 homers and drove in 92 runs for the Padres in 1997.

After being drafted by the Baltimore Orioles in the 13th round of the 1987 draft, it didn't take Finley long to find his place in the big leagues. Finley played 81 games with the Orioles in 1989 and was in their every-day lineup the following season. In one of the biggest deals of that offseason, Finley and pitchers Pete Harnisch and Curt Schilling were traded to the Houston Astros for Glenn Davis, one of the best first basemen in baseball at the time.

The Astros got the better end of the deal by far. Finley was their every-day center fielder the next four seasons before being involved in a huge 11-player trade between Houston and San Diego on December 28, 1994.

Career milestones

1996 Had a career-high 195 hits

1997 Became the first player in Padres history to score 100 or more runs in three consecutive seasons

1998 Hit ninth-inning, two-out grand slam to give San Diego a 6–4 win over Arizona, April 10

1999 Won National League Gold Glove for third time in career

Batting

Year	G	AB	R	H	HR	RBI	BB	SO	SB	CS	OBP	SLG	AVG
1999	**156**	**590**	**100**	**156**	**34**	**103**	**63**	**94**	**8**	**4**	**.336**	**.525**	**.264**
Career	**1538**	**5788**	**905**	**1586**	**153**	**649**	**469**	**766**	**242**	**82**	**.329**	**.430**	**.274**

Fielding

Year	Posn	G	GS	TC	PO	A	E	DP	FLD%
1999	**OF**	**155**	**149**	**404**	**397**	**5**	**2**	**0**	**.995**
Career		**1504**	**1395**	**3628**	**3487**	**89**	**52**	**22**	**.986**

Profile

Name: Todd Randolph Hundley **Height:** 5–11 **Weight:** 199 **Throws:** Right **Bats:** Both **Position:** Catcher **Born:** May 27, 1969, Martinsville, Virginia **Drafted:** Selected by the New York Mets in the second round of the 1987 free-agent draft **Acquired:** Traded by the New York Mets to the Los Angeles Dodgers, December 1, 1998 **Pre-Majors Highlight:** Named to International League All-Star team, 1991 **Personal Information:** Son of former Major League catcher Randy Hundley

Todd Hundley

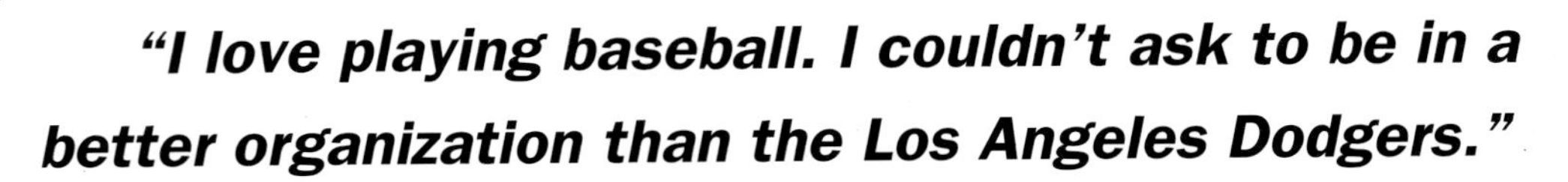

"I love playing baseball. I couldn't ask to be in a better organization than the Los Angeles Dodgers."

Los Angeles Dodgers catcher, Todd Hundley

Career milestones

1992 Set New York Mets club record with .996 fielding percentage

1996 Set Major League record for most home runs by a catcher in one season (41). Named to National League All-Star team.

1997 Had four consecutive multi-hit games, May 24–31. Named to National League All-Star team

Switch-hitting catchers capable of big offensive production don't exactly fall out of trees.

That's what made the season Todd Hundley had in 1996 especially noteworthy. In fact, it was history making.

Hundley, playing for the New York Mets at the time, hit 41 homers and drove in 112 runs in 1996. That set a Major League record for home runs by a catcher in one season, previously held by Hall of Famer Roy Campanella. Hundley also set a National League record for most home runs by a switch-hitter—in any position—in one season.

"I always knew I had power, but if someone had told me I was going to break the record, I would have said they were crazy," said Hundley, whose father, Randy, was a 14-year Major League catcher from 1964–77. "It was a great time and I learned a lot from it, but it also got nerve-racking when I got close to the record."

After that record-breaking season, Hundley's encore wasn't too bad, either. He hit 30 homers and drove in 86 runs in 132 games for the Mets, becoming the third player in franchise history to hit at least 30 homers in consecutive seasons.

Hundley definitely was at the top of his game. He led the Major Leagues in games caught with 150 in 1996 and was putting together another solid year in 1997 when disaster struck. Persistent pain in Hundley's right elbow finally forced him to call it a season after playing 132 games. That led to reconstructive surgery on the ligament after the season.

Hundley then started a long rehabilitation program. He started the 1998 season on the disabled list and lost his catcher's job when the Mets acquired All-Star Mike Piazza from the Los Angeles Dodgers. Hundley, who appeared in only 53 games, was moved to the left field, but had problems defensively while hitting only .161 with three homers and 12 RBIs.

With Piazza around, it was obvious Hundley's time with the Mets was over. Ironically, Hundley, along with pitcher Arnold Gooch, was traded to the Dodgers for catcher Charles Johnson and outfielder Roger Cedeno on December 1, 1998.

Hundley hoped the trade would be a new beginning, but he struggled with his batting average, hitting .207 and made 16 errors. His power stroke returned with 24 homers and 55 RBIs in 114 games.

Hundley continued to work on strengthening his elbow last season.

"It took a year and a half to get close to where I felt before I got hurt," he said. "This is as close to 100 percent as I've ever felt where I could get back to playing every day. Physically, it takes time to get back. I know it's going to take time."

Batting

Year	G	AB	R	H	HR	RBI	BB	SO	SB	CS	OBP	SLG	AVG
1999	**114**	**376**	**49**	**78**	**24**	**55**	**44**	**113**	**3**	**0**	**.295**	**.436**	**.207**
Career	**943**	**2925**	**389**	**690**	**148**	**452**	**343**	**737**	**14**	**9**	**.319**	**.438**	**.236**

Fielding

Year	Posn	G	GS	TC	PO	A	E	DP	FLD%
1999	**C**	**108**	**99**	**748**	**681**	**51**	**16**	**5**	**.979**
Career		**887**	**780**	**5237**	**4805**	**368**	**64**	**37**	**.988**

Barry Larkin

"Barry Larkin is what the Cincinnati Reds are all about. The fans here love him. Barry has done everything for this franchise and he deserves all the praise he's been getting."

Cincinnati Reds general manager, Jim Bowden

Profile

Name: Barry Louis Larkin
Height: 6–0 **Weight:** 185
Throws: Right **Bats:** Right
Position: Shortstop **Born:** April 28, 1964, Cincinnati, Ohio **Drafted:** Selected by the Cincinnati Reds in the first round (fourth pick overall) of the 1985 free-agent draft **Pre-Majors Highlights:** Compiled a .361 average in three seasons at the University of Michigan. Two-time Big Ten Player of the Year and All-American selection **Personal Information:** Married (Lisa) with three children (Brielle, Cymber and DeShane)

Barry Larkin and the Cincinnati Reds have lived a perfect marriage.

Very few players make it to the Major Leagues with their hometown team, but it's a dream Larkin has lived. Both player and team have benefited greatly from the relationship.

"Playing for your hometown team is a dream come true," said Larkin. "I know how lucky I've been to do it. Not many players can experience the things I have."

Larkin signed with the Reds after being drafted in 1985. Larkin has been the Reds' starting shortstop since 1987. He was a key member of the Reds team that won the World Series in 1990 and was named the National League's Most Valuable Player in 1995.

At 35 years old, he shows no signs of letting up. Larkin had another solid season in 1999 as the Reds surprised the baseball world by almost making the playoffs. He batted .293 with 12 homers and 52 RBIs in 161 games.

Larkin's list of accomplishments in Cincinnati is a long one. His finest moment came in 1995, his MVP year. Larkin did just about everything a player could do that season. He hit .319 with 15 homers, 66 runs batted in, 98 runs scored and 51 stolen bases. Larkin also was at his best defensively. He made 11 errors in 131 games and won a Gold Glove.

Larkin helped the Reds win the National League West title, their first playoff appearance since winning the World Series, and hit .385 in the Division Series against Los Angeles and .389 in the League Championship Series against Atlanta.

Larkin was a key player in 1990 when the Reds won the World Series. He hit .301 with seven homers. 67 RBIs and 30 stolen bases. Larkin committed 17 errors in 158 games and led National League shortstops with 469 assists.

Larkin was at his best when the Reds swept the heavily favored Oakland A's in the World Series. He hit .353, drove in a run and didn't make an error in the field.

Larkin hit a career-high .342 in 1989 when he appeared in 97 games because of injury. He set a career-high with 33 homers in 1996, while hitting .298 with 36 stolen bases. That included a three-homer game against Houston on June 28.

Larkin has hit .300 or better seven times in his career. He has made the National League All-Star team in 1988, 1989, 1990, 1991, 1993, 1994, 1995, 1996, 1997 and 1999. He has won the Gold Glove in 1994, 1995, and 1996.

"To play your whole career with one team is special," said Larkin. "To do it in your hometown in front of your family and friends makes it even better."

Career milestones

1990 World Series ring as Cincinnati swept Oakland

1994 Won National League Gold Glove

1995 Named National League Most Valuable Player. Won National League Gold Glove

1996 Won National League Gold Glove

1998 Led National League shortstops with a .309 average, 17 homers and 72 runs batted in

1999 Named to National League All-Star team for 10th time

Batting

Year	G	AB	R	H	HR	RBI	BB	SO	SB	CS	OBP	SLG	AVG
1999	**161**	**583**	**108**	**171**	**12**	**75**	**93**	**57**	**30**	**8**	**.390**	**.420**	**.293**
Career	**1707**	**6291**	**1063**	**1884**	**168**	**793**	**764**	**633**	**345**	**65**	**.376**	**.454**	**.299**

Fielding

Posn	G	GS	TC	PO	A	E	DP	FLD%	
1999	**SS**	**161**	**160**	**635**	**220**	**401**	**14**	**77**	**.978**
Career		**1661**	**1642**	**7520**	**2568**	**4762**	**190**	**869**	**.975**

Scott Brosius

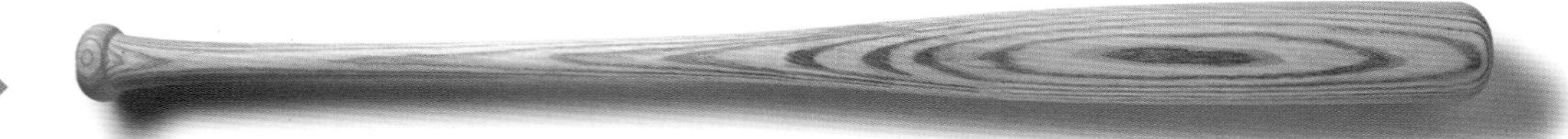

Profile

Name: Scott David Brosius **Height:** 6–1 **Weight:** 202 **Throws:** Right **Bats:** Right **Position:** Third Base **Born:** August 15, 1966, Hillsboro, Oregon **Drafted:** Selected by the Oakland Athletics in the 20th round of the 1987 free-agent draft **Acquired:** Traded by the Oakland Athletics to the New York Yankees, November 7, 1997 **Pre-Majors Highlight:** Finished second in Midwest League with .304 average in 1988 **Personal Information:** Resides in McMinnville, Ore. with wife (Jennifer) and their children (Allison, Megan and David)

"Scott has done the job for us. He's been very steady. He's done a solid job offensively and defensively." **New York Yankees manager, Joe Torre**

Career milestones

1991 Went 2-for-4 in his Major League debut August 7
1996 Led the American League with a .365 average with runners in scoring position
1997 Ranked second in the American League with .977 fielding percentage at third base
1998 Named Most Valuable Player of World Series
1999 Won his first American League Gold Glove as the Yankees won back-to-back World Series

The turning point of Scott Brosius' career had nothing to do with getting a clutch hit or making a great defensive play.

In fact, it didn't even come on the baseball field or during the baseball season. On November 18, 1997, Brosius, coming off the worst season of his career, was traded by the Oakland Athletics to the New York Yankees.

The trade didn't grab a lot of headlines. Brosius had just completed a terrible year with the A's. He hit a career-low .203 with 11 homers and 41 runs batted in with 102 strikeouts in 479 at-bats. So when the Yankees sent left-hander Kenny Rogers to Oakland for the struggling third basemen, the general reaction was a yawn, even in the media capital of the world.

Two years later, the trade has brought a different conclusion. The deal has turned into the biggest break of Brosius' career and has turned out to be a steal for the Yankees. Not only has Brosius turned his career around, he helped New York win back-to-back World Series titles.

"Sometimes I have to pinch myself to make sure this has all really happened," said Brosius. "Sometimes it's hard to believe. To be a part of such a special team is something I'll never forget."

Brosius had the kind of seasons most players can only dream about in 1998. Although not known as a power-hitting third baseman, he finished with a career-high 98 RBIs—shattering his previous best mark by 27—while batting .300 with 19 homers.

Hitting at the bottom of the order, Brosius made the potent Yankees' lineup even more dangerous as New York overpowered opponents all season. He was named to the All-Star team for the first time in his career and also earned a spot on the Sporting News All-Star team. The Yankees won a Major League record 114 regular-season game and rolled to the American League East title.

Brosius' dream season didn't stop there. He batted .400 with a homer and three RBIs as the Yankees swept the Texas Rangers in the Division Series. As the Yankees eliminated the Cleveland Indians in six games in the League Championship Series, Brosius batted .300 with a homer and six RBIs.

The story got better as the Yankees swept the San Diego Padres in the World Series. Brosius hit .471 with two home runs and six RBIs. The storybook season featured a fitting ending. Brosius homered in the seventh and eighth innings of Game 3 to cap a Yankees' rally. That also tied a Series record for most home runs in two consecutive innings and Brosius' was named the Series' Most Valuable Player Award.

While Brosius' numbers fell off in 1999, the season was still a huge success for him and the Yankees. Brosius batted .247, hit 17 homers, 71 RBIs and earned his first Gold Glove as New York won its second straight World Series.

Batting

Year	G	AB	R	H	HR	RBI	BB	SO	SB	CS	OBP	SLG	AVG
1999	**133**	**473**	**64**	**117**	**17**	**71**	**39**	**74**	**9**	**3**	**.307**	**.414**	**.247**
Career	**891**	**2991**	**430**	**770**	**112**	**418**	**269**	**543**	**54**	**26**	**.324**	**.426**	**.257**

Fielding

Year	Posn	G	GS	TC	PO	A	E	DP	FLD%
1999	**3B**	**132**	**130**	**339**	**87**	**239**	**13**	**20**	**.962**
Career		**873**	**801**	**2471**	**1033**	**1352**	**86**	**178**	**.965**

Bernard Gilkey

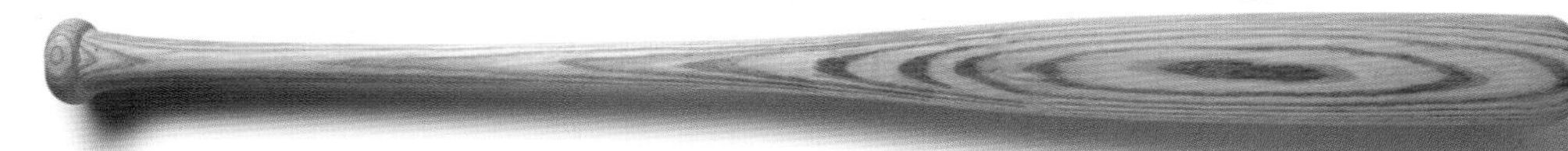

"Bernard has a lot of talent. He has good power, he can run and he's a good defensive player."

Arizona Diamondbacks manager, Buck Showalter

Profile

Name: Otis Bernard Gilkey **Height:** 6–0 **Weight:** 198 **Throws:** Right **Bats:** Right **Positions:** Right Field, Left Field **Born:** September 24, 1966, St. Louis, Missouri **Drafted:** Signed as an undrafted free agent by the St. Louis Cardinals, August 22, 1984 **Acquired:** Traded by the New York Mets to the Arizona Diamondbacks, July 31, 1998 **Pre-Majors Highlight:** Led Texas League in runs scored (104) in 1989 **Personal Information:** Married (Patrice) with two sons (Jaelen) and (Dawson)

Bernard Gilkey is proof positive that a player can go on to have a solid Major League career without being drafted.

The 1984 Major League draft came and went without Gilkey's name getting called, but that didn't stop him from giving up his dream to play in the big leagues. Gilkey was a star athlete in baseball and basketball at University City High School in St. Louis.

His basketball talent earned him a scholarship at Drake University, but Gilkey turned it down to pursue his goal of not only making it to the Majors, but doing it with the Cardinals, his hometown team. He signed with the Cardinals as a free agent on August 22, 1984.

Gilkey wasn't an immediate success. He spent five years in the minor leagues in stops such as Erie, Pennsylvania, Savannah, Georgia, Springfield, Missouri and Lousiville. Gilkey persevered and was finally called up to St. Louis late in the 1990 season. He picked up his first Major League hit on September 5 against Montreal and hit his first home run on October 1, also against the Expos.

Gilkey spent most of the 1991 season with the Cardinals. The rookie batted just .216, but stole 14 bases and showed enough for the Cardinals to put him in their plans for the future. As it turned out, the kid nobody drafted became a fixture in the St. Louis outfield for the next four years.

From 1992–95, Gilkey averaged 12 home runs, 57 RBIs, 54 runs scored and 15 stolen bases while hitting .292. His best season with St. Louis came in 1993 when he hit .305 with 40 doubles, 16 homers, 70 RBIs, 99 runs scored and 15 stolen bases. Gilkey also cracked the .300 mark in 1992, hitting .302, and fell a bit short in 1995, hitting .298.

The 1995 season was Gilkey's last with his hometown team. The Cardinals traded him to the New York Mets on January 22, 1996. He put together a career season in 1996, hitting .317 with 108 runs, 44 doubles, 30 homers, 117 RBI, 73 walks, and 17 steals. Gilkey reached career highs in all categories except stolen bases and led National League outfielders with 18 assists.

Gilkey had another productive season with the Mets in 1997, hitting 18 homers with 78 RBIs while batting .249. He began the 1998 season with the Mets before being traded to the Arizona Diamondbacks on July 31. His season ended after 29 games with Arizona when he had laser eye surgery.

Gilkey didn't get much playing time in the Diamondbacks' talented outfield during the 1999 season, but he led Arizona with 13 pinch-hits. He batted .294 with eight homers and 39 RBIs in 94 games.

He will only be 33 when the 2000 season opens, so any thoughts that Gilkey's career is winding down are almost certainly false. Solid, experienced, power-hitting outfielders are always in demand.

Career milestones

1991 Stole 14 bases in rookie season, despite hitting just .216

1996 Posted career highs in batting average, runs scored, doubles, homers and runs batted in. Led the National League with 18 outfield assists

1997 Led the National League with 17 outfield assists.

1998 Led Arizona Diamondbacks with 13 pinch-hits

Batting

Year	G	AB	R	H	HR	RBI	BB	SO	SB	CS	OBP	SLG	AVG
1999	**94**	**204**	**28**	**60**	**8**	**39**	**29**	**42**	**2**	**2**	**.379**	**.500**	**.294**
Career	**1096**	**3791**	**581**	**1057**	**113**	**517**	**438**	**649**	**115**	**70**	**.356**	**.442**	**.279**

Fielding

Year	Posn	G	GS	TC	PO	A	E	DP	FLD%
1999	**OF**	**53**	**49**	**96**	**90**	**3**	**3**	**0**	**.969**
Career		**1003**	**949**	**2015**	**1873**	**106**	**36**	**22**	**.982**

Al Leiter

Profile

Name: Alois Terry Leiter **Height:** 6–3 **Weight:** 220 **Throws:** Left **Bats:** Left **Positions:** Pitcher **Born:** October 23, 1965, Toms River, New Jersey **Drafted:** Selected by the New York Yankees in the second round of the 1984 free-agent draft **Acquired:** Traded by the Florida Marlins to the New York Mets, February 6, 1998 **Personal Information:** Brother Kurt was a pitcher with the Baltimore organization while brother Mark has pitched for seven Major League teams

"I've been through a lot in my career. That makes the last few years very rewarding for me."

New York Mets pitcher, Al Leiter

Career milestones

1989 Traded from the New York Yankees to the Toronto Blue Jays, April 30

1995 Led the American League with 14 wild pitches

1996 Pitched a no-hitter against the Colorado Rockies, May 11

1998 His 17 victories were the most by a New York Mets pitcher since 1990

1999 Was the winning pitcher as the New York Mets defeated the Cincinnati Reds 8–0 in the National League Wild Card playoff game

The early portion of Al Leiter's career featured more injuries than victories.

The left-handed pitcher was considered to be one of the top prospects in baseball when the New York Yankees took him in the second round of the 1984 draft. The Yankees thought it was only a matter of time until Leiter was a star in the Major Leagues.

Leiter picked up his first Major League win in 1987 and began the 1988 season in the Yankees' rotation. However, a seemingly endless string of injuries kept him from fulfilling that promise. Shoulder, elbow and blister problems landed Leiter on the disabled list in 1988, 1989, 1990, 1991, 1993 and 1994.

The injuries caused the Yankees to give up on him. New York traded Leiter to the Toronto Blue Jays for outfielder Jesse Barfield on April 30, 1989. However, the pitcher's luck didn't change. Leiter didn't win a game for Toronto from 1989–92. In fact, because of injuries and ineffective pitching in the minors when he wasn't hurt, Leiter appeared in only nine games for the Blue Jays in those four years.

Although the injuries still dogged Leiter in 1993 and 1994, he was able to get on the mound. He went 9–6 with a 4.11 ERA in 34 games (12 starts) in the '93 season. Leiter also made six postseason appearances as the Blue Jays won the World Series.

Finally in the rotation for the first time since the early part of the 1988 season, Leiter started 20 games in 1994, going 6–7 with a 5.08 ERA.

At that point, his career finally began to take off. Over the last four years, he has a 68–50 record with a 3.48 ERA, has pitched a no-hitter, has made the National League All-Star team and been a key component of two playoff teams, including another World Series champion in 1997.

Leiter went 11–11 with a 3.64 ERA in 28 starts for the Blue Jays in 1995. That earned him a big free-agent contract from the Florida Marlins. Leiter paid immediate dividends, pitching the first no-hitter in Marlins' history against the Colorado Rockies on May 11, 1996. He pitched a career-high 215.1 innings, went 16–12, had a 2.93 ERA and made the All-Star team.

As the Marlins won the World Series the following year, Leiter was 11–9 with a 4.34 ERA and appeared in five postseason games (four starts). Florida traded him to the New York Mets after the season and his return to the Big Apple has been a success.

Leiter won a career-high 17 games, while losing only six and had a 2.47 ERA in 1998. He was 13–12 with a 4.23 ERA last season as the Mets won the National League wild card spot and advanced to the League Championship Series.

Pitching

Year	W	L	ERA	G	GS	CG	SHO	SV	SVO	INN	H	R	ER	HR	HBP	BB	SO
1999	**13**	**12**	**4.23**	**32**	**32**	**1**	**1**	**0**	**0**	**213.0**	**209**	**107**	**100**	**19**	**9**	**93**	**162**
Career	**90**	**71**	**3.82**	**233**	**203**	**11**	**6**	**2**	**5**	**1294.2**	**1136**	**586**	**549**	**94**	**62**	**683**	**1107**

Batting

Year	G	AB	R	H	HR	RBI	BB	SO	SB	CS	OBP	SLG	AVG
Career	**233**	**232**	**7**	**24**	**0**	**11**	**16**	**131**	**0**	**0**	**.161**	**.125**	**.103**

Fielding

Year	Posn	G	GS	TC	PO	A	E	DP	FLD%
1999	**P**	**32**	**32**	**25**	**3**	**18**	**4**	**1**	**.840**
Career		**233**	**203**	**168**	**31**	**129**	**8**	**9**	**.952**

Javy Lopez

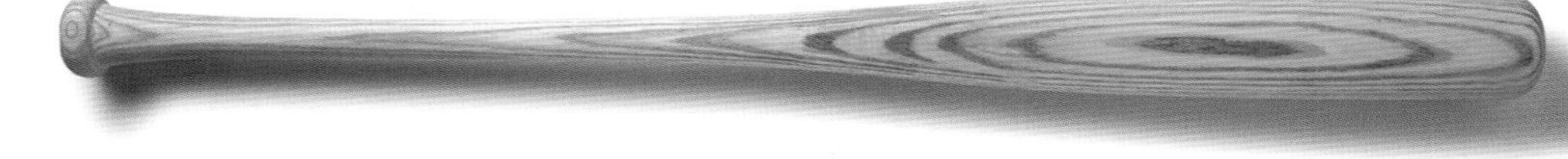

Profile

Name: Javier Torres Lopez
Height: 6–3 **Weight:** 200
Throws: Right **Bats:** Right
Position: Catcher **Born:** November 5, 1970, Ponce, Puerto Rico **Drafted:** Signed by the Atlanta Braves as an undrafted free agent to a minor-league contract on November. 6, 1987
Pre-Majors Highlight: Hit 17 home runs at Class AAA Richmond, 1993
Personal Information: Named Ponce's Athlete-of-the-Year from 1984–87

"Javy gets better every year. He has improved offensively and made himself into a top catcher."

Atlanta Braves manager, Bobby Cox

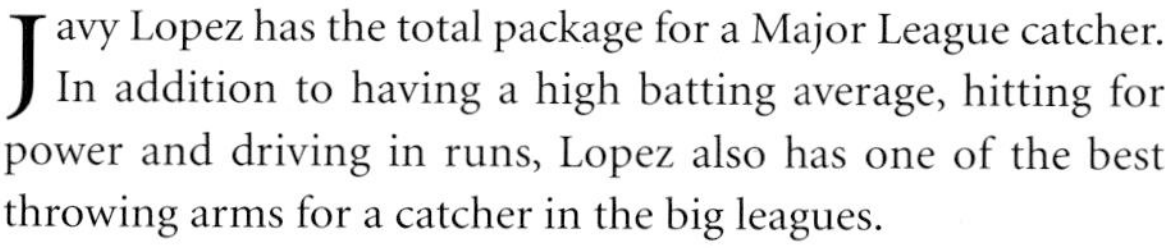

Javy Lopez has the total package for a Major League catcher. In addition to having a high batting average, hitting for power and driving in runs, Lopez also has one of the best throwing arms for a catcher in the big leagues.

That's why Lopez has been the Atlanta Braves' regular catcher for the last five years and is one of the top players in his position in baseball.

A knee injury brought Lopez's 1999 season to an early end. He tried to play through the injury early in the season, but finally had to have surgery in July. Lopez still put up solid numbers. He hit .317 with 11 homers and 45 RBIs in 65 games. The Braves expect Lopez to make a full recovery for the 2000 season.

It will be hard for Lopez to top what he did in 1998. He set career highs in home runs (34) and runs batted in (106) while batting .284. The season earned him his second spot on the National League All-Star team.

Lopez was the Braves' best clutch hitter. He led the team with a .336 average and 58 RBIs with runners in scoring position. He also tied for the team lead with 13 homers with runners in scoring position.

Lopez also had a career-high 13-game hitting streak, homered in four straight games, had the most RBIs by a Braves catcher since Joe Torre in 1964 and hit his 100th career home run on August 24. Lopez, who homered in four straight games, was sixth in the National League in at-bats per home run (14.4) and tied for sixth in at-bats per RBI (4.6).

In addition to his numbers, Lopez also did the job behind the plate. He led all National League catchers by throwing out 33.8 percent of would-be base stealers. Lopez also led all Major League catchers in fielding percentage (.995).

Lopez's career-high in home runs had previously come in 1996 and 1997 when he hit 23 in each season. He batted a career-high .315 in 1995, becoming the first Braves catcher since Torre in 1966 to hit over .300. His first All-Star appearance came in 1997.

Lopez also has been a clutch performer in the playoffs. He has a career average of .333 in nine Division Series games, and a career average of .329 with four homers in 22 League Championship Series games. Lopez was named the Most Valuable Player of the 1996 LCS when he batted .542 with two homers and six RBIs. He had five straight hits and scored right runs in that series, a playoff record.

Even though the Braves reached the World Series for the fifth time in the 1990s, they missed Lopez in the batter's box and behind the plate.

Lopez will be only 29 years old when the 2000 season starts. For the Braves, his return to the starting line-up—along with Andres Galarraga at first base—will be like two free agants strengthening an already potent force.

Career milestones

1992 Picked up first Major League hit, Sept. 18

1994 Selected to Topps Rookie All-Star Team

1996 Set Atlanta club record with 135 games caught

1997 Had 10-game hitting streak June 4–16 and had two four-RBI games, April 5 and 19

1998 Led all major league catchers in fielding percentage (.995)

Batting

Year	G	AB	R	H	HR	RBI	BB	SO	SB	CS	OBP	SLG	AVG
1999	**65**	**246**	**34**	**78**	**11**	**45**	**20**	**41**	**0**	**3**	**.375**	**.533**	**.317**
Career	**656**	**2280**	**283**	**662**	**119**	**378**	**149**	**413**	**7**	**16**	**.338**	**.503**	**.290**

Fielding

Year	Posn	G	GS	TC	PO	A	E	DP	FLD%
1999	**C**	**60**	**56**	**446**	**413**	**29**	**4**	**3**	**.991**
Career		**624**	**575**	**4780**	**4424**	**323**	**33**	**33**	**.993**

Fred McGriff

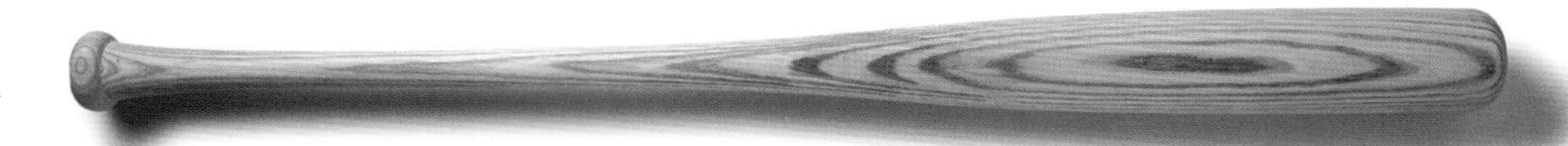

Profile

Name: Frederick Stanley McGriff **Height:** 6-3 **Weight:** 215 **Throws:** Left **Bats:** Left **Positions:** First Base, Designated Hitter **Born:** October 31, 1963, Tampa, Florida **Drafted:** Selected by the New York Yankees in the ninth round of the 1981 free-agent draft **Acquired:** Traded from the Atlanta Braves to the Tampa Bay Devil Rays, November 18, 1997 **Pre-Majors Highlight:** Hit 21 home runs for Class A Kinston, 1987 **Personal Information:** Nickname is "The Crime Dog"

"Fred has been a dangerous hitter for a long time. He fits in very well with our franchise and what we're trying to do." **Tampa Bay Devil Rays manager, Larry Rothschild**

Career milestones

1989 Led American League in home runs

1991 Shares Major League record for most grand slams (two) in two straight games, August 13-14

1992 Led National League in home runs

1994 Named Most Valuable Player of the All-Star Game. Had best batting average of career (.318) with the Atlanta Braves

1995 Won World Series ring with Atlanta Braves

Fred McGriff's Major League career has been all about power. And few players have put up power numbers that can match the man known by fans as the "Crime Dog".

McGriff's numbers say it all. Since becoming a regular with the Toronto Blue Jays in 1987, he has hit 390 home runs, an average of 28 home runs a season. It hasn't mattered where McGriff has played. He has pounded the ball with the Blue Jays (1986–90), San Diego (1991–93), Atlanta (1993–97) and Tampa Bay (1998–99).

The homer numbers are impressive: 20 in 1987, 34 in 1988, 36 in 1989, 35 in 1990, 31 in 1991, 35 in 1992, 37 in 1993, 34 in 1994, 27 in 1995, 28 in 1996, 22 in 1997, 19 in 1998 and 32 in 1999.

McGriff led the American League in home runs with the Blue Jays in 1989 and 1990. He also has topped the 100-RBI mark four times: 106 in 1991, 104 in 1992, 107 in 1996 and 104 in 1999.

Just how impressive is McGriff's consistent home run production? He had his string of 20 or more homer seasons snapped at 11 in 1998. He didn't homer in May, the first homerless month in his career.

McGriff, who has 10 postseason home runs, including four in 1995 when the Braves won the World Series, and has made four All-Star teams, had another big season in 1999 with the hometown Devil Rays. His 32 homers were second on the team behind Jose Canseco. McGriff led Tampa Bay in hitting (.310), games (144), total bases (292), doubles (30), RBI (104), walks (86), on-base percentage (.405) and hitting with men in scoring position (.324).

The New York Yankees will always look at McGriff as one who got away. He was New York's ninth-round draft pick in 1981, but never got past the rookie league level in two seasons in the Yankees' minor league system. In a deal that always will be remembered in both cities, New York traded McGriff, pitcher Mike Morgan and outfielder Dave Collins to Toronto for pitcher Dale Murray and catcher/outfielder Tom Dodd on December 9, 1982.

McGriff belted 125 home runs for the Blue Jays between 1987 and 1990. He topped the 30-homer mark every season and led the American League in 1989.

Considering those numbers, one would say the edge in the deal goes to Toronto, but that wasn't the last big trade McGriff would be involved in. On December 5, 1990, the Blue Jays traded McGriff and shortstop Tony Fernandez to the San Diego Padres for outfielder Joe Carter and second baseman Roberto Alomar.

The trade was a memorable one. All four players were stars at the time and it's rare players of that caliber are involved in the same trade.

When McGriff's career is finally over, he'll be remembered for a lot of memorable home runs, too.

Batting

Year	G	AB	R	H	HR	RBI	BB	SO	SB	CS	OBP	SLG	AVG
1999	**144**	**529**	**75**	**164**	**32**	**104**	**86**	**107**	**1**	**0**	**.405**	**.552**	**.310**
Career	**1897**	**6786**	**1094**	**1946**	**390**	**1192**	**1045**	**1472**	**68**	**34**	**.382**	**.517**	**.287**

Fielding

Year	Posn	G	GS	TC	PO	A	E	DP	FLD%
1999	**1B**	**125**	**124**	**1138**	**1038**	**87**	**13**	**132**	**.989**
Career		**1749**	**1735**	**16344**	**15037**	**1178**	**129**	**1401**	**.992**

Larry Walker

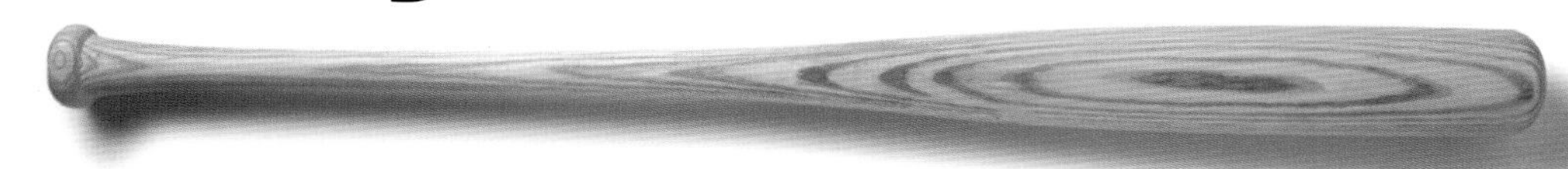

"When you look at Larry's numbers, they are unbelievable. He does it every season, year after year."

Former Colorado Rockies manager, Jim Leyland

Profile

Name: Larry Kenneth Robert Walker **Height:** 6–3 **Weight:** 237 **Throws:** Right **Bats:** Left **Positions:** Right Field **Born:** December 1, 1966, Maple Ridge, British Columbia **Drafted:** Signed as an undrafted free agent by the Montreal Expos, November 14, 1984 **Acquired:** Signed by the Colorado Rockies as a free agent on April 8, 1995 **Pre-Majors Highlight:** Hit 29 home runs for Class A Burlington, 1986 **Personal Information:** Was a hockey goaltender while growing up and played on the same team as former Boston Bruin Cam Neely

It's the dream of every kid growing up in Canada to become a star player in the National Hockey League.

Larry Walker got half of the dream right. He went on to become a star all right, but it turned out to be with a baseball bat instead of a hockey stick.

Instead of winning a Stanley Cup, he might be setting a new trend for Canadian kids. Walker, the star right fielder for the Colorado Rockies, became the first native Canadian to win the National League Most Valuable Player Award in 1997. A year later, he became the first Canadian-born player to win the National League batting title before leading the league again in 1999.

Walker's production in 1997 was one for the books. He came within four hits and 10 RBIs of winning the league's first Triple Crown in 60 years.

Walker led the league with 49 homers, ranked second with a .366 batting average, and finished third with 130 RBIs. He also led the league with a .720 slugging percentage, the sixth highest in league history, and became only the 15th player to top 400 total bases in a single season (409). Only 10 players in the history of the game have amassed more total bases in a single season. Walker ranked second in the league with 143 runs, the 10th highest total in Major League history, and finished second in the NL with 208 hits.

His season didn't stop there. With 33 steals in 41 attempts he became only the fifth player (Hank Aaron, Jose Canseco, Barry Bonds and Ellis Burks) with at least 40 homers and 30 steals in a season.

Walker batted .363 in 1998 to win his first batting title and became only the third player in the past 60 years to post consecutive seasons of .360 or better. He also earned his second straight Gold Glove, the fourth of his career.

Walker did it again in 1999. He batted .379 with 37 homers, 115 RBIs, 108 runs scored and a .710 slugging percentage. He was named to the National League All-Star team for the fourth time.

Walker reached stardom with the Montreal Expos from 1990–94. He hit between 16 and 23 homers every year for the Expos, with top batting averages of .322 in 1994 and .301 in 1992. He also stole 29 bases in 1993. Walker also led the National League with 16 outfield assists in 1992, and was awarded Gold Glove that season and again in 1993.

On paper, some of Walker's numbers look like impossible achievements. Considering what he's done, he might accomplish what looks like another impossibility: getting Canadian kids to trade in their skates and pucks for bats and gloves.

Career milestones

1992 Won National League Gold Glove

1993 Won National League Gold Glove

1995 Hit .306 with 36 home runs after signing with the Colorado Rockies as a free agent

1997 Named National League Most Valuable Player, led league in home runs and won Gold Glove

1998 Won National League batting title and won Gold Glove

1999 Won second straight National League batting title and earned his fourth All-Star selection

Batting

Year	G	AB	R	H	HR	RBI	BB	SO	SB	CS	OBP	SLG	AVG
1999	**127**	**438**	**108**	**166**	**37**	**115**	**57**	**52**	**11**	**4**	**.458**	**.710**	**.379**
Career	**1298**	**4592**	**886**	**1431**	**262**	**855**	**532**	**807**	**190**	**56**	**.389**	**.567**	**.312**

Fielding

Year	Posn	G	GS	TC	PO	A	E	DP	FLD%
1999	**OF**	**114**	**110**	**221**	**204**	**13**	**4**	**3**	**.982**
Career		**1252**	**1202**	**3088**	**2884**	**163**	**41**	**76**	**.987**

Curt Schilling

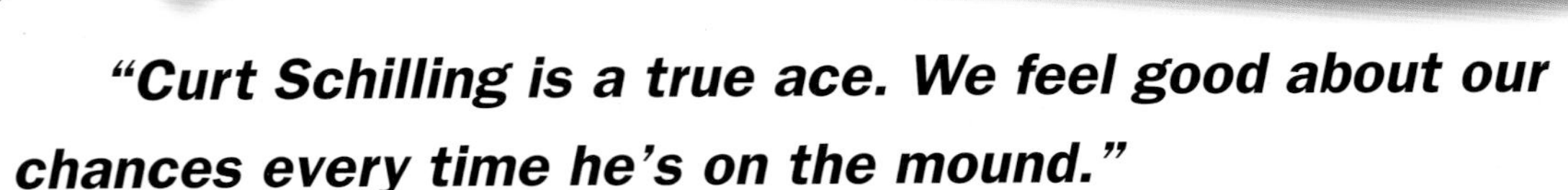

Profile

Name:
Curtis Montague Schilling
Height: 6-4 **Weight:** 230
Throws: Right **Bats:** Right **Position:** Pitcher
Born: November 14, 1966, Anchorage, Alaska
Drafted: Selected by the Boston Red Sox in the second round of the 1986 free-agent draft **Acquired:** Traded by the Houston Astros to the Philadelphia Phillies for Jason Grimsley on April 2, 1992 **Personal Information:** Initiated "Curtis Pitch for ALS" (Lou Gehrig's Disease) and has helped raise over $1,000,000 since 1993

"Curt Schilling is a true ace. We feel good about our chances every time he's on the mound."

Philadelphia Phillies manager, Terry Francona

Career milestones

1993 Named Most Valuble Player of the National League Championship Series

1996 Led the National League with eight complete games

1997 Led the National League in strikeouts and named to the All-Star team

1998 Led the National League in strikeouts and complete games. Named to the All-Star team

1999 Named to the All-Star team for the third straight season

The trade the Philadelphia Phillies and Houston Astros made on April 2, 1992 will go down as one of the biggest deals in baseball history.

Or maybe one of the biggest steals.

On that day, the Phillies and Astros swapped right-handed pitchers. Curt Schilling went to Philadelphia and Jason Grimsley headed to Houston.

Eight years later, it's advantage, Phillies. Make that big advantage, Phillies. While Grimsley has been a journeyman, bouncing from team to team during the decade, Schilling has developed into one of the best pitchers in the Major Leagues.

It didn't take Schilling very long to make the trade look good for the Phillies. After going 14–11 with a 2.35 earned run average and 10 complete games in 1992, Schilling and the Phillies had a memorable season in 1993. He finished with a 16–7 record while the Phillies won the National League East and advanced to the World Series for the first since 1980. Schilling made four starts in the postseason and won Game 5 of the World Series against the Toronto Blue Jays.

Schilling's list of accomplishments since the trade is a long one. He was especially effective in 1998, going 15–14 with a 3.25 earned run average. He led the majors in complete games (15) and innings pitched (268.2) and led the National League in strikeouts (300). Schilling also tied for the league lead in starts (35), was second in strikeouts per nine innings (10.0) and ninth in fewest walks per nine innings (2.0) and ERA (3.25). Opposing batters hit just .236 against him.

Schilling also became just the fifth pitcher in Major League Baseball history to strike out 300 batters in back-to-back seasons. Schilling had 15 double-figure strikeout games and his 15 complete games were the most for a Phillies pitcher since Hall of Famer Steve Carlton had 19 in 1982.

Schilling was equally dominating in 1997. He led the Majors with 319 strikeouts—10th all-time on the single-season strikeouts list—and set the National League record for strikeouts by a right-hander. He surpassed Carlton's team record of 310 strikeouts and reached 300 strikeouts quicker than any pitcher in history, (236.2) innings.

The strikeouts were accompanied by good control. Schilling tied Hall of Famer Sandy Koufax (1963) for fewest walks (58) among pitchers with 300 or more strikeouts Schilling also set a career-high with 16 strikeouts against the New York Yankees on September 1.

Schilling was having another strong season in 1999 before being limited to 24 starts because of shoulder problems. He was 15–6 with a 3.54 ERA while striking out 152 in 180.1 innings while pitching eight complete games.

Pitching

Year	W	L	ERA	G	GS	CG	SHO	SV	SVO	INN	H	R	ER	HR	HBP	BB	SO
1999	**15**	**6**	**3.54**	**24**	**24**	**8**	**1**	**0**	**0**	**180.1**	**159**	**74**	**71**	**25**	**5**	**44**	**152**
Career	**99**	**83**	**3.38**	**326**	**215**	**57**	**13**	**13**	**23**	**1691.2**	**1483**	**688**	**635**	**153**	**31**	**454**	**1571**

Batting

Year	G	AB	R	H	HR	RBI	BB	SO	SB	CS	OBP	SLG	AVG
Career	**328**	**480**	**22**	**72**	**0**	**21**	**16**	**176**	**1**	**0**	**.177**	**.173**	**.150**

Fielding

Year	Posn	G	GS	TC	PO	A	E	DP	FLD%
1999	**P**	**24**	**24**	**30**	**11**	**19**	**0**	**1**	**1.000**
Career		**326**	**215**	**274**	**91**	**172**	**11**	**9**	**.960**

Steve Trachsel

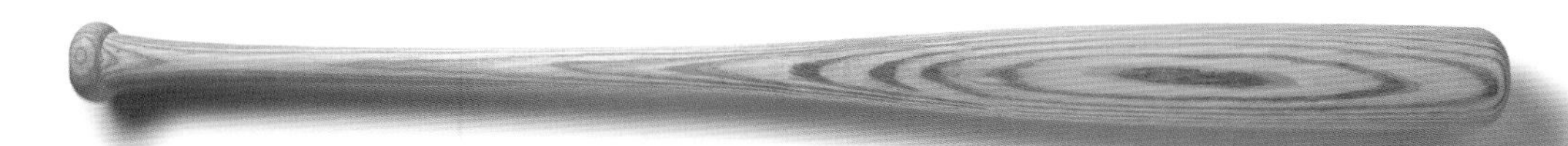

"Steve gives you innings. That's his biggest plus. He takes the ball and doesn't miss his turn."

Chicago Cubs general manager, Ed Lynch

Profile

Name: Stephen Christopher Trachsel
Height: 6–4 **Weight:** 205
Throws: Right **Bats:** Right **Position:** Pitcher
Born: October 31, 1970, Oxnard, California
Drafted: Selected by the Chicago Cubs in the eighth round of the 1991 free-agent draft **Pre-Majors Highlight:** Led Southern League in innings pitched, 1992
Personal Information: Gives time to such charitable organizations such as the March of Dimes and the Crohn's and Colitis Foundation

Steve Trachsel will always be remembered as the pitcher who made history.

On September 8, 1998, the Chicago Cubs right-hander gave up Mark McGwire's record-setting 62nd home run. The homer broke Roger Maris' mark that had stood since 1961.

So while Trachsel will always be the answer to one of baseball's most popular trivia questions, he should be known for more than just the man who put McGwire in the record book. Despite a poor season in 1999, in which he went 8–18 with a 5.56 earned run average, Traschel has been a solid pitcher for the Cubs since joining their rotation full-time in 1994.

In fact, Trachsel accomplished more than just his link with McGwire in 1998. He finished the season with a 15–8 record and a 4.46 ERA in 33 starts. Trachsel also started the Cubs' biggest game of the season. The Cubs and San Francisco Giants ended the season tied for the wild card spot in the National League. When the two met for a one-game, winner-take-all playoff, Cubs manager Jim Riggelman gave the ball to Trachsel. The decision was a wise one.

In what might have been his finest game of the season, Trachsel was the winning pitcher in the Cubs' 5–3 victory that put them in the National League Division Series. He took a no-hitter into the seventh and pitched 6.1 scoreless innings.

The victory capped Trachsel's finest season in his Major League career, which began when he was called up during the 1993 season. He established career highs in wins and innings pitched, and had a five-game winning streak, another career best.

Despite his poor record in 1999, Trachsel still led the Cubs in starts (34), complete games (four) and innings pitched (205.2).

After getting off to a 2–12 start, Trachsel finished up 6–6 in the closing weeks of the season. At one point, he won three of four decisions and was 3–1 with a 2.81 ERA over five starts.

Durability is another Trachsel asset. He's been healthy his entire career, having been on the disabled list only once, with a blister on his finger in 1994. He has been a 200-plus innings man the last four years. Trachsel pitched 205 innings in 1996, 201.1 in 1997 and 208 in 1998 (a career high) before cracking the 200-mark again in 1999.

If Trachsel follows his trend of pitching well in even-numbered years, he is due for a good season in 2000. He has finished 9–7 in 1994, 13–9 in 1996 and 15–8 in 1998. In odd-numbered years, he has gone 0–2 in 1993, 7–13 in 1995, 8–12 in 1997 and 8–18 in 1999.

Career milestones

1993 Made Major League debut, September 17

1994 Named the National League Rookie Pitcher of the Year by The Sporting News

1997 Tied for third in the National League with 34 games started

1998 Was one of baseball's top hitting pitchers, batting .266 (17-for-64) with one homer and eight RBIs

Pitching

Year	W	L	ERA	G	GS	CG	SHO	SV	SVO	INN	H	R	ER	HR	HBP	BB	SO
1999	**8**	**18**	**5.56**	**34**	**34**	**4**	**0**	**0**	**0**	**205.2**	**226**	**133**	**127**	**32**	**3**	**64**	**149**
Career	**60**	**69**	**4.35**	**187**	**186**	**11**	**2**	**0**	**0**	**1146.1**	**1159**	**603**	**554**	**169**	**27**	**412**	**829**

Batting

Year	G	AB	R	H	HR	RBI	BB	SO	SB	CS	OBP	SLG	AVG
Career	**187**	**351**	**30**	**60**	**2**	**23**	**17**	**110**	**1**	**1**	**.211**	**.222**	**.171**

Fielding

Year	Posn	G	GS	TC	PO	A	E	DP	FLD%
1999	**P**	**34**	**34**	**38**	**18**	**20**	**0**	**3**	**1.000**
Career		**187**	**186**	**261**	**92**	**161**	**8**	**4**	**.969**

Profile

Name: Carlos Juan Delgado
Height: 6–3 **Weight:** 225
Throws: Right **Bats:** Left
Positions: First Base, Designated Hitter
Born: June 25, 1972, Aguadilla, Puerto Rico
Drafted: Not drafted. Signed by the Toronto Blue Jays as a free agent, October. 9, 1988
Pre-Majors Highlight: Drove in 100 runs at Class A Dunedin in 1992 and 102 at Class AA Knoxville in 1993 **Personal Information:** Participated in baseball and track and field in high school

Carlos Delgado

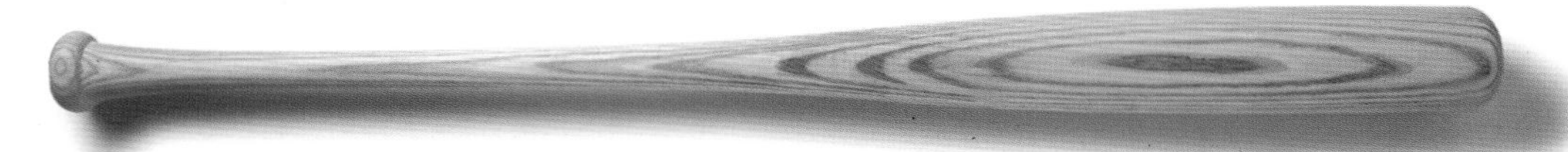

"He's got raw power. You can't make a mistake against him or he'll he hit it out."

Cleveland Indians pitcher, Charles Nagy

Career milestones

1994 Hit nine homers with 24 runs batted in in rookie season

1998 Homered in three consecutive at-bats and became sixth Blue Jay to hit three home runs in a game. Had 19-game hitting streak, May 21-June 9

1999 His 44 homers and 134 RBIs were personal bests and Blue Jays records

When it comes to raw power, few Major League players can top Carlos Delgado.

The bad news for American League pitchers: Delgado keeps getting better and better every season.

The Toronto Blue Jays' first baseman/designated hitter has put together four outstanding power seasons in a row and had another big year in 1999. Delgado blasted 44 home runs with 134 runs batted in, both career highs, while hitting a steady .272 in 152 games. He finished tied for third in the American League in homers and RBIs and was eighth in slugging percentage (.571).

Delgado began his run of solid years in 1996, his first full season with the Blue Jays. He hit .270 with 25 homers, 28 doubles and 92 RBIs in serving notice that he had arrived as an every-day player.

That was only the beginning of Delgado's power show. In 1997, he hit .262 in 153 games for Blue Jays, with 42 doubles, 30 home runs and 91 RBIs. That included three grand slams and homers in four consecutive games, which tied a club record.

Even offseason surgery couldn't stop Delgado from continuing his power emergence. He had arthroscopic surgery on January 19, 1998 to repair a torn labrum suffered in winter ball, missed the first 20 games of the season and wasn't activated until April. 24.

Despite the missed time, Delgado's numbers got better. While hitting a career-high 292, he belted 38 home runs, a career-high 43 doubles and drove in 115 runs.

Delgado ranked fifth in the league in doubles, tied for fourth in extra base hits (82), was fifth in slugging percentage (.592) and ninth in home runs. His biggest night of the season came on August 4 at Texas when he became the sixth Blue Jay to hit three home runs in a game and the third Toronto player to hit three home runs in three consecutive at-bats.

Long home runs have become Delgado's specialty. In 1997, he hit a homer over the roof in right field at Tiger Stadium in Detroit, making him the 29th player in Major League history to perform that feat. In 1994, he hit a 445-foot homer off the glass of the Windows Restaurant in center field at Toronto's Sky Dome.

It wouldn't show by Delgado's numbers now, but he struggled in his early big league seasons. He started the 1994 and 1995 seasons with the Blue Jays, but was sent back to Class AAA Syracuse both years. Delgado hit nine homers with 24 RBIs and batted .215 in 43 games in 1994. He had more problems in 1995, batting .165 with three homers and 11 RBIs in 37 games.

Unfortunately for American League pitchers, it's obvious Delgado's days of struggling are over.

Batting

Year	G	AB	R	H	HR	RBI	BB	SO	SB	CS	OBP	SLG	AVG
1999	**152**	**573**	**113**	**156**	**44**	**134**	**86**	**141**	**1**	**1**	**.377**	**.571**	**.272**
Career	**667**	**2332**	**378**	**622**	**149**	**467**	**313**	**624**	**5**	**5**	**.361**	**.531**	**.267**

Fielding

Year	Posn	G	GS	TC	PO	A	E	DP	FLD%
1999	**1B**	**147**	**147**	**1404**	**1306**	**84**	**14**	**134**	**.990**
Career		**495**	**485**	**4063**	**3766**	**255**	**42**	**366**	**.990**

Jeff Fassero

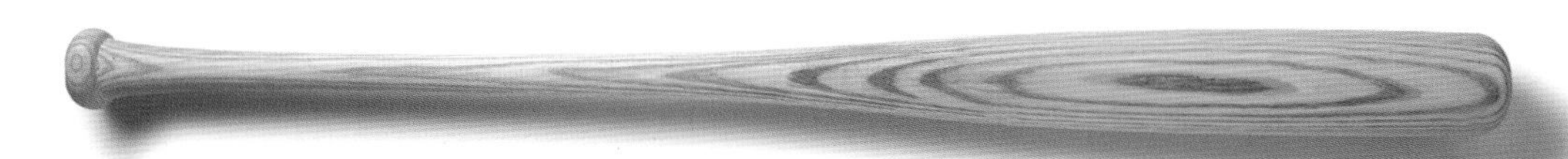

"I can describe the year (1999) in one word—frustrating. And I haven't figured out why."

Pitcher, Jeff Fassero

Profile

Name: Jeffrey Joseph Fassero
Height: 6–1 **Weight:** 195
Throws: Left **Bats:** Left **Position:** Pitcher
Born: January 5, 1963, Springfield, Illinois
Drafted: Selected by the St. Louis Cardinals in the 22nd round of the 1984 free-agent draft **Acquired:** Traded by the Seattle Mariners to the Texas Rangers, August 27, 1999 **Pre-Majors Highlight:** Saved 17 games at Class AA Arkansas in 1988
Personal Information: Married (Cathy) with two sons (Trevor Ryan, Blake Andrew)

If baseball handed out an award for perseverance, Jeff Fassero would win it.

A 22nd round draft pick of the St. Louis Cardinals in 1984, Fassero bounced around four organizations, was released twice and spent his first nine years in professional baseball in the minor leagues.

A lot of players would give up their dream of playing in the Major Leagues, but Fassero didn't. He finally reached the big leagues in 1991 and was one of the best left-handed starters in the game by the middle of the decade.

Fassero spent four years in St. Louis' minor league system, but never advanced past the Double-A level before being taken by the Chicago White Sox in the Rule 5 draft after the 1989 season. He was released before the next season began and signed a minor league contract with the Cleveland Indians. Back at the Double-A level again, Fassero lasted exactly one season before the Indians let him go.

After being signed by the Montreal Expos in 1991, Fassero finally got his first shot at the big leagues. The Expos called him up and he appeared in 51 games out of the bullpen, going 2–5 with a 2.44 earned run average.

Once Fassero got his chance, he wasn't about to go back to the minors. In 70 relief appearances in 1992, he was 8–7 with a 2.84 ERA. The Expos moved him into the rotation in 1993 and Fassero compiled a 12–5 record and a 2.29 ERA in 56 games (15 starts).

Fassero wouldn't leave the rotation for the next five years. Between 1994 and 1998, he compiled a 65–52 record while averaging 30 starts a season. Fassero was 36–31 with the Expos from 1994–96. His best season with Montreal came in 1996 when he went 15–11 with a 3.30 ERA in 34 starts. Fassero pitched five complete games and logged 231.2 innings.

Several contenders around the Major Leagues had taken notice of Fassero's good work and he was traded to Seattle after the 1996 season. The trade paid off for the Mariners. Starting a league-high 35 games in 1997, Fassero was 16–9, a career high in wins, with a 3.61 ERA. He also pitched a career-high 234.1 innings. After Seattle won the American League West title, Fassero picked up a win in the Division Series, holding the Baltimore Orioles to one run and three hits in eight innings.

After another solid season in 1998—13–12 with a 3.97 ERA—Fassero struggled last season and was traded to the Texas Rangers. He finished with a 5–14 record and a 7.20 ERA.

Despite the poor showing, don't be surprised if Fassero turns things around. It wouldn't be the first time he overcame big odds. Texas, however, declined to offer him arbitration.

Career milestones

1991 Pitched in first Major League game with the Montreal Expos

1996 Traded from the Montreal Expos to the Seattle Mariners, October 29, 1996.

1997 Was the winning pitcher victor of Game 3 in the Division Series against Baltimore, his first post-season appearance

1998 Threw a career-high seven complete games

1999 Traded to the Texas Rangers and pitched for American League West Division champions

Pitching

Year	W	L	ERA	G	GS	CG	SHO	SV	SVO	INN	H	R	ER	HR	HBP	BB	SO
1999	**5**	**14**	**7.20**	**37**	**27**	**0**	**0**	**0**	**0**	**156.1**	**208**	**135**	**125**	**35**	**4**	**83**	**114**
Career	**92**	**83**	**3.81**	**366**	**194**	**17**	**2**	**10**	**26**	**1465.1**	**1439**	**711**	**620**	**146**	**26**	**507**	**1229**

Batting

G	AB	R	H	HR	RBI	BB	SO	SB	CS	OBP	SLG	AVG	
Career	**366**	**222**	**15**	**17**	**0**	**5**	**17**	**125**	**1**	**0**	**.142**	**.095**	**.077**

Fielding

Year	Posn	G	GS	TC	PO	A	E	DP	FLD%
1999	**P**	**37**	**27**	**33**	**4**	**29**	**0**	**2**	**1.000**
Career		**366**	**194**	**333**	**67**	**254**	**12**	**8**	**.964**

Profile

Name: Andrew Jason Ashby
Height: 6–5 **Weight:** 202
Throws: Right **Bats:** Right
Position: Pitcher **Born:** July 11, 1967, Kansas City, Missouri **Drafted:** Signed as an undrafted free agent by the Philadelphia Phillies, May 4, 1986 **Acquired:** Traded by the San Diego Padres to the Philadelphia Phillies, 1999 **Pre-Majors Highlight:** Led the International League in complete games and shutouts 1991
Personal Information: Attended Crowder Junior College (Missouri)

Andy Ashby

"To add Andy Ashby to our pitching staff certainly validates what we're trying to do."

Philadelphia Phillies general manager, Ed Wade

Career milestones

1992 Selected by the Colorado Rockies in the expansion draft, November 17
1993 Traded to the San Diego Padres, July 27
1997 Came within three outs of the first no-hitter in San Diego Padres' history in a 6–2 win against Atlanta, September 5
1998 Named to the National League All-Star for the first time. Pitched in the World Series for the Padres
1999 Named to National League All-Star team for the second time

Andy Ashby's career has come full circle. Ashby spent the first seven years of his career with the Philadelphia Phillies' organization before being taken by the Colorado Rockies in the expansion draft following the 1992 season.

Ashby was traded to San Diego in 1993 and spent the next six years with the Padres, helping them reach the World Series in 1998. The right-hander was traded back to the Phillies following the 1999 season in a trade that sent pitchers Carlton Loewer, Adam Eaton and Steve Montgomery to San Diego.

"You hate to leave somewhere where you've been so long and what we've been through there, but I knew it was going to happen," said Ashby. "It's going to be nice, I hope. I want to go back and definitely help them go where they want to go and help them win."

The Ashby coming back to Philadelphia is a much different pitcher than the one who left town. Signed as a non-drafted free agent by the Phillies in 1986, Ashby toiled in Philadelphia's minor league organization before finally reaching the big leagues in 1991. He also spent part of the 1992 season with the Phillies, but his two-year numbers were unimpressive: 1–5 with a 6.00 ERA in 1991 and 1–3 with a 7.54 ERA in 1992.

The Phillies left Ashby unprotected in the expansion draft and the Rockies took him with the 25th overall pick. It's a move the Phillies turned out to regret.

"This is a homecoming for Andy Ashby," said Philadelphia general manager Ed Wade. "We let him get by in the expansion draft, and obviously it turned out to be a mistake on our part."

Ashby didn't spend much time with the Rockies. They traded him to San Diego on July 27, 1993, where he developed into one of the most dependable starters in the National League over the next six seasons. Ashby averaged 29 starts a season and has pitched over 200 innings in each of the last three last three years.

Ashby went 70–62 with the Padres, but is still under .500 for his career at 72–74.

He helped San Diego win the National League West title in 1996 and 1998. Ashby was 9–5 with a 3.23 ERA in 24 starts and started a game in the Division Series in '96. He was 17–9 —a career-high in wins—with a 3.34 ERA when the Padres reached the World Series in 1998. Ashby also set career highs in starts (33), complete games (five) and innings pitched (226.2). The Padres were 23–10 in games he started.

Another steady season followed in 1999, as Ashby went 14–10 with a 3.80 ERA and threw a career-high three shutouts.

Pitching

Year	W	L	ERA	G	GS	CG	SHO	SV	SVO	INN	H	R	ER	HR	HBP	BB	SO
1999	**14**	**10**	**3.80**	**31**	**31**	**4**	**3**	**0**	**0**	**206.0**	**204**	**95**	**87**	**26**	**7**	**54**	**132**
Career	**72**	**74**	**3.98**	**223**	**210**	**18**	**6**	**1**	**1**	**1343.0**	**1357**	**666**	**594**	**146**	**44**	**396**	**910**

Batting

Year	G	AB	R	H	HR	RBI	BB	SO	SB	CS	OBP	SLG	AVG
Career	**225**	**396**	**18**	**54**	**0**	**15**	**11**	**165**	**1**	**0**	**.159**	**.169**	**.136**

Fielding

Year	Posn	G	GS	TC	PO	A	E	DP	FLD%
1999	**P**	**31**	**31**	**51**	**14**	**35**	**2**	**4**	**.961**
Career		**223**	**210**	**309**	**97**	**205**	**7**	**13**	**.977**

Marquis Grissom

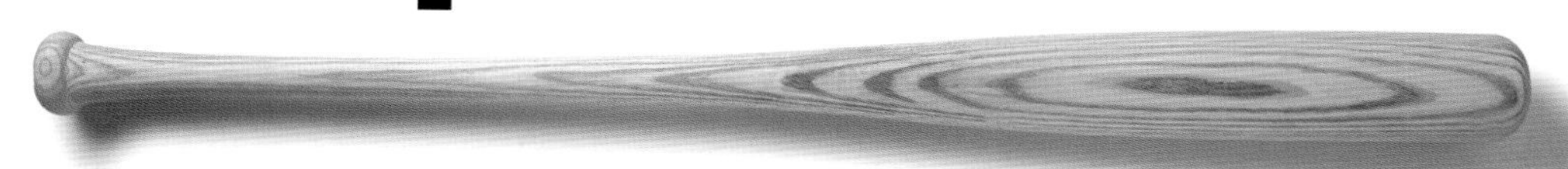

Profile

Name: Marquis Deon Grissom **Height:** 5–11 **Weight:** 188 **Throws:** Right **Bats:** Right **Position:** Center Field **Born:** April 17, 1967, Atlanta, Georgia **Drafted:** Selected by the Montreal Expos in the third round of the 1988 free-agent draft **Acquired:** Traded by the Cleveland Indians to the Milwaukee Brewers, December 8, 1997 **Pre-Majors Highlights:** Attended Florida A&M University in Tallahassee, where he excelled in 1988 as a pitcher and outfielder **Personal Information:** He is one of 15 children

"You've got to love to have Marquis on your team. He plays hard all the time, he plays every day and he's a leader in the clubhouse." **Cleveland Indians outfielder, David Justice**

There isn't anything spectacular or flashy about the way Marquis Grissom plays baseball, but anyone interested in winning will take the veteran outfielder any day.

Baseball people know the talents Grissom brings to a team. He's one of the few players around who can hit for power, drive in runs, steal bases and play outstanding defense in center field.

Grissom has reached double figures in homers eight times in the nine full seasons he's been in the Major Leagues. He's also reached double figures in stolen bases each season from 1990–99 and stolen over 50 bases three times. Grissom also won a Gold Glove for his defensive play from 1993–96.

Grissom's finest years came while playing for the Montreal Expos from 1990–94. He stole 76 bases during the 1991 season—his first full year in the Majors—and followed that by stealing 78, a career high, in 1992. Both marks led the National League. His 15 outfield assists in 1991 also led the league.

His best overall season came in 1993. He batted .298 with 19 homers, 95 RBIs, 104 runs scored and 53 stolen bases while winning his first Gold Glove. He'd have a lock on that award the next three years.

As most of the Expos' stars neared free agency, team management made the decision to trade them instead of paying out big contracts. Grissom was one of the players to go, being traded to the Atlanta Braves for outfielders Roberto Kelly, Tony Tarasco and pitchers Esteban Yan on April 6, 1995.

The trade was special to Grissom for two reasons. Not only was he joining one of the best teams in baseball, he was also returning to the city he was born and raised in. The 1995 season turned out to be special for the player and the team. Grissom batted .258 with 12 homers, 42 RBIs and 36 stolen bases while winning his third straight Gold Glove.

Meanwhile, the Braves won the franchise's first World Series since moving to Atlanta in 1966. Fittingly, Grissom caught the final out in the clinching game against Cleveland. While the Braves lost the Series to the New York Yankees in 1996, Grissom's numbers improved. He hit a career-high .308 with 106 runs scored, 32 doubles, 10 triples, 23 homers, 74 RBIs and his fourth straight Gold Glove.

Ironically, Grissom was traded to the Indians days before the 1997 season with outfielder David Justice for outfielder Kenny Lofton and pitcher Alan Embree. His numbers slipped in Cleveland, but he helped the Indians reach the World Series. Grissom was traded to the Brewers after the season and he has had two solid years in Milwaukee.

Career milestones

1993 Won National League Gold Glove Award. Also won Gold Glove in 1994, 1995 and 1996

1995 Traded by the Montreal Expos to the Atlanta Braves for Roberto Kelly, Tony Tarasco, Esteban Yan and cash, April 6

1997 Named Most Valuable Player of American League Championship Series

1999 Got his 1,000th career hit off Houston's Mike Hampton, August 18

Batting

Year	G	AB	R	H	HR	RBI	BB	SO	SB	CS	OBP	SLG	AVG
1999	**154**	**603**	**92**	**161**	**20**	**83**	**49**	**109**	**24**	**6**	**.320**	**.415**	**.267**
Career	**1435**	**5603**	**839**	**1550**	**131**	**601**	**412**	**783**	**382**	**95**	**.327**	**.410**	**.277**

Fielding

Year	Posn	G	GS	TC	PO	A	E	DP	FLD%
1999	**OF**	**149**	**145**	**380**	**374**	**1**	**5**	**2**	**.987**
Career		**1395**	**1353**	**3500**	**3379**	**78**	**43**	**17**	**.988**

Derek Jeter

"To win the World Series three times in my first four years is unbelievable. I never dreamed anything like this would happen to me." New York Yankees shortstop, Derek Jeter

Profile

Name: Derek Sanderson Jeter
Height: 6–3 **Weight:** 195 **Throws:** Right
Bats: Right **Position:** Shortstop
Born: June 26, 1974, Pequannock, New Jersey
Drafted: Selected by the New York Yankees in the first round (sixth pick overall) of the 1992 free-agent draft
Pre-Majors Highlight: Led the International League in runs scored in 1995 **Personal Information:** Attends the University of Michigan in the offseason

Career milestones

1995 Made Major League debut May 29, 1995
1996 Named the American League Rookie of the Year
1998 Had 50 hits in August, making him the first Yankee to accomplish a 50-hit month since Joe DiMaggio in July of 1941
1999 Named to the American League All-Star team for the second straight year. Won his third World Series in four years

If baseball ever filmed a version of the movie It's a Wonderful Life, Derek Jeter would be perfect for the leading role.

Since becoming the New York Yankees every-day shortstop in 1996, life has been wonderful for Jeter. In those four years, he has won the American League Rookie of the Year Award, hit well over .300 three straight years, developed into one of the top players in the game today and been a big part of a team that has won three straight World Series titles.

Obviously, the man is doing something right.

When it comes to helping the Yankees win, Jeter does it all. Offensively, he hits for a high batting average, he scores runs, he hits home runs, he drives in runs and he steals bases. Defensively, he is one of the best shortstops in the Major Leagues.

All this, and he's only 25 years old.

The scary thing about Jeter is there appears to be no limit on how good he will become. He keeps topping himself, as 1999 showed. Jeter batted .349 with 37 doubles, 24 homers, 102 RBIs, 134 runs scored and 19 stolen bases. He reached career highs in all of the categories except steals. Jeter led the American League with 219 hits (another career high) and was beaten out for the league's batting title by Boston shortstop Nomar Garciaparra, who hit .357.

The Yankees, meanwhile, swept the Atlanta Braves for their second straight World Series title and third in four years.

"Derek is a rare talent," said Yankees manager Joe Torre. "It doesn't seem possible, but he keeps getting better."

The Yankees thought enough of Jeter to take him in the first round of the 1992 draft, even though he was only 17 years old. In 1994, he batted .329, .377 and .349 at three minor league levels and was in the Majors by the end of the 1995 season.

By 1996, the Yankees' shortstop position was his. Jeter, who became New York's first rookie Opening Day shortstop since Tom Tresh in 1962, proved he was ready for the job. He batted .314 with 10 homers and 78 RBIs while being named the American League Rookie of the Year. The season ended with the Yankees beating the Atlanta Braves in the World Series.

In 1997, Jeter hit .291 with 10 homers and 70 RBIs. He took a step to the next level in 1998, batting .324 with 19 homers, 84 RBIs, a league-high 127 runs scored and a career-high 30 stolen bases. The Yankees regained their World Series title by sweeping the San Diego Padres.

With the Yankees and Jeter at the top of their games, there's no telling what they'll accomplish in the future.

Batting

Year	G	AB	R	H	HR	RBI	BB	SO	SB	CS	OBP	SLG	AVG
1999	**158**	**627**	**134**	**219**	**24**	**102**	**91**	**116**	**19**	**8**	**.438**	**.552**	**.349**
Career	**638**	**2537**	**486**	**807**	**63**	**341**	**273**	**473**	**86**	**33**	**.389**	**.465**	**.318**

Fielding

Year	Posn	G	GS	TC	PO	A	E	DP	FLD%
1999	**SS**	**158**	**158**	**635**	**230**	**391**	**14**	**87**	**.978**
Career		**637**	**635**	**2742**	**958**	**1719**	**65**	**346**	**.976**

Dean Palmer

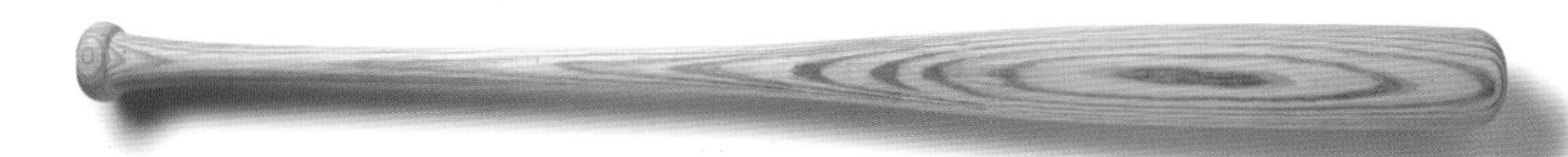

"Dean did the things we brought him here to do. He gave us a big bat in the middle of our lineup."

Detroit Tigers general manager, Randy Smith

Profile

Name: Dean William Palmer **Height:** 6–1 **Weight:** 210 **Throws:** Right **Bats:** Right **Positions:** Third Base **Born:** December 27, 1968, Tallahassee, Florida **Drafted:** Selected by the Texas Rangers in the third round of the 1986 free-agent draft **Acquired:** Signed by the Detroit Tigers as a free agent, November 13, 1998 **Pre-Majors Highlight:** Led the Texas League with 25 home runs in 1989 **Personal Information:** Hosted Palmer's Pals, youngsters from Los Barios Unidos Community Clinic, to home games in 1996 while playing for Texas

After losing 97 games in 1998, the Detroit Tigers went looking for some help. They needed a veteran player who would provide some production for their lineup, play every day and give some leadership to a young team.

The Tigers found exactly what they were looking for when they signed third baseman Dean Palmer on November 13, 1998.

Palmer did everything the Tigers asked. In 150 games, he batted .263 with a career-high 38 home runs and 100 runs batted in while providing leadership for a team that improved to a 69–92 record.

Putting up solid power numbers is nothing new for Palmer. He's been doing it since coming to the Major Leagues in 1991 with the Texas Rangers, who drafted him in 1986. On his way to the Majors, Palmer led the Texas League (25 in 1989) and the American Association (22 in less than half a season 1991) in home runs. Although he batted only .187 after being called up midway through the '91 season, Palmer hit 15 home runs with 37 RBIs in 81 games.

Palmer was the Rangers' starting third baseman for the next six seasons and was a consistent power source each year. His first full year in the big leagues saw him hit 26 homers with 72 RBIs while his batting average improved to .229. A breakthrough year followed in 1993. Palmer belted 33 homers, drove in 96 runs and upped his average to .245.

A 19-homer, 59-RBI season in 1994 was cut short by a stay on the disabled list and the players' strike that ended the season in August. Palmer batted a career-high .336 in 1995, but he was limited to just 36 games by a ruptured biceps tendon. He hit nine homers and drove in 24.

Palmer made a strong comeback from the injury the following year, his best season with the Rangers. He hit .280 with a career-high 98 runs scored, 38 homers and 107 RBIs in 154 games in 1996.

However, Palmer's days with the Rangers were numbered. After hitting .245 with 14 homers and 55 RBIs in 94 games, he was traded to Kansas City on July 26, 1997. Palmer hit .278 with nine homers and 31 RBIs in 49 games for the Royals.

Palmer recorded the best power numbers in Royals' history the following season, slamming 34 homers with 119 RBIs (a career high) in 152 games. He also hit .278 and ranked second in the American League with 13 sacrifice flies.

Those numbers caught the Tigers' attention and earned Palmer a big payday on the free-agent market. Judging by the results in 1999, it looks like a good arrangement for both sides.

Career milestones

1991 Was second among American League rookies in homers (15) and runs batted in (37)

1997 Traded by the Texas Rangers to the Kansas City Royals for outfielder Tom Goodwin, July 25

1998 Named as third baseman on American League Silver Slugger team selected by The Sporting News

1999 Tied his career-high mark of 38 home runs

Batting

Year	G	AB	R	H	HR	RBI	BB	SO	SB	CS	OBP	SLG	AVG
1999	**150**	**560**	**92**	**147**	**38**	**100**	**57**	**153**	**3**	**3**	**.339**	**.518**	**.263**
Career	**1125**	**4064**	**624**	**1035**	**235**	**701**	**399**	**1094**	**40**	**28**	**.325**	**.483**	**.255**

Fielding

Year	Posn	G	GS	TC	PO	A	E	DP	FLD%
1999	**3B**	**141**	**140**	**348**	**89**	**240**	**19**	**24**	**.945**
Career		**1071**	**1043**	**2612**	**713**	**1734**	**165**	**143**	**.937**

Profile

Name: Kenneth Scott Rogers **Height:** 6–1 **Weight:** 217 **Throws:** Left **Bats:** Left **Position:** Pitcher **Born:** November 10, 1964, Savannah, Georgia **Drafted:** Selected by the Texas Rangers in the 39th round of the 1982 free-agent draft **Acquired:** Traded by the Oakland Athletics to the New York Mets, July 23, 1999 **Pre-Majors Highlight:** Appeared in 39 games for Class A Burlington in 1994 **Personal Information:** Did not play organized baseball until his senior year of high school, when he was used exclusively as an outfielder

Kenny Rogers

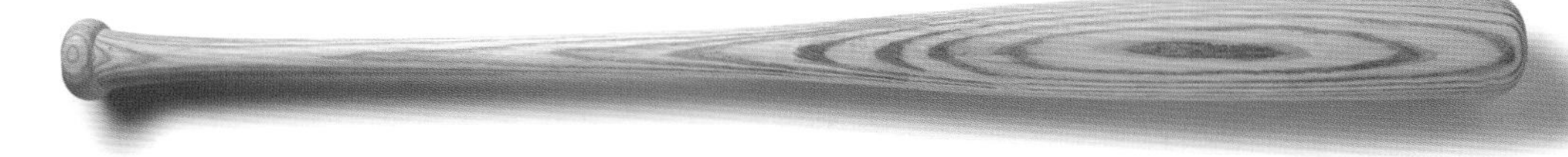

"I don't overpower anyone. I need to hit my spots and throw strikes."

New York Mets pitcher, Kenny Rogers

Career milestones

1992 Led the American League with 81 appearances

1994 Pitched a perfect game in a 4-0 victory vs California, the 11th regular-season perfect game since 1900 and the first ever by an American League left-hander, July 28

1996 Won a World Series ring

1998 Posted second-best win total in his career and had third-best ERA in the American League

1999 Had a perfect home record with both Oakland and New York until late September. Even when he did not get the win, the A's and Mets won the games he started

The road to the Major Leagues certainly wasn't an easy one for Kenny Rogers.

Unless you call making it to the big leagues after being a 39th round draft pick and spending seven full years in the minors easy.

Somehow, Rogers survived and has turned into a solid Major League starting pitcher. He finished the 1999 season with a 112–78 lifetime record, which includes a perfect game. It's a pretty safe bet to say not many pitchers taken in the 39th round can make such statements.

Rogers' long road started almost as an afterthought by the Texas Rangers in the 1982 draft. Texas was definitely taking a flier on Rogers, who didn't even pitch on his high school team in Plant City, Florida. Rogers played the outfield, but the Rangers had good reports on his throwing arm and decided to try him as a pitcher.

Rogers spent the next seven years trying to be a pitcher, but the results weren't there. Between 1982 and 1988, he compiled a 19–38 record as a minor league pitcher and never won more than four games in a season.

Rogers never advanced beyond the Class AA level in the minors, but a funny thing happened in spring training of 1989. The left-hander actually made the Rangers' pitching staff. Then an even funnier thing happened. Rogers never went back to the minors. He spent his first four Major League seasons primarily as a reliever, recording 15 saves with a 10–6 record and a 3.13 ERA in 1990. Rogers also won 10 games in 1991 and led the American League with 81 appearances in 1992.

The Rangers made Rogers a starter in 1993 and he was the ace of their staff the next three years, going 44–25. Rogers has the highest career winning percentage in Rangers history (.579) and ranks among the club's all-time leaders in games (second), wins (fourth), walks (fifth), innings (sixth), strikeouts (seventh) and saves (tied for seventh).

The high point of his career came on July 28, 1994 when he pitched a perfect game against the California Angels. Rogers struck out eight and threw only 98 pitches.

Rogers left Texas after the 1995 season to sign with the New York Yankees. He went 18–15 in two years before being traded to the Oakland Athletics. Rogers was the ace of the A's pitching staff in 1998. He led the club in wins (16), starts (34), complete games (seven), ERA (3.17), innings (238.2) and strikeouts (138).

Rogers was 5–3 with the A's in 1999 before being traded to the New York Mets on July 23. He went 5–1 and helped the Mets win the wild card playoff spot in the National League.

Pitching

Year	W	L	ERA	G	GS	CG	SHO	SV	SVO	INN	H	R	ER	HR	HBP	BB	SO
1999	10	4	4.19	31	31	5	1	0	0	195.1	206	101	91	16	13	69	126
Career	114	78	4.05	502	217	29	6	28	57	1701.1	1686	862	766	166	55	651	1114

Batting

Year	G	AB	R	H	HR	RBI	BB	SO	SB	CS	OBP	SLG	AVG
Career	502	35	3	3	0	2	2	13	0	0	.135	.086	.086

Fielding

Year	Posn	G	GS	TC	PO	A	E	DP	FLD%
1999	P	31	31	76	10	62	4	4	.947
Career		502	217	532	111	394	27	25	.949

Kevin Appier

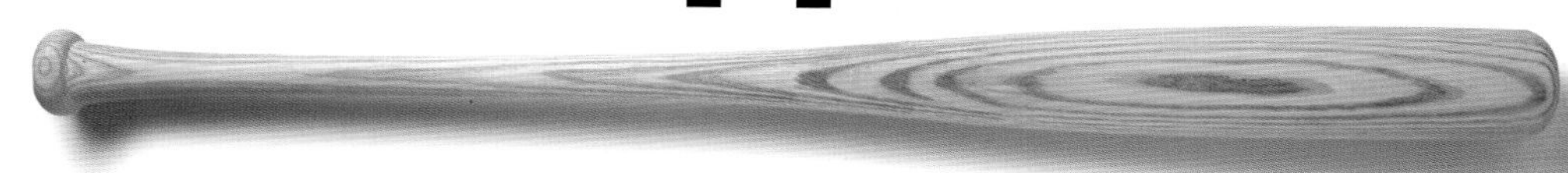

"No one thought we'd get Kevin Appier and that's what's fun about this. We got him. We got him over everybody."

Oakland Athletics general manager, Billy Beane

Profile

Name: Robert Kevin Appier **Height:** 6–2 **Weight:** 200 **Throws:** Right **Bats:** Right **Position:** Pitcher **Born:** December 6, 1967, Lancaster, California **Drafted:** Selected by the Kansas City Royals in the first round (ninth pick overall) of the 1987 free-agent draft **Acquired:** Traded by the Kansas City Royals to the Oakland Athletics, July 31, 1999 **Pre-Majors Highlight:** Led the Northwest League in games started, 1987 **Personal Information:** Received the 1996 Kansas City Roberto Clemente Award for his service in the community

When Kevin Appier missed most of the 1998 season because of shoulder surgery, many wondered if his career was over.

Appier proved them wrong in 1999.

"I feel if I'm healthy, I'll be able to pitch a lot of innings," said Appier. "Then the rest will take care of itself."

Although Appier's earned run average was a career-high 5.17, he finished the season with a 16–14 record, started 34 games and pitched 209 innings.

Apparently, many teams in baseball think Appier has a chance to regain the form that made him one of the best right-handers in baseball throughout most of the 1990s. As the trading deadline approached last July, several teams contending for playoff spots talked to the Kansas City Royals about acquiring Appier. In the end, the Oakland Athletics, who were trying to win the wild card race in the American League won the bidding war. The A's traded right-handers Blake Stein, Jeff D'Amico and Brad Rigby for Appier, who turned 32 at the end of 1999.

Although the A's didn't make the playoffs, they saw enough of Appier to pick up the option on his contract for the 2000 season.

If Appier regains his past form, the A's could have a No. 1 starter. He was one of the most effective pitchers in the league from 1990 through 1996. Appier pitched over 200 innings five times and had an earned run average under 3.00 three times.

His best season came in 1993 when his 2.56 earned run average was the lowest in the league, the first Royal to achieve that honor since Bret Saberhagen. Appier finished that season with an 18–8 record (a career-high in wins) and pitched 238.2 innings, another career best. He finished third in the Cy Young Award voting behind Jack McDowell and Randy Johnson.

Appier struck out a career-high 207 in 1996. Although his record slipped to 9–13 in 1997—his first losing season since his rookie year in 1989—his ERA was a solid 3.40 and he pitched 235.2 innings.

Appier had surgery to repair a torn labrum in his right shoulder on March 24, 1998. Doctors also trimmed frayed edges of the rotator cuff. He was on the disabled list from March 20 until September 1. He finished with a 1–3 record and a 7.80 ERA. On September 18, he struck out Cleveland's Jim Thome for career strikeout No. 1,367, passing Mark Gubicza on the team's career list for No. 1.

Appier ranks among the Royals' career top 10 in a number of pitching categories, including victories, innings, ERA, starts, complete games and shutouts. The A's are confident Appier will now start writing his name in their record book.

Career milestones

1990 Threw a one-hit shutout against the Detroit Tigers, July 7

1993 Had the lowest earned run average in the American League. Finished third in the voting for the American League Cy Young Award. Threw a one-hit shutout against the Texas Rangers, July 27

1996 Struck out a career-best 207

1998 Set a new Kansas City Royals record for strikeouts

1999 Returned from 1998 shoulder surgery to win 16 games

Pitching

Year	W	L	ERA	G	GS	CG	SHO	SV	SVO	INN	H	R	ER	HR	HBP	BB	SO
1999	**16**	**14**	**5.17**	**34**	**34**	**1**	**0**	**0**	**0**	**209.0**	**230**	**131**	**120**	**27**	**7**	**84**	**131**
Career	**121**	**94**	**3.54**	**293**	**281**	**32**	**10**	**0**	**0**	**1889.1**	**1726**	**804**	**743**	**143**	**40**	**657**	**1504**

Batting

Year	G	AB	R	H	HR	RBI	BB	SO	SB	CS	OBP	SLG	AVG
Career	**293**	**8**	**0**	**0**	**0**	**0**	**0**	**6**	**0**	**0**	**.000**	**.000**	**.000**

Fielding

Year	Posn	G	GS	TC	PO	A	E	DP	FLD%
1999	**P**	**34**	**34**	**35**	**13**	**21**	**1**	**2**	**.971**
Career		**293**	**281**	**338**	**160**	**169**	**9**	**22**	**.973**

Profile

Name: Jose Antonio Dono Offerman **Height:** 6–0 **Weight:** 190 **Throws:** Right **Bats:** Both **Positions:** Second Base, Designated Hitter, First Base **Born:** November 8, 1968, San Pedro de Macoris, Dominican Republic **Drafted:** Not drafted. Signed by the Los Angeles Dodgers as a free agent, July 24, 1986 **Acquired:** Signed as a free agent by the Boston Red Sox, November 16, 1998 **Pre-Majors Highlight:** Batted .326 at Class AAA Albuquerque, 1990 **Personal Information:** Married, two children

Jose Offerman

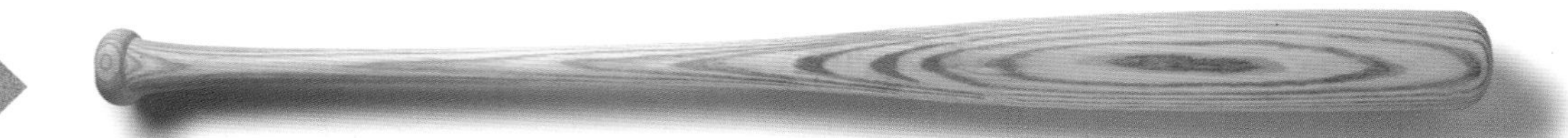

"Jose can do a lot of things with the bat. You can move him around in the lineup. That's why we got him."

Boston Red Sox manager, Jimmy Williams

Career milestones

1990 Became the first Los Angeles Dodgers player to homer in his first Major League at-bat, August 19, 1990
1995 Traded from the Los Angeles Dodgers to the Kansas City Royals for pitcher Billy Brewer, December 17
1998 Led the Major Leagues with 13 triples. Had a 27-game hitting streak from July 11–August 7
1999 Had career best season in runs scored (107), doubles (37), home runs (8), runs batted in (96) in his first season

The Boston Red Sox brought Jose Offerman to town for one reason and one reason only: To hit.

Fortunately for the Sox and Offerman, that's exactly what he did during the 1999 season.

Batting from the leadoff spot, Offerman gave the Sox the spark they were looking from when they signed him to a four-year contract on November 16, 1998.

Switch-hitting leadoff men who combine the ability to get on base, with good speed, extra-base punch and the talent to drive in runs don't come along every day, but that's what the Red Sox found in Offerman. He hit .294 with 107 runs scored, 37 doubles, 11 triples, eight homers, 37 doubles, 69 runs batted in and 18 stolen bases.

Offerman's presence at the top of the lineup helped set the table for the meat of the Boston batting order. Thanks to big bats of teammates Nomar Garciaparra, Troy O'Leary and Brian Dabauch, Offerman often got knocked home when he did get on. His 107 runs scored were a career high. He also reached career bests in doubles, homers, RBIs and walks (96).

Defense has always been a different story with Offerman, but that's all right with the Red Sox. He began the season as the designated hitter, was moved to first base for a while and then became the every-day second baseman. He committed 14 errors in 149 games.

Hitting has been Offerman's forte his entire professional career, which began when he signed with the Los Angeles Dodgers in 1987. He batted over .300 three times in the minor leagues, but his defensive problems at shortstop kept him from becoming a solid all-around player for the Dodgers. He made the National League All-Star team in 1995, hitting .287, his best season with Los Angeles.

The Dodgers traded Offerman to the Kansas City Royals for left-hander Billy Brewer on December 17, 1995. He found the American League to his liking, hitting .303 in 1996 and .297 in 1997.

His 1998 numbers while playing for the Royals earned him his contract with the Red Sox. Offerman had a career-high 27-game hitting streak from July 11 to August 7, the third longest streak in the American League in 1998, and the second longest in Royals history.

Offerman's 13 triples led the league and he became the first Kansas City player to lead the league since Willie Wilson in 1998. He also had a career-high 191 hits, the most by a Royals player in 21 years.

For the season, Offerman hit .313 with seven homers and 66 RBIs while being named to the American League All-Star team.

Offerman signed with the Red Sox following the '98 season, a move that looks good for both parties.

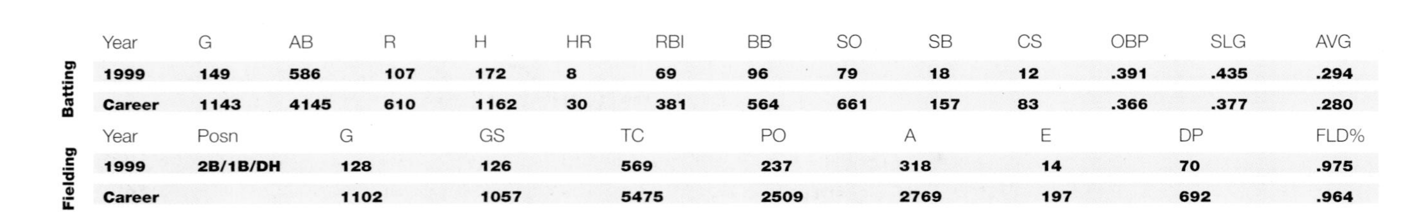

Batting

Year	G	AB	R	H	HR	RBI	BB	SO	SB	CS	OBP	SLG	AVG
1999	**149**	**586**	**107**	**172**	**8**	**69**	**96**	**79**	**18**	**12**	**.391**	**.435**	**.294**
Career	**1143**	**4145**	**610**	**1162**	**30**	**381**	**564**	**661**	**157**	**83**	**.366**	**.377**	**.280**

Fielding

Year	Posn	G	GS	TC	PO	A	E	DP	FLD%
1999	**2B/1B/DH**	**128**	**126**	**569**	**237**	**318**	**14**	**70**	**.975**
Career		**1102**	**1057**	**5475**	**2509**	**2769**	**197**	**692**	**.964**

Trevor Hoffman

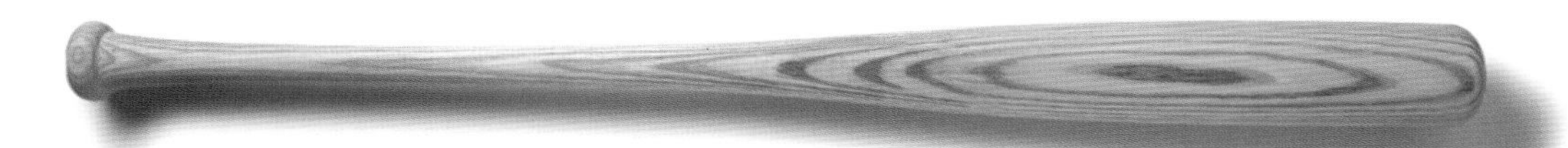

"With Trevor Hoffman, you know it's an eight-inning game when you play San Diego."

Former Colorado manager, Jim Leyland

Profile
Name:
Trevor William Hoffman
Height: 6-0 **Weight:** 215 **Throws:** Right **Bats:** Right **Position:** Pitcher
Born: October 13, 1967, Bellflower, California **Drafted:** Selected by the Cincinnati Reds in the 11th round of the 1989 free-agent draft.
Acquired: Traded by the Florida Marlins to the San Diego Padres, June 24, 1993. **Personal Information:** Brother Glenn is a former Major Leaguer infielder and former manager of the Los Angeles Dodgers. He is now a coach for the Dodgers

Trevor Hoffman is as close to automatic as it gets in baseball these days.

When Hoffman comes into the game, opposing teams know it's time to pack up the equipment and head for home.

Yes, the San Diego Padres closer is that good.

A year after blowing one save in 54 chances the entire season in leading his team to the World Series, Hoffman was almost as good in 1999.

The right-hander converted 40 of 43 save opportunities, including 31 in a row to end the season. Hoffman finished second in the National League in saves to Montreal's Ugueth Urbina. He had a 2–3 record, which meant he earned the win or the save in 42 of the Padres' 74 victories (57 percent). He allowed 16 earned runs and struck out 73 in 67.1 innings.

Hoffman, who didn't blow a save after June 2, was nearly unhittable after the All-Star break. He was 2–0 with 19 saves and a 0.92 ERA. In his final 20 appearances, he saved 14 games and allowed one earned run in 22 innings.

As good as Hoffman was last season, he was even better in 1998 when he converted 53 of 54 save opportunities to establish a new Major League single-season record for save percentage (.981). That earned him the National League Rolaids Relief Award. He had a 4–2 record and a 1.48 ERA, allowing 12 earned runs and striking out 86 in 73 innings.

His 53 saves matched the National League record for most saves in a single season (Randy Myers had 53 with Chicago in 1993). The Padres were 85–0 when leading after eight innings in the 1998 regular season.

Hoffman became one of only five closers to collect 50 or more saves in a single season. He earned the win or save in 58 of San Diego's 98 wins. The Padres were 62–1 in games in which he pitched. He converted 41 consecutive save opportunities between September 1997 and July 1998.

Since Opening Day 1998, Hoffman has 93 saves in 97 opportunities, a 96 percent success rate. He has converted 60 of his last 63 save chances, 101 of his last 105 and 120 of his last 125.

Hoffman has been golden since the Padres acquired him from the Florida Marlins on June 24, 1993, a deal that sent outfielder Gary Sheffield to the Marlins. He saved 20 games in 1994, 31 in 1995 and 43 in 1996.

As if facing Hoffman isn't bad enough, here are two more scary thoughts for opposing teams. He only turned 32 years old during the 1999 playoffs and has remained-injury throughout his career, which means he should continue to be automatic for a long time.

Career milestones

1997 Finished second in the National League with 37 saves

1998 Converted 53 of 54 save opportunities to establish a new Major League single-season record for save percentage (.981) . Named winner of the National League Rolaids Relief Award.

1999 Named to the National League All-Star team for the second year in a row

Pitching

Year	W	L	ERA	G	GS	CG	SHO	SV	SVO	INN	H	R	ER	HR	HBP	BB	SO
1999	**2**	**3**	**2.14**	**64**	**0**	**0**	**0**	**40**	**43**	**67.1**	**48**	**23**	**16**	**5**	**0**	**15**	**73**
Career	**36**	**28**	**2.69**	**439**	**0**	**0**	**0**	**228**	**260**	**509.0**	**365**	**167**	**152**	**46**	**4**	**164**	**580**

Batting

Year	G	AB	R	H	HR	RBI	BB	SO	SB	CS	OBP	SLG	AVG
Career	**439**	**29**	**1**	**4**	**0**	**5**	**0**	**9**	**0**	**0**	**.138**	**.207**	**.138**

Fielding

Year	Posn	G	GS	TC	PO	A	E	DP	FLD%
1999	**P**	**64**	**0**	**8**	**3**	**5**	**0**	**0**	**1.000**
Career		**439**	**0**	**69**	**31**	**37**	**1**	**2**	**.986**

Manny Ramirez

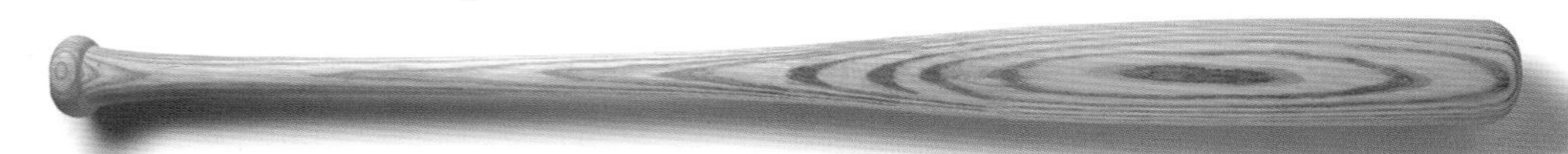

Profile

Name: Manuel Aristides Ramirez **Height:** 6–0 **Weight:** 205 **Throws:** Right **Bats:** Right **Position:** Right Field **Born:** May 30, 1972, Santo Domingo, Dominican Republic **Drafted:** Selected by the Cleveland Indians in the first round (13th pick overall) of the 1991 free-agent draft. Pre-Majors **Highlight:** Led the Eastern League with a 340 batting average, 1993 **Personal Information:** Named New York Public Schools "High School Player of the Year" in 1991.

"Manny is a very special talent. He is a great pure hitter. He has grown as a player every year."

Cleveland Indians general manager, John Hart

Career milestones

1994 Finished second in voting for American League Rookie of the Year Award

1997 Hit 100th career home run, August 8

1998 Ranked fourth in the American League in home runs and runs batted in

1999 Drove in 165 runs, the most in the Major Leagues since Jimmie Foxx drove in 175 in 1938

When it comes to driving in runs, Manny Ramirez is a machine. And the machine shows no signs of letting up anytime soon.

Ramirez, the right fielder for the Cleveland Indians, led the Major Leagues with 165 runs batted in last season. In leading the Indians to their fifth straight American League Central Division title, Ramirez had one of the most dominating offensive seasons baseball has witnessed over the last 60 years.

"Manny is an unbelievable talent," said Indians first baseman Jim Thome. "Just look at his numbers. He just keeps putting up the numbers every year. It's a thrill just watching him."

In 1999, Ramirez became the first Major League player in over 60 years to top the 160-RBI mark. Hall of Famer Jimmie Foxx, who had 175 RBIs in 1938, was the last to do it. Ramirez's total ranks him 12th on the all-time list for the most RBIs in one season. At one point, Ramirez was on pace to break Hack Wilson's record of 191 RBIs in a season.

Ramirez's name can be found among the leaders in several offensive categories in the American League from last season. He was first in RBIs and slugging percentage (.663), second in on-base percentage (.442), third in home runs (44) and extra-base hits (81), fourth in runs scored (131) and fifth in batting average (.333) and total bases (346).

Ramirez made the American League All-Star team for the third time in his career and the second year in a row. His biggest game came on September 24 against Toronto when he homered twice and drove in eight runs

In another big season in 1998, Ramirez hit .294 with 45 homers and 145 RBIs. He ranked among the top 10 in the league in average, home runs, runs scored, total bases and slugging percentage. He tied a Major League record with eight homers in five games, only the second player to do so.

Ramirez also topped the 100-RBI mark in 1995 (107) and in 1996 (112). In six big-league seasons, he already has 10 career grand slams. He is a .402 career hitter with 117 RBIs with the bases loaded.

Ramirez first made the All-Star team in 1995, when he hit .308 with 31 homers and 107 RBIs. In 1994, he finished second in the American League Rookie of the Year voting, hitting .269 with 17 homers in 91 games.

Ramirez also has 13 career postseason home runs, ranking him fifth on the all-time list in Major League history.

Ramirez finished fourth in the voting for the American League Most Valuable Player Award in 1998 and was third in 1999.

Batting

Year	G	AB	R	H	HR	RBI	BB	SO	SB	CS	OBP	SLG	AVG
1999	**147**	**522**	**131**	**174**	**44**	**165**	**96**	**131**	**2**	**4**	**.442**	**.663**	**.333**
Career	**849**	**3031**	**573**	**932**	**198**	**682**	**455**	**663**	**27**	**23**	**.399**	**.576**	**.307**

Fielding

Year	Posn	G	GS	TC	PO	A	E	DP	FLD%
1999	**OF**	**145**	**144**	**281**	**267**	**7**	**7**	**2**	**.975**
Career		**804**	**791**	**1554**	**1462**	**56**	**36**	**13**	**.977**

Tony Gwynn

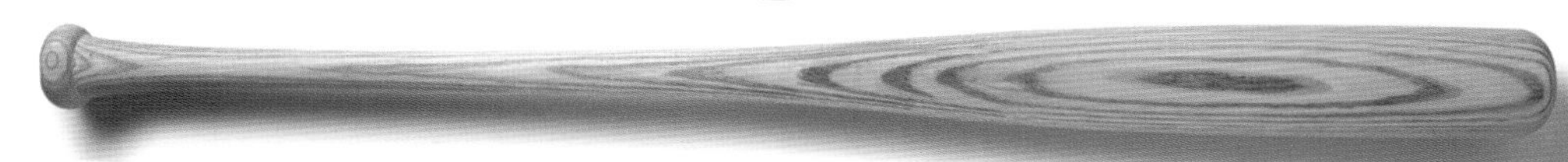

"He's so great with two strikes, that's almost when he's the most dangerous."

San Diego Padres manager, Bruce Bochy

Profile

Name: Anthony Keith Gwynn **Height:** 5–11 **Weight:** 220 **Throws:** Left **Bats:** Left **Position:** Right Field **Born:** May 9, 1960, Los Angeles, California **Drafted:** Selected by the San Diego Padres in the third round of the 1981 free-agent draft **Pre-Majors Highlight:** Played both baseball and basketball at San Diego State University Drafted by the then-San Diego Clippers in the 10th round of the 1981 NBA draft **Personal Information:** Brother, Chris, played in the Major Leagues from 1987–96

Career milestones

1984 Won first National League batting title. Also led league in hitting in 1987–89 and 1994–97.

1986 Won first National League Gold Glove. Also won award in 1987 and 1989–91

1994 His .394 average was the highest by a National League hitter since Bill Terry hit .401 in 1930

1999 Recorded 3,000th career hit against Montreal, August 6

It's not every day an umpire hugs a player in the middle of a Major League baseball game and nobody complains.

Then again, it's not every day a player gets his 3,000th career hit.

That's what happened on August 6 of last season in Olympic Stadium when the San Diego Padres played the Montreal Expos. Gwynn slapped a single to center field off rookie pitcher Dan Smith to become the 22nd Major Leaguer to reach 3,000 hits.

As Gwynn rounded the base, his teammates rushed to congratulate him. Before they could get there, first base umpire Kerwin Danley—Gwynn's college teammate at San Diego State University—gave him a hug.

Danley, as well as baseball fans everywhere, had good reason to be excited. Gwynn reached the 3,000-mark in 2,284 games, the third-fastest in Major League history behind Ty Cobb and Nap Lajoie. Gwynn is the seventh player to reach 3,000 hits who spent his entire Major League career with one team.

To Gwynn, a San Diego native, that means everything. The 18 straight years he has batted over .300, all eight of his National League record-tying eight batting championships (1984, 1987–89, 1994–97) and all five of his Gold Gloves (1986–87, 1989–91) have come wearing a Padres uniform.

"I've been a Padre my whole career, and I'm proud of that," Gwynn said. "Everything I've done, I've done in a Padre uniform. If my career is over and they look back and they see San Diego all the way down the line, that means a lot to me."

Only six other members of the 3,000 club spent their entire careers with the same team: Stan Musial (Cardinals), Roberto Clemente (Pittsburgh Pirates), Al Kaline (Detroit Tigers), Carl Yastrzemski (Boston Red Sox), Robin Yount (Milwaukee Brewers) and George Brett (Kansas City Royals).

Not surprisingly, Gwynn is the all-time club leader in batting, hits, runs, doubles, triples, stolen bases, RBIs and games played.

Gwynn, who turned 40 in May, also became the first National League player to get 3,000 hits since Lou Brock in 1979. He began his odyssey on July 19, 1982. He got his 1,000th hit on April 22, 1988 and reached his 2,000th on August 6, 1993 exactly six years before No. 3,000.

Gwynn has made the National League All-Star team 15 times and has been voted to start 12 times, including each of the last six seasons. He led the Padres to two World Series appearances (1984 and 1998) and has hit .371 in the two Fall Classics. In his career he's batted .347 with men in scoring position.

"He's going to go down as one of the greatest hitters of all time," Padres manager Bruce Bochy said.

Batting

Year	G	AB	R	H	HR	RBI	BB	SO	SB	CS	OBP	SLG	AVG
1999	**111**	**411**	**59**	**139**	**10**	**62**	**29**	**14**	**7**	**2**	**.381**	**.477**	**.338**
Career	**2333**	**9059**	**1361**	**3067**	**133**	**1104**	**771**	**421**	**318**	**124**	**.389**	**.459**	**.339**

Fielding

Year	Posn	G	GS	TC	PO	A	E	DP	FLD%
1999	**OF**	**104**	**104**	**152**	**147**	**4**	**1**	**0**	**.993**
Career		**2283**	**2261**	**4683**	**4464**	**157**	**62**	**26**	**.987**

Profile

Name: Mariano Rivera
Height: 6–2 **Weight:** 170
Throws: Right **Bats:** Right
Position: Pitcher **Born:** November 29, 1969, Panama City, Panama **Drafted:** Not drafted. Signed by the New York Yankees as a free agent to a minor-league contract February. 17, 1990
Pre-Majors Highlight: Had a 0.17 earned run average for the Gulf Coast Yankees, 1990
Personal Information: Is first cousin of San Diego Padres outfielder Ruben Rivera

Mariano Rivera

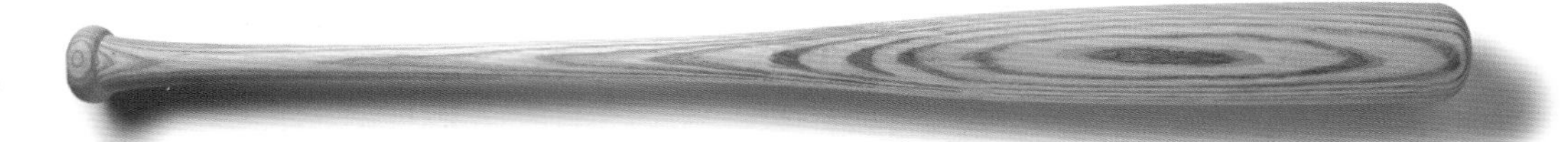

"He's the best. He's the best closer I've ever seen."

New York Yankees catcher, Joe Girardi

Career milestones

1995 Made 10 starts in 19 appearances in rookie season with the New York Yankees
1996 Threw 26 consecutive scoreless innings, April 19–May 21
1998 Converted 22 consecutive save opportunities before streak ended in a 6–5 victory vs. Texas, August 16
1999 Led the American League with 45 saves. Did not allow an earned run after July 2 and won the World Series Most Valuable Player Award with a win and two saves as the Yankees swept Atlanta

At some time in every player's career, there comes a challenge.

Some players answer the challenge. Others don't.

The challenge for New York Yankees reliever Mariano Rivera came during Game 4 of the 1997 Division Series against the Cleveland Indians. In his first season as the Yankees closer he saved 43 games and had a 6–4 record with a 1.88 earned run average.

Four outs from eliminating the Indians, the Yankees gave the ball to Rivera, but he didn't finish the job. Cleveland catcher Sandy Alomar Jr. homered to tie the game, which the Indians won in the ninth inning. The Indians won Game 5 the next night and the Yankees were finished.

Even though Rivera was so dominating during the regular season, Yankees fans wondered how he would respond to letting the season slip away.

Well, Rivera has shown them. Not only has he saved 81 games the last two seasons, he has been unhittable in the playoffs.

In fact, Rivera hasn't allowed a postseason run since Alomar's homer, a span of 25.2 innings. He has two victories and 12 saves since the home run. Rivera's postseason earned-run average of 0.38—two earned runs allowed in 47.1 innings —is the lowest for any pitcher with at least 30 innings pitched in postseason history.

Alomar's homer is now a distant memory.

"I love the challenge," said Rivera. "I love to be in that situation. I guess that's my motivation. Once you're there, you have butterflies in your stomach. You know you're there for real. You just want to do it."

Rivera has been particularly awesome in the Yankees' World Series sweeps the last two seasons. He saved three games against San Diego in 1998 and had two saves and a win against Atlanta in 1999, while being named the Most Valuable Player.

Rivera has been on the mound for the Series-clinching games the last two seasons. His Game 4 save over Atlanta extended his streak to 12.1 consecutive scoreless innings over eight games in three World Series. The last time he gave up a run in a Series game was the eighth inning of Game 3 in 1996. Rivera was the Yankees set-up man at the time.

"I want to be there when this happens," said Rivera. "I was the guy throwing the last pitch. And I had the last out. It feels tremendous."

Rivera wasn't too shabby in the regular season, either. He finished with a 4–3 record and 1.83 ERA, converting 45 of 49 save opportunities. while leading the league in saves, he ended the regular season with a scoreless streak of 30.2 innings over 28 games and converted his last 22 save chances.

Pitching

Year	W	L	ERA	G	GS	CG	SHO	SV	SVO	INN	H	R	ER	HR	HBP	BB	SO
1999	**4**	**3**	**1.83**	**66**	**0**	**0**	**0**	**45**	**49**	**69.0**	**43**	**15**	**14**	**2**	**3**	**18**	**52**
Career	**26**	**13**	**2.58**	**266**	**10**	**0**	**0**	**129**	**153**	**376.2**	**300**	**113**	**108**	**22**	**8**	**119**	**337**

Batting

Year	G	AB	R	H	HR	RBI	BB	SO	SB	CS	OBP	SLG	AVG
Career	**266**	**0**	**0**	**0**	**0**	**0**	**0**	**0**	**0**	**0**	**-**	**-**	**-**

Fielding

Year	Posn	G	GS	TC	PO	A	E	DP	FLD%
1999	**P**	**66**	**0**	**22**	**12**	**10**	**0**	**2**	**1.000**
Career		**266**	**10**	**92**	**32**	**60**	**0**	**4**	**1.000**

Alex Rodriguez

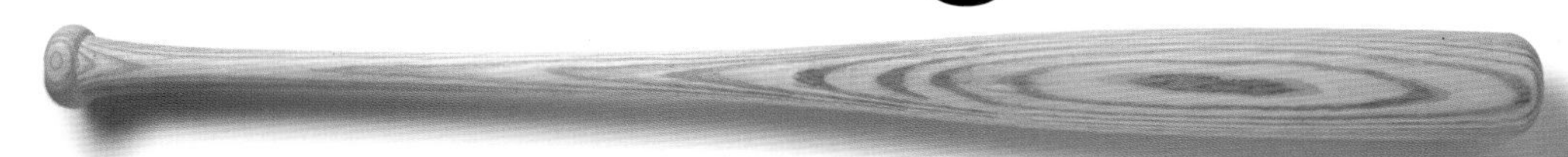

"Alex is a special player."

Seattle Mariners manager, Lou Piniella

Profile

Name: Alexander Emmanuel Rodriguez **Height:** 6–3 **Weight:** 195 **Throws:** Right **Bats:** Right **Position:** Shortstop **Born:** July 27, 1975, New York, New York **Drafted:** Selected by the Seattle Mariners in the first round (first pick overall) of the 1993 free-agent draft **Pre-Majors Highlight:** Batted .360 at Class AAA Tacoma, 1995 **Personal Information:** Visits grade schools and holds assemblies to promote his Grand Slam for Kids program, which encourages kids to work hard in school

Alex Rodriguez has had the word "superstar" written all over him since he came to the Major Leagues.

And the Seattle Mariners shortstop has lived up to every word of the hype.

In fact, if there's something Rodriguez doesn't do well on the baseball field, please contact all the opposing teams in the American League. They'd appreciate the information.

Rodriguez has hit .300 or better and cracked the 100-mark in RBIs in three of his four full seasons in the big leagues. He has hit 42 homers in each of the last two seasons and stolen at least 15 bases three times in the last four years.

Oh, and then there's his defense. At 6-foot-3 and 195 pounds, Rodriguez has outstanding range and a strong throwing arm.

"I feel very good about my defense," he said. "Unfortunately, I think my defense is overlooked because of my offense. I think my defense is as good as my offense. It won't get the recognition unless people watch me play."

The numbers Rodriguez put together in 1996—his first full year in the big leagues—were staggering. It might have been the best offensive season of any shortstop in Major League history. Rodriguez led the American League with a .356 batting average, scored 141 runs, hit 36 homers and drove in 123 runs. He also had 54 doubles, 215 hits, 36 homers, 59 walks and 15 stolen bases.

The .356 average was highest by a right-handed hitter since Joe DiMaggio hit .381 in 1939. Rodriguez was named to the American League All-Star Team and finished second to Texas outfielder Juan Gonzalez in the league's Most Valuable Player Award voting. He was named the Player of the Year in The Sporting News poll of Major League players and won the Silver Slugger Award.

Incredibly, he was only 20 years old when the season started, turning 21 on July 27.

Rodriguez's numbers the last two seasons have also set a new plateau for offensive production by a shortstop. In 1998, he led the league with 213 hits, batted .310, hit 42 homers and drove in 124 runs. Despite not playing until May 15, 1999, after having knee surgery in April, he hit 42 home runs again and became the first American League shortstop to reach the 40-homer mark twice.

Ernie Banks, who set the Major League mark for shortstops with 47 homers in 1958, reached 40 in 1955 and from 1957–60. The only other shortstop to hit 40 home runs was Rico Petrocelli, who had 40 in 1969.

Rodriguez is expected to hit the free-agent market when the 2000 season is over. With his numbers, he's guaranteed to become a very rich young man. It is possible that Seattle may trade him before he becomes a free agent when they would get nothing if he signs for another team.

Career milestones

1996 Led the American League in hitting with a .358 batting average

1997 Became the first American League shortstop other than Cal Ripken to start an All-Star Game since 1983

1998 Became just the third player in major league history with more than 40 homers and 40 stolen bases in one season

Batting

Year	G	AB	R	H	HR	RBI	BB	SO	SB	CS	OBP	SLG	AVG
1999	129	502	110	143	42	111	56	109	21	7	.357	.586	.285
Career	642	2572	493	791	148	463	210	495	118	32	.363	.551	.308

Fielding

Year	Posn	G	GS	TC	PO	A	E	DP	FLD%
1999	SS	129	129	609	213	382	14	103	.977
Career		638	629	2865	1004	1776	85	391	.970

Profile

Name: Larry Wayne Jones **Height:** 6–4 **Weight:** 210 **Throws:** Right **Bats:** Both **Position:** Third Base **Born:** April 24, 1972, DeLand, Florida **Drafted:** Selected by the Atlanta Braves in the first round (first pick overall) of the 1990 free-agent draft **Pre-Majors Highlight:** Led the International League in hits in 1993 **Personal Information:** Was honored as the Florida High School Player-of-the-Year in 1990

Chipper Jones

"It's awfully hard to believe. To have this in your corner, to always be able to say you won an MVP, is a tremendous honor." **Atlanta Braves third baseman, Chipper Jones**

Career milestones

1996 Became the first Braves players since Dale Murphy in 1985 to hit .300, hit 30 homers, and drive in and score 100 runs

1997 Hit three grand slams in a 13 game stretch in late June and early July

1999 Named the Most Valuable Player in the National League

The Atlanta Braves have always been about pitching. Greg Maddux. Tom Glavine. John Smoltz.

But as the 1999 season unfolded, the Braves needed some help in another area. First baseman Andres Galarraga was out for the season after being diagnosed with cancer in the offseason. Catcher Javy Lopez went out in midseason with a knee injury.

When the Braves needed some offense, Chipper Jones stepped up. Jones stepped up so much, he was named the Most Valuable Player in the National League.

"Most people who watched our team play know what a significant role he played in our success, especially when the season wore down and the pressure got great," Braves general manager John Schuerholz said. "He showed he was a leader of this team and he had what it takes to be recognized as the MVP of the league."

Jones hit .319 with 45 home runs, 110 runs batted in, 116 run scored, 25 stolen bases and 126 walks. He finished third in the league in homers behind Mark McGwire (65) and Sammy Sosa (63) and third in walks; fourth in slugging percentage (.633), on-base percentage (.441) and total bases (359); seventh in runs; and 10th in batting.

After June 15, he hit 30 homers and drove in 79 runs. The NL East race and the MVP race were decided when the New York Mets visited Atlanta for a three-game series September 21–23. The Mets had cut the Braves' lead in the division to one game before Jones took over. He hit four home runs, the Braves swept the series and wrapped up their eighth straight division title while Jones got ready for a new piece of hardware.

"Any time I read anything pertaining to the MVP race, they point directly back to that Mets' series," Jones said. "I think those four home runs were huge. I'd like to think my name was already on the map before that, but that kind of jump-started everything."

Jones has become one of the most productive hitters in baseball the last four years. In 1996, he batted .309 with 30 homers and 110 RBIs. He followed that by hitting .295 with 21 homers and 111 RBIs in 1996. Jones had another big year in 1998 in home runs (34), games (160), hits (188), runs (123), batting average (.313) and RBIs (107).

Jones was runner-up in the NL Rookie of the Year voting in 1995 after batting .265 with 23 homers and 86 RBIs.

Jones was the Braves' No.1 draft pick in 1990—the first pick overall. After four years in the minors, Jones was expected to be a regular in the Braves lineup in 1994, but he missed the entire season after injuring his knee in spring training.

Opponents have discovered Jones hasn't missed much since.

Batting

Year	G	AB	R	H	HR	RBI	BB	SO	SB	CS	OBP	SLG	AVG
1999	**157**	**567**	**116**	**181**	**45**	**110**	**126**	**94**	**25**	**3**	**.441**	**.633**	**.319**
Career	**779**	**2890**	**542**	**871**	**153**	**524**	**459**	**463**	**83**	**19**	**.394**	**.529**	**.301**

Fielding

Year	Posn	G	GS	TC	PO	A	E	DP	FLD%
1999	**SS**	**1**	**0**	**1**	**0**	**1**	**0**	**0**	**1.000**
Career		**766**	**761**	**1883**	**483**	**1314**	**86**	**110**	**.954**

Jeromy Burnitz

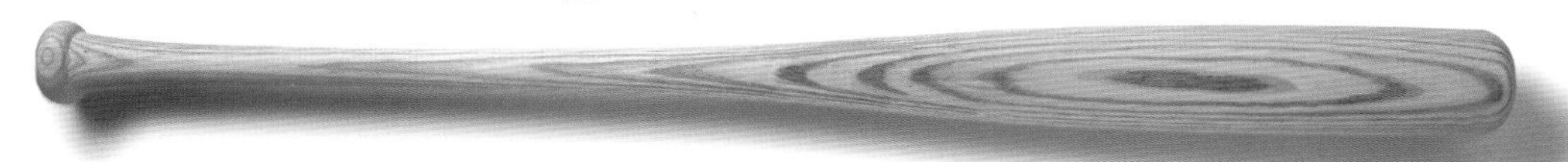

"I always thought I could up good numbers if I got the chance. That was the key for me."

Milwaukee Brewers outfielder, Jeromy Burnitz

Profile

Name: Jeromy Neal Burnitz
Height: 6–0 **Weight:** 205
Throws: Right **Bats:** Left **Position:** Right Field **Born:** April 15, 1969, Westminster, California **Drafted:** Selected by the New York Mets in the first round (17th pick overall) of the 1990 free-agent draft **Acquired:** Traded by the Cleveland Indians to the Milwaukee Brewers, August 31, 1996 **Pre-Majors Highlight:** Led the Eastern League in home runs and runs batted in in 1991 **Personal Information:** Attended Oklahoma State University

For Jeromy Burnitz, the game of baseball has all been about opportunity.

After languishing in the New York Mets and Cleveland Indians organizations, Burnitz finally has gotten his opportunity with the Milwaukee Brewers.

And he's taken advantage of his chance to play every day in the Major Leagues. Burnitz has been the Brewers' regular right fielder the last three years. He has averaged 33 home runs and 104 runs batted in a season.

"Jeromy's our offensive thrust," said former Milwaukee manager Phil Garner "When he's swinging the bat and hitting home runs, we do well."

Though Garner was fired during the 1999 season, he got a close look at just how Burnitz developed into a very productive player.

Burnitz's big break came on August 31, 1996. He spent the first five months of the season with the Indians, but was buried behind an outfield that consisted of stars like Albert Belle, Kenny Lofton and Manny Ramirez. On that day, the Indians traded Burnitz to the Brewers for Kevin Seitzer. Although Burnitz batted .236 with two homers and 14 RBIs in the final 22 games with Milwaukee, it didn't take long for the Brewers to get the big edge in the trade.

Burnitz had a breakthrough season in 1997. Playing in 153 games, he hit 27 homers, drove in 85 runs, batted .281 and stole 20 bases. He led the team in runs scored, triples, RBIs, total bases (273) and on-base percentage (.382). Burnitz was the first Brewer to have 20 home runs and 20 stolen bases in a season since Robin Yount in 1980.

That was only a preview for the 1998 season, the best year of Burnitz's career. He reached career highs in games played (161), hits (160), runs (92), homers (35) and RBIs (125). His RBI total led all left-handed hitters in the National League and his home run total was the most for a Brewer since Gorman Thomas slugged 39 in 1982. Burnitz also moved into second place all-time on the club's single-season RBI list behind Cecil Cooper (126). He set the club record with 24 RBIs in April and compiled a personal-best 12-game hitting streak (August 22–September 3).

Despite missing 30 games because of injuries, Burnitz had another good season in 1999 with 33 homers, 103 RBIs and a .270 average while being named to his first All-Star team.

Burnitz also is a good outfielder. He led the team with 10 outfield assists in 1997 and had 13 in 1998.

The Brewers, who are scheduled to move into a new ballpark in 2001, think Burnitz is the cornerstone of their franchise. And it all goes back to his opportunity to finally play in the big leagues.

Career milestones

1997 Homered in five straight games, August 1–5

1998 Tied for sixth in the National League in home runs (38) and fifth in RBIs (125)

1999 Named to National League All-Star team for the first time. Named National League Player of the Month for June with 12 homers and 31 runs batted in

Batting

Year	G	AB	R	H	HR	RBI	BB	SO	SB	CS	OBP	SLG	AVG
1999	**130**	**467**	**87**	**126**	**33**	**103**	**91**	**124**	**7**	**3**	**.402**	**.561**	**.270**
Career	**678**	**2183**	**381**	**580**	**123**	**406**	**330**	**551**	**42**	**28**	**.367**	**.508**	**.266**

Fielding

Year	Posn	G	GS	TC	PO	A	E	DP	FLD%
1999	**OF**	**127**	**127**	**275**	**262**	**8**	**5**	**2**	**.982**
Career		**616**	**569**	**1211**	**1144**	**39**	**28**	**10**	**.977**

Brian Jordan

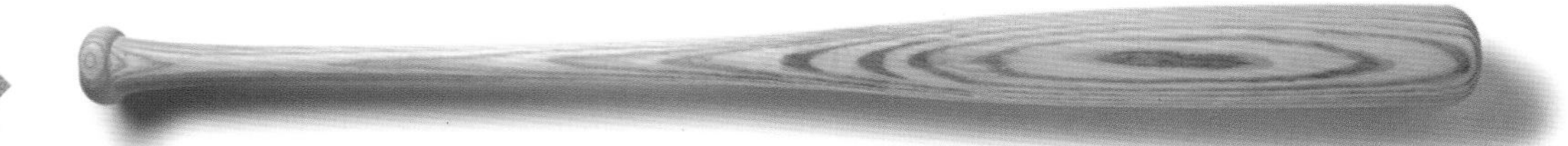

Profile

Name: Brian O'Neal Jordan
Height: 6–1 **Weight:** 205
Throws: Right **Bats:** Right
Position: Right Field **Born:** March 29, 1967, Baltimore, Maryland **Drafted:** Selected by the St. Louis Cardinals in the supplemental round of the 1988 free-agent draft **Acquired:** Signed by the Atlanta Braves as a free agent, November 23, 1998
Pre-Majors Highlight: Played defensive back for the Atlanta Falcons of the National Football League, 1989–91
Personal Information: Attended the University of Richmond

"Brian is a great athlete. He was a big addition for us. He was a boost to our lineup all season."

Atlanta Braves manager, Bobby Cox

Career milestones

1996 Led the National League with .422 average with runners in scoring position

1997 Matched known modern record with 13 bases-loaded hits, set by Mike Devereaux in 1989

1998 Named National League Player of the Week, May 11–17

1999 Named to the National League All-Star team for the first time

Brian Jordan takes the old phrase about players who can do it all a bit farther than most athletes.

Jordan has been an All-Star player in both Major League Baseball and the National Football League.

Jordan, an outfielder for the Atlanta Braves, is one of the best all-around players in baseball today. He has hit over .300 three times in his eight-year career while cracking the 100-run batted in mark twice. Jordan also has stolen more than 20 bases twice and has one of the best outfield arms in the National League, registering nine assists in 1999.

Jordan, who appeared in his first All-Star Game in 1999, showed the same kind of ability when he played in the NFL for the Atlanta Falcons from 1989–1991 as a defensive back. He was named an alternate for the 1992 Pro Bowl.

For now, Jordan is sticking with baseball. While that's good news for wide receivers in the National Football League, who no longer have to deal with a well-built 6-foot-1, 205-pound safety with excellent speed, it's bad news for pitchers around baseball.

Jordan turned in a solid year for the Braves in 1999, hitting .283 with 23 homers and a career-high 115 RBIs while scoring 100 runs for the second straight season.

Jordan hit over .300 three times between 1993 and 1998 while playing for the St. Louis Cardinals. His best season with the Cardinals came in 1998 when he led St. Louis in batting average (.316), at-bats (564), hits (178) and multi-hit games (52). He also drove in 91 runs and hit 25 homers.

Before suffering through an injury-plagued season in 1997 when he was limited to 47 games, Jordan had another big year in 1996. He hit .310 with 82 runs scored, 159 hits, 36 doubles, 17 homers, 104 RBIs, and 22 stolen bases. The RBI and stolen base totals are career highs. Jordan helped the Cardinals win the National League Central title that season. He also hit over .300 in 1993, with a .309 average.

Jordan spent the 1989, 1990 and 1991 seasons splitting his time between baseball and football. He was drafted by baseball's St. Louis Cardinals in 1988 and was also selected by football's Buffalo Bills in the seventh round of the 1989 NFL draft after playing at the University of Richmond.

The Falcons claimed Jordan on waivers early in the 1989 NFL season. After appearing in four games that year, he started all 16 games for Atlanta the next two seasons. He was a force in the Falcons' secondary, intercepting three passes and recovering a fumble in 1990 while intercepting two passes, recovering a fumble and being credited with two safeties in 1991. Jordan also returned punts and kickoffs.

Jordan decided to play baseball exclusively in 1992.

Batting

Year	G	AB	R	H	HR	RBI	BB	SO	SB	CS	OBP	SLG	AVG
1999	**153**	**576**	**100**	**163**	**23**	**115**	**51**	**81**	**13**	**8**	**.346**	**.465**	**.283**
Career	**796**	**2882**	**446**	**834**	**107**	**482**	**190**	**454**	**99**	**39**	**.340**	**.472**	**.289**

Fielding

Year	Posn	G	GS	TC	PO	A	E	DP	FLD%
1999	**OF**	**150**	**148**	**307**	**295**	**9**	**3**	**3**	**.990**
Career		**762**	**719**	**1655**	**1584**	**50**	**21**	**12**	**.987**

Shawn Green

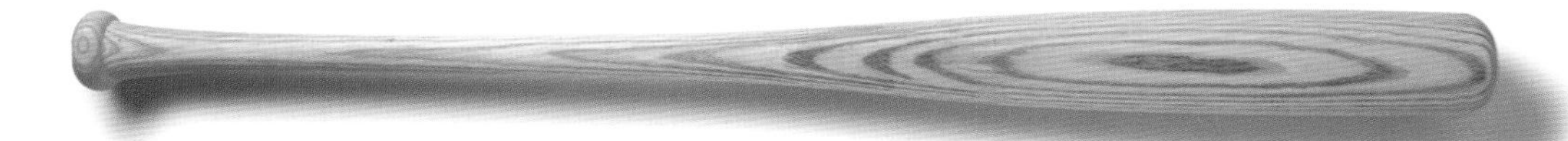

"Playing for the Dodgers is like a dream come true."

Los Angeles Dodgers outfielder, Shawn Green

Profile

Name: Shawn David Green **Height:** 6–4 **Weight:** 200 **Throws:** Left **Bats:** Left **Position:** Right Field **Born:** November 10, 1972, Des Plaines, Illinois **Drafted:** Selected by the Toronto Blue Jays in the first round (16th pick overall) of the 1991 free-agent draft **Acquired:** Traded by the Toronto Blue Jays to the Los Angeles Dodgers, November 10, 1999 **Pre-Majors Highlight:** Led the International League in hitting, 1994 **Personal Information:** Gives $250,000 yearly to the Dodgers Dream Foundation in Los Angeles

For Shawn Green, the 1999 season couldn't have worked out better.

First, he had the best season of his seven-year Major League career. Then he was traded to the team he rooted for growing up. On top of that, he signed a contract that will pay him $84 million over the next six years.

Yes, the man had a good year.

Green's run of good fortune began when he hit .309 with 42 home runs and 123 runs batted in with the Toronto Blue Jays. The season earned the right fielder, who reached career highs in all three categories and won a Gold Glove, a spot on the American League All-Star team and made him one of the top all-around players in the game today.

Since Green could be a free agent after the 2000 season, the Blue Jays began exploring trade possibilities. They found one on November 10 when they traded Green and infielder Jorge Nunez to the Los Angeles Dodgers for outfielder Raul Mondesi and pitcher Pedro Borbon. Green signed a new contract with the Dodgers.

The trade also put Green on the team he's been wanting to play for his entire career. Although he was born in Illinois, he grew up in the Los Angeles area and the Dodgers were his favorite team.

"I remember going to games at Dodger Stadium when I was a kid," he said. "I always dreamed about playing there."

Green, who will not turn 28 until after the end of the 2000 season, will now get the chance to live out his dream. And after the back-to-back seasons Green put together with the Blue Jays, it will be a nice dream for the Dodgers, who are in need of an obvious boost after the team's disastrous season in 1999. Green hit .278 with 35 homers and 100 RBIs in 1998. He also stole a career-high 35 bases in '98 and stole 20 in '99.

"I've been an admirer of Shawn Green for a long time," Dodgers manager Davey Johnson said. "He does a lot of things well and the left-handed bat gives you some options. He's going to help us do some things that will improve our lineup. He's the type of guy who adds to the whole team with everything he brings. You can envision a lot of possibilities."

Green's new teammates in Los Angeles also are looking forward to his arrival.

"Shawn Green is a great fit for our team," said left fielder Gary Sheffield. "Left-handed power is the main thing in the game today, and he's one of those guys teams have to pay attention to. He can create havoc in the middle of the batting order, and that just helps improve everything else. This can really help us turn the corner."

Green's career has already turned the corner. Maybe the Dodgers will be next.

Career milestones

1995 Led the Toronto Blue Jays in slugging percentage, the first rookie in Blue Jay history to do so

1998 Became first Blue Jays player to collect more than 30 home runs and 30 stolen bases in one season

1999 Selected to the American League All-Star team for the first time

Batting

Year	G	AB	R	H	HR	RBI	BB	SO	SB	CS	OBP	SLG	AVG
1999	**153**	**614**	**134**	**190**	**42**	**123**	**66**	**117**	**20**	**7**	**.384**	**.588**	**.309**
Career	**716**	**2513**	**402**	**718**	**119**	**376**	**206**	**510**	**76**	**25**	**.344**	**.505**	**.286**

Fielding

Year	Posn	G	GS	TC	PO	A	E	DP	FLD%
1999	**OF**	**152**	**152**	**346**	**340**	**5**	**1**	**1**	**.997**
Career		**652**	**600**	**1363**	**1298**	**46**	**19**	**14**	**.986**

Brad Radke

Profile

Name: Brad William Radke
Height: 6–2 **Weight:** 188
Throws: Right **Bats:** Right
Position: Pitcher **Born:** October 27, 1972, Eau Claire, Wisconsin **Drafted:** Selected by the Minnesota Twins in the eighth round of the 1991 free-agent draft **Pre-Majors Highlight:** Led the Southern League in games started, 1991
Personal Information: Married (Heather) with son (Kasey)

"An ace is someone like Pedro Martinez. I'm just a guy who goes out there every five days."

Minnesota pitcher, Brad Radke

Career milestones

1996 Was the youngest Opening Day starter for Minnesota since Bert Blyleven in 1974
1997 First 20-game winner for the Minnesota Twins since Scott Erickson in 1991, and the 14th pitcher to do so in club history
1998 Named to the American League All-Star team

If Brad Radke played on a contending team, he'd be recognized as one of the top starting pitchers in the American League.

Unfortunately for Radke, he pitches for the Minnesota Twins, so his name isn't as well-known as other starters with poorer records and less ability.

However, that doesn't take away from the fact the right-hander is a consistent and reliable pitcher.

Despite the fact the Twins fight a yearly battle to stay out of the cellar in the American League Central, Radke still puts up good numbers. He is 44–38 over the last three seasons with a 3.96 earned run average, 13 complete games, 135 walks and 441 strikeouts in 100 games.

On a team that featured 18 rookies on its roster at various times during the 1999 season, Radke was 12–14 with a solid 3.75 ERA. Radke, who was third in the league with just 1.8 walks per nine innings. He had four complete games, walked 44 and struck out 121 in 33 starts for the Twins. Radke led the staff in wins and innings pitched (218.1), and had the fourth-best ERA in the American League.

While the rest of the Twins struggle, Radke continues to be the mainstay of their staff. He eats up innings and consistently gives the Twins a chance to win.

Another plus for Radke is his durability. He has missed just one start in his five seasons with the Twins. Since joining the Twins' rotation in 1995, he has averaged 33 starts and 217 innings pitched a season.

Soon after the 1999 season ended, the Twins picked up the $3.5 million option on Radke's contract for 2000. Considering Radke's production, the Twins are getting a quality pitcher for a very reasonable rate in today's market.

That's one reason why contending teams often inquire about Radke's availability in a trade. He's not a prototype No.1 starter, but he would fit in very well as a No. 2 or No. 3 starter on a contender. The fact he will be only 27 on Opening Day 2000 is another reason why contending teams like him.

Radke's best season came in 1997. He finished the year with a 20–10 record and a 3.87 ERA while leading the league with 35 games started, a career high. Radke also pitched 239.2 innings, another career high and threw four complete games. His record would have been better with some run support from his teammates. The Twins managed only 2.6 runs a game in his 14 losses.

Selected by the Twins in the eighth round of the 1991 draft, Radke progressed quickly through Minnesota's farm system and was in the big leagues for the beginning of the 1995 season. He started the Twins' season opener at 22 years old and was 11–14 as a rookie.

Pitching

Year	W	L	ERA	G	GS	CG	SHO	SV	SVO	INN	H	R	ER	HR	HBP	BB	SO
1999	**12**	**14**	**3.75**	**33**	**33**	**4**	**0**	**0**	**0**	**218.2**	**239**	**97**	**91**	**28**	**1**	**44**	**121**
Career	**66**	**68**	**4.30**	**164**	**163**	**18**	**3**	**0**	**0**	**1085.0**	**1141**	**557**	**518**	**151**	**21**	**239**	**664**

Batting

Year	G	AB	R	H	HR	RBI	BB	SO	SB	CS	OBP	SLG	AVG
Career	**164**	**10**	**0**	**0**	**0**	**0**	**0**	**3**	**0**	**0**	**.000**	**.000**	**.000**

Fielding

Year	Posn	G	GS	TC	PO	A	E	DP	FLD%
1999	**P**	**33**	**33**	**57**	**21**	**36**	**0**	**5**	**1.000**
Career		**164**	**163**	**224**	**87**	**136**	**1**	**12**	**.996**

Orlando Hernandez

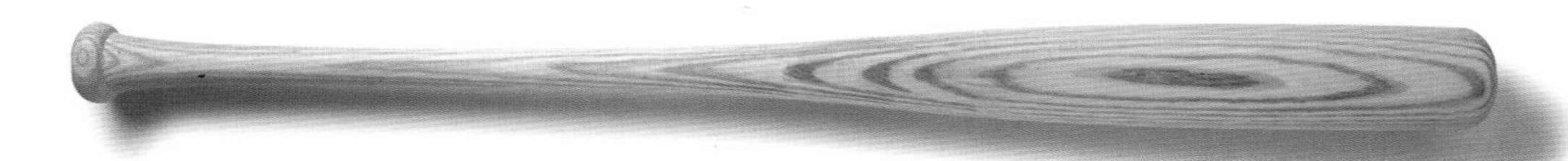

"He continues to just make you shake your head."

New York Yankees manager, Joe Torre

Profile

Name: Orlando P. Hernandez
Height: 6–2 **Weight:** 210
Throws: Right **Bats:** Right **Position:** Pitcher **Born:** October 11, 1969, Villa Clara, Cuba **Drafted:** Signed as an undrafted free agent by the New York Yankees, March 23, 1998
Pre-Majors Highlight: The ace pitcher on the Cuban National Team for many years, he had the best win-loss record in Cuban amateur history, 129–47
Personal Information: Half-brother of Florida Marlins pitcher Livan Hernandez

Two years ago, Orlando Hernandez was an unknown commodity to the New York Yankees.

That certainly isn't the case anymore. The right-hander, who defected from Cuba in December 1997 and was signed by the Yankees a few months later, is one of the top pitchers in the Major Leagues today. On a team with such pitching aces as David Cone and Roger Clemens, it was Hernandez who became the No. 1 pitcher on the best team in baseball. The pitcher nicknamed "El Duque", finished the 1999 season with a 17–9 record and a 4.12 ERA. He led the staff in wins, starts (33) and innings pitched (214.1).

Hernandez has been a major reason why the Yankees have won back-to-back World Series titles. In fact, the postseason has become his own personal stage. Hernandez was 3–0 in the 1999 postseason and is 5–0 overall with a 1.02 ERA in six career starts in the postseason the last two years.

"He really likes his pressure situations," Yankees catcher Jorge Posada said. "It's a lot of fun to see a guy so intense, so aggressive. He wants the ball. He wants to be the guy."

Hernandez started last season's playoffs by beating the Texas Rangers in Game 1 of the Division Series. After getting a no-decision in Game 1 of the League Championship Series against Boston, he finished off the Sox by winning Game 5. Hernandez was named the Most Valuable Player of the series.

In Game 1 of the World Series against Atlanta, Hernandez out-pitched Greg Maddux in a classic duel. Hernandez allowed one hit in seven innings—a home run by National League Most Valuable Player Chipper Jones—and struck out 10.

After going 12–4 in his rookie season, Hernandez showed he could handle the pressure when the Yankees needed him the most. Trailing Cleveland 2–1 in games in the 1998 League Championship Series, Hernandez came through with seven innings of shutout ball as the Yankees tied the series.

"Ever since that day, he has stepped up," said Posada.

The Yankees didn't lose another game in the postseason. Hernandez got another win in the World Series against the San Diego Padres.

Hernandez baffles hitters with a high leg-kick and a dazzling assortment of pitches and deliveries.

"It seems like 100 years ago when I saw him in spring training of '98 and watched him throw on the side," said Yankees manager Joe Torre. "Wow! That big leg kick!"

There's even mystery about Hernandez's age. When he defected, the Yankees officially listed him as being born in 1969. Court documents filed in Havana in connection to the divorce case from his ex-wife, Norma, say he was born in 1965. Hernandez's age won't be an issue for the Yankees if he continues to pitch as he has done since arriving in New York.

Career milestones

1998 Made Major League debut, June 3, picking up a 7–1 win over Tampa Bay. Tossed first complete game in an 11–1 victory over Montreal, June 9. Threw first shutout, September 14 vs. Boston

1999 Led the Yankees in wins, starts and innings pitched. Was the winning pitcher in Game 1 of the World Series against Atlanta

Pitching

Year	W	L	ERA	G	GS	CG	SHO	SV	SVO	INN	H	R	ER	HR	HBP	BB	SO
1999	**17**	**9**	**4.12**	**33**	**33**	**2**	**1**	**0**	**0**	**214.1**	**187**	**108**	**98**	**24**	**8**	**87**	**157**
Career	**29**	**13**	**3.72**	**54**	**54**	**5**	**2**	**0**	**0**	**355.1**	**300**	**161**	**147**	**35**	**14**	**139**	**288**

Batting

Year	G	AB	R	H	HR	RBI	BB	SO	SB	CS	OBP	SLG	AVG
Career	**54**	**10**	**1**	**1**	**0**	**0**	**0**	**5**	**0**	**0**	**.100**	**.100**	**.100**

Fielding

Year	Posn	G	GS	TC	PO	A	E	DP	FLD%
1999	**P**	**33**	**33**	**44**	**17**	**25**	**2**	**3**	**.955**
Career		**54**	**54**	**77**	**27**	**48**	**2**	**3**	**.974**

Profile

Name:
Anthony Nomar Garciaparra
Height: 6–0 **Weight:** 180
Throws: Right **Bats:** Right **Position:** Shortstop **Born:** July 23, 1973, Whittier, California
Drafted: Selected by the Boston Red Sox in the first round (12th pick overall) of the 1994 June draft
Pre-Majors Highlights: A member of the 1992 United States Olympic Team in Barcelona, Spain
Personal Information: Attended Georgia Tech University for three years. His name Nomar comes from his father, who reversed his first name, Ramon

Nomar Garciaparra

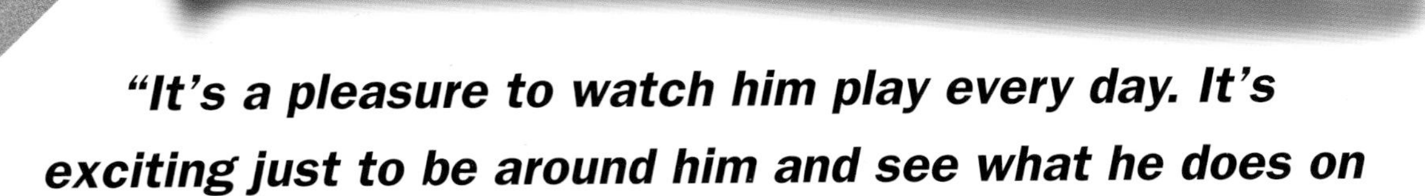

"It's a pleasure to watch him play every day. It's exciting just to be around him and see what he does on the field." **Boston Red Sox outfielder, Troy O'Leary**

Career milestones

1997 Named American League Rookie of the Year. First Red Sox rookie since Fred Lynn (1975) to be named to a American League All-Star team

1998 Had hitting streaks of 24, 16 and 11 games

1999 Led American League in hitting and named to American League All-Star team for the second time

If the first three years of his career are any indication, there's no telling what kind of numbers Nomar Garciaparra will put up.

"It's really incredible what Nomar's been able to do," Boston Red Sox manager Jimy Williams said of his shortstop. "He's only been in the league for three years and he's done so much already."

The scary thing for opposing teams in the American League is that Garciaparra keeps getting better.

It all started in 1996 when he won the American League Rookie of the Year honors. Garciaparra hit 30 home runs and batted .306 with 98 runs batted in. He was unanimously voted as the league's top rookie, becoming only the sixth player to do so.

Garciaparra led the league with 684 at-bats, 209 hits, and 11 triples. He led American League rookies in 13 offensive categories and set the league rookie record with a 30-game hitting streak (July 26–Aug. 29). His first Major League hit was a home run.

Garciaparra followed that up by hitting .323 with 35 homers and 122 RBIs. He became only the fifth player in Major League Baseball history with 30 or more home runs in each of his first two major league seasons. Garciaparra was among the league leaders in hits (195), batting average, RBIs and triples (8). He also led Boston with 20 game-winning RBIs and finished second in the American League Most Valuable Player Award.

A closer look at the numbers show how good his season really was. He was only the fifth Red Sox shortstop in franchise history to record 100 or more RBIs, went hitless in two straight games only twice and had hitting streaks of 24, 16 and 11 games. The 24-game hitting streak was the 10th-longest in Red Sox history. It ran from June 7–July 3. Garciaparra batted .387 during the streak.

Garciaparra topped himself again in 1999. He led the American League in hitting with a .357 batting average. He also had 42 doubles, 27 home runs, 104 runs batted in, 14 stolen bases and a .603 slugging percentage. He finished the season third in the league in slugging percentage and fourth in doubles. Despite all that production, Garciaparra struck out only 39 times. He did all this despite having two spells on the disabled list, helping Boston to win its second straight wild card berth.

Garciaparra's season is more amazing considering the Red Sox lost Mo Vaughn to free agency before the 1999 season. Many believed Garciaparra's production would go down without a big threat behind him in the lineup, but instead his batting average went up 34 points.

Along with the New York Yankees' Derek Jeter and the Seattle Mariners' Alex Rodriguez, Garciaparra is part of the new breed of shortstops who put up big offensive numbers, but are also good defensive players. Garciaparra, who has excellent range, quick reflexes and a strong arm, although he did make 17 errors in 1999.

Batting

Year	G	AB	R	H	HR	RBI	BB	SO	SB	CS	OBP	SLG	AVG
1999	**135**	**532**	**103**	**190**	**27**	**104**	**51**	**39**	**14**	**3**	**.418**	**.603**	**.357**
Career	**455**	**1907**	**347**	**615**	**96**	**340**	**123**	**207**	**53**	**18**	**.367**	**.566**	**.322**

Fielding

Year	Posn	G	GS	TC	PO	A	E	DP	FLD%
1999	**SS**	**134**	**133**	**606**	**232**	**357**	**17**	**72**	**.972**
Career		**453**	**449**	**2070**	**746**	**1260**	**64**	**264**	**.969**

Jason Kendall

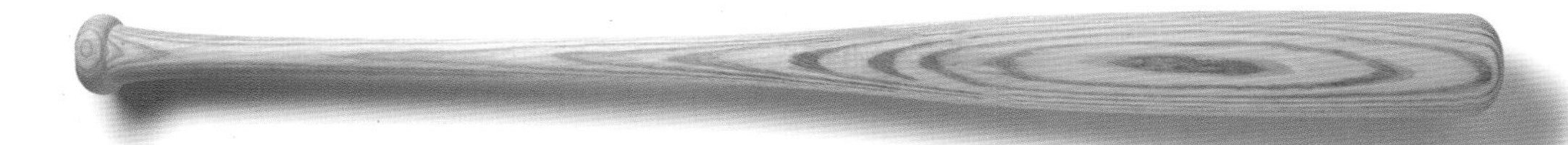

"I don't want to ever get hurt again. It's not fun. It's work. But I knew it was going to be hard."

Pittsburgh Pirates catcher, Jason Kendall

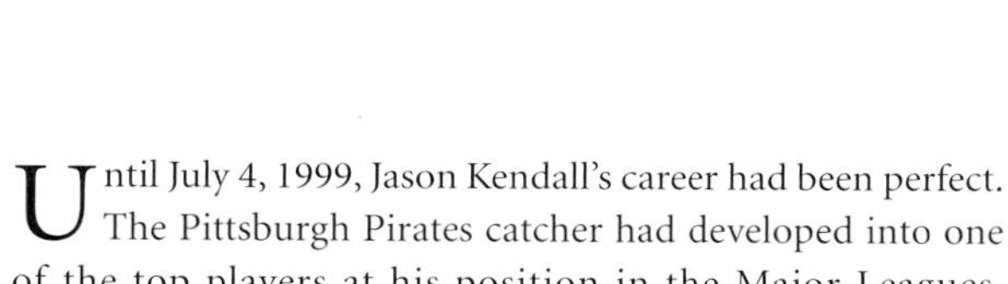

Profile

Name:
Jason Daniel Kendall
Height: 6–0 **Weight:** 193
Throws: Right **Bats:** Right **Position:** Catcher
Born: June 26, 1974, San Diego, California
Drafted: Selected by the Pittsburgh Pirates in the first round (23rd pick overall) in the 1992 free agent draft
Pre-Majors Highlight: Tied a national high school record when he hit safely in 43 straight games (dating back to his junior year)
Personal Information: Son of former catcher, Fred Kendall, who spent 12 years in the Major Leagues

Until July 4, 1999, Jason Kendall's career had been perfect. The Pittsburgh Pirates catcher had developed into one of the top players at his position in the Major Leagues. Kendall had hit .300 or better two times in his first three seasons and had made the National League All-Star team twice (1996 and 1998). He was about to be nominated for a third time.

Kendall, the Pirates' No. 1 draft pick in 1992, was on his way to another big season in 1999. Going into a game against the Milwaukee Brewers, he was hitting .332 with eight home runs and 41 runs batted in.

However, then came a moment that put Kendall's career in jeopardy. While racing to first base trying to beat out a bunt, Kendall suffered a devastating injury to his right ankle. He severely dislocated the ankle when he stumbled over the bag and had to be carried from the field on a stretcher.

The injury was so gruesome several players from both teams had to look away. In one horrible mis-step Kendall's season was over. His place on the All-Star team was taken—ironically—by the man who was behind the plate for the Brewers that day, Dave Nilsson.

Following surgery, Kendall began the long rehabilitation process to get back on the field for the 2000 season. He began running in November. He also was practicing his catcher's stance, which was to be followed by hitting and throwing. Kendall thought the process was going well during the offseason.

"That's behind me," he said. "It happened. It's over with. I honestly felt like I haven't missed a beat."

Kendall is encouraged by the fact New York Mets third baseman Robin Ventura came back from a similar injury suffered in 1997 to have productive seasons. The fact Kendall's legs suffer the wear and tear of catching makes his situation different, however.

Kendall was one of the top defensive catchers in the league before the injury. He led the league in assists in 1997 and putouts in 1998. In 1997, he threw out 40 percent of baserunners attempting to steal.

It remains to be seen how the injury affects Kendall's speed. Showing surprising speed for a catcher, Kendall stole 18 bases in 1997, 26 in 1998 and 22 in 1999 at the time of his injury.

Kendall set career highs in runs scored (95), hits (175), home runs (12) and RBIs (75) in 1998. He also appeared in a career-high 149 games, making 143 starts at catcher. His .327 batting average, another career high, was good for fifth in the National League, and he showed his great eye by striking out only 51 times in 535 at-bats.

Kendall also had a solid season in 1997. He hit .294 in 144 games, with eight homers and 49 RBIs. He batted .300 with three homers and 42 RBIs in his rookie year.

Career milestones

1996 Was named to the National League All-Star Team, becoming just the fifth rookie catcher so honored. Finished third in the Rookie of the Year voting

1997 Was hit by 31 pitches, setting a club record

1998 Set the National League record for most stolen bases in a season by a catcher (26)

Batting

Year	G	AB	R	H	HR	RBI	BB	SO	SB	CS	OBP	SLG	AVG
1999	**78**	**280**	**61**	**93**	**8**	**41**	**38**	**32**	**22**	**3**	**.428**	**.511**	**.332**
Career	**501**	**1715**	**281**	**535**	**31**	**207**	**173**	**166**	**71**	**16**	**.399**	**.451**	**.312**

Fielding

Year	Posn	G	GS	TC	PO	A	E	DP	FLD%
1999	**C**	**75**	**74**	**560**	**505**	**48**	**7**	**13**	**.988**
Career		**490**	**473**	**3594**	**3269**	**280**	**45**	**53**	**.987**

Profile

Name: Vladimir Alvino Guerrero
Height: 6–3 **Weight:** 205
Throws: Right **Bats:** Right **Position:** Right Field **Born:** February 9, 1976, Nizao Bani, Dominican Republic **Drafted:** Signed by the Montreal Expos as an undrafted free agent on March 1, 1993 **Pre-Majors Highlight:** Named Minor League Player of the Year by the Sporting News **Personal Information:** Brother, Wilton, is a second baseman for the Montreal Expos

Vladimir Guerrero

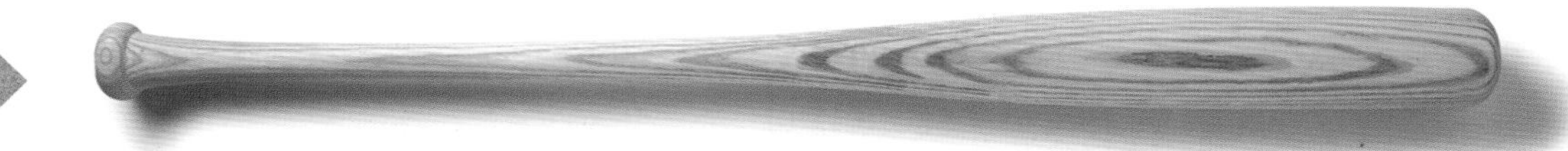

"Vladimir is one of the most exciting young players I've ever seen."

Montreal Expos manager, Felipe Alou

Career milestones

1996 Appeared in nine games with the Montreal Expos

1998 Ranked in the top 10 of the National League in 10 major offensive categories. Was one of only 10 players to reach the 200-hit plateau with 202

1999 Named to the National League All-Star team for the first time

The fact Vladimir Guerrero plays in the relative obscurity of Montreal should not overshadow the fact that he is one of the most exciting players in the Major Leagues today.

In fact, the 24-year-old Guerrero might be the best player fans never get a chance to see. A lack of ability isn't his problem. Guerrero's problem is a lack of exposure. The Expos draw poorly in Montreal and the team is rarely on television in the United States. Other than nightly highlight shows, fans don't get to see how good the Expos' right fielder is.

If someone takes a look at the stat sheet, they'll see Guerrero's name all over the place. He had another outstanding season in 1999. He finished fifth in the National League in runs batted in (131), fifth in hits (193), sixth in homers (42) and sixth in slugging percentage (.600).

Guerrero also batted .316 with 102 runs scored, 193 hits, 37 doubles and 14 stolen bases. He set single-season club records in homers and extra base hits (84). He also struck out just 62 times in 610 at-bats and played in 160 games.

Guerrero emerged as one baseball's top players in his first full season of big league experience in 1998. His name appeared in the top 10 in 10 offensive categories. He finished third in the league in multi-hit games (63), fourth in total bases (367), hits (202) and extra-base hits (82), sixth in homers (38) and intentional walks (13), seventh in batting (.324), eighth in triples (7) and slugging percentage (.589) and 10th in at-bats (623).

Guerrero has scored 100 runs and driven in 100 runs in each of the last two seasons. He set club single-season records for home runs, extra-base hits and total bases in 1998 and set new records in 1999.

Guerrero's rookie season in 1997 was marred by a broken foot, a broken hand and a strained hamstring. He played in only 90 games, but hit .302 with 11 homers and 40 RBIs

Guerrero also possesses one of the strongest throwing arms in baseball. The arm makes baserunners cautious, but it's also erratic and gets him in trouble sometimes. Guerrero has committed 12, 17 and 19 errors the last three seasons.

It didn't take long for the Expos to discover what a special talent Guerrero was after they signed him in 1993. In 1994, he had one of the greatest half-season performances in the 10-year history of the Dominican Summer League, hitting .424 with 12 homers and 35 RBIs in 25. Guerrero became the youngest player to win a batting title in the Eastern League (.360) while playing for Class AA Harrisburg in 1994. He was called up to the Expos later that season, which was the last he would see of the minor leagues.

Batting

Year	G	AB	R	H	HR	RBI	BB	SO	SB	CS	OBP	SLG	AVG
1999	**160**	**610**	**102**	**193**	**42**	**131**	**55**	**62**	**14**	**7**	**.378**	**.600**	**.316**
Career	**418**	**1585**	**256**	**498**	**92**	**281**	**116**	**199**	**28**	**20**	**.367**	**.567**	**.314**

Fielding

Year	Posn	G	GS	TC	PO	A	E	DP	FLD%
1999	**OF**	**160**	**159**	**366**	**332**	**15**	**19**	**3**	**.948**
Career		**410**	**406**	**896**	**814**	**34**	**48**	**9**	**.946**

Wade Boggs

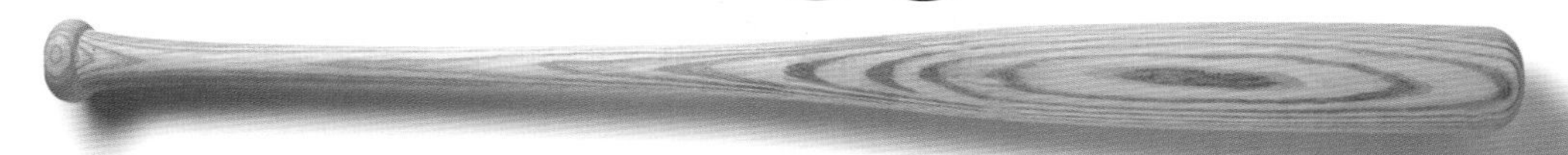

"I can still play. I had one style and took it to the max."

Former Major Leaguer, Wade Boggs

Profile

Name: Wade Anthony Boggs **Height:** 6–2 **Weight:** 197 **Throws:** Right **Bats:** Left **Positions:** Third Base, Designated Hitter, First Base **Born:** June 15, 1958, Omaha, Nebraska **Drafted:** Selected by the Boston Red Sox in the seventh round of the 1976 free-agent draft **Acquired:** Signed with the Tampa Bay Devil Rays as a free agent, December 9, 1998 **Pre-Majors Highlight:** Led the International League in hitting (.335) in 1981 **Personal Information:** Known for his superstitions, such as eating chicken before every game

Career milestones

1983 Won his first American League batting title. Also led the league in hitting from 1985–1988

1994 Won his first American League Gold Glove. Also won the award in 1995

1998 Hit first home run in Tampa Bay Devils Rays history

1999 Recorded his 3,000th career hit against Cleveland, August 7. Announced his retirement after the season

When Wade Boggs does something big, he does it with style. Boggs reached the 3,000-hit mark in style last season and, two months later, bowed out in style by retiring.

The fact Boggs joined the 3,000-hit club wasn't a surprise. He was one of the best hitters in baseball over the last 18 years and it was only a matter of time until he reached the historic mark. It was how Boggs, who played for the Tampa Bay Devil Rays the last two seasons, reached it that will always be memorable.

The milestone hit on August 7 off Cleveland Indians left-hander Chris Haney was a home run. That made Boggs the first player to reach 3,000 with a home run. Even more surprising is the fact Boggs was never known as a home-run hitter. That homer was his second—and last—of the season and he finished his career with 117.

After rounding the bases, Boggs dropped to his hands and knees and kissed home plate.

"I finally put my flag in that mountain," said Boggs. "So many guys have tried and come up short. It was like the longest mile to walk up to the plate."

Boggs finished the season on the disabled list after surgery to repair torn cartilage in his right knee on September 7. He ends his career with 3,010 career hits, good for 21st on the all-time hit list, 13 behind Hall of Famer Lou Brock.

Boggs, who played with the Boston Red Sox from 1982–1992, won five American League batting titles, was selected to 12 All-Star Games and earned two Gold Gloves. He posted a career-best .368 average for the Red Sox in 1985. Two years later, he slugged an atypical 24 home runs, 13 more than in any other season.

After six years in the minors, Boggs batted .349 in his rookie season. He batted over .300 the next nine straight seasons from 1983-1991 and set an American League record with seven straight seasons of 200 or more hits from 1983–1989.

Boggs slumped to a career-worst .259 in 1992 and signed a free agent contract with the Yankees following the season. He spent five seasons in New York, hitting over .300 four times. The highlight of his career came while he was in New York. In 1996 he won a World Series championship

Boggs signed with the expansion Devil Rays on December 9, 1997, batting .280 and .301 in his final two years.

Boggs will be a favorite for election to the Hall of Fame in 2005, his first year of eligibility. All members of the 3,000-hit club who are eligible have been elected to the Hall.

Boggs, who retires with a .328 average, will move into the Devil Rays' front office as a special assistant to general manager Chuck LaMar. In his new position, Boggs will be involved in both baseball and business operations.

Batting

Year	G	AB	R	H	HR	RBI	BB	SO	SB	CS	OBP	SLG	AVG
1999	**90**	**292**	**40**	**88**	**2**	**29**	**38**	**23**	**1**	**0**	**.377**	**.377**	**.301**
Career	**2440**	**9180**	**1513**	**3010**	**118**	**1014**	**1412**	**745**	**24**	**35**	**.415**	**.443**	**.328**

Fielding

Year	Posn	G	GS	TC	PO	A	E	DP	FLD%
1999	**3B/1B**	**78**	**75**	**186**	**77**	**100**	**9**	**17**	**.952**
Career		**1564**	**1522**	**6651**	**2115**	**4304**	**232**	**472**	**.965**

Profile

Name:
Matthew Bruce Mantei
Height: 6–1 **Weight:** 190
Throws: Right **Bats:** Right **Position:** Pitcher
Born: July 7, 1973, Tampa, Florida **Drafted:** Selected by the Seattle Mariners in the 25th round of the 1991 free-agent draft **Acquired:** Traded by the Florida Marlins to the Arizona Diamondbacks, July 10, 1999
Pre-Majors Highlight: Saved 26 games for Class A Appleton, 1994
Personal Information:
Played baseball at River Valley High School, Three Oaks, Michigan

Matt Mantei

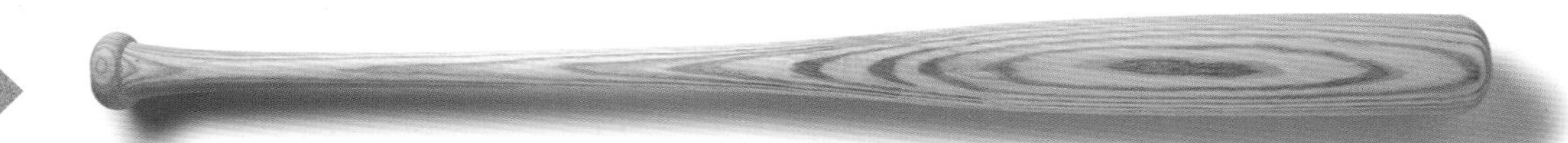

"He was somebody that a lot of clubs were trying to acquire, and we were lucky enough to put something together. He's got great stuff." **Arizona Diamondbacks manager, Buck Showalter**

Career milestones

1993 Led the Northwest League with 12 saves while playing for Bellingham.

1994 Selected by the Florida Marlins from the Seattle Mariners in the 1994 Rule 5 Major-League Draft.

1995 Made 12 relief appearances for the Florida Marlins

1998 Split the season between Class AAA Charlotte and the Florida Marlins

1999 Traded to the Arizona Diamondbacks and recorded 22 saves, helping his team win the National League West Division

Signing Randy Johnson after the 1998 season might have put the Arizona Diamondbacks on the baseball map, but the team still had a big problem.

By midseason, their bullpen was a mess. Arizona's relievers had blown 14 of 29 save opportunities and the Diamondbacks trailed San Francisco by 2.5 games in the National League West. Arizona management spent millions to acquire stars such as Johnson, third baseman Matt Williams and second baseman Jay Bell, but it looked like an ineffective bullpen was going to keep the team from reaching the top.

That problem was solved on July 10 when Arizona acquired closer Matt Mantei from the Florida Marlins for pitchers Vlade Nunez and Brad Penny. Mantei converted 22 of 25 save opportunities for the Diamondbacks, who ended up winning the division by 14 games.

Mantei, a hard-throwing right-hander who can reach a 100 miles-per-hour on the radar gun, ended the season with 32 saves, good for eighth in the National League. He blew five saves all season and had a 2.76 earned run average.

Mantei, 26, is one of the most overpowering relief pitchers in baseball. He struck out 95 and allowed only 44 hits in 65.1 innings. Opponents batted .189 against him. Mantei's 21 saves after the All-Star break tied him with the Atlanta Braves' John Rocker for the second-highest total in the majors, just one behind the New York Yankees' Mariano Rivera and the Montreal Expos' Ugueth Urbina

Mantei was 1–2 with 10 saves and a 2.72 ERA for the Marlins at the time of the trade. He had 50 strikeouts in 36.1 innings. Mantei saved nine games for Florida in 1998.

Mantei has had a history of arm problems. He underwent arthroscopic surgery in 1996 to repair a partially torn rotator cuff. He spent the entire 1997 season on the Marlins' disabled list and also missed most of the 1995 season because of arm problems.

"I knew I was going to be able to pitch again. I just didn't know I'd be as strong," he said. "But I'm stronger than I was before I had the surgery. I thank God every morning when I wake up and I feel great."

The Seattle Mariners selected Mantei in the 25th round of the 1991 draft. He pitched in their minor league system for four years before the Marlins took him in the Rule 5 Major League draft after the 1994 season. Mantei appeared in 12 games for the Marlins in 1995 before his arm problems began.

If Mantei stays away from injuries, he has a bright future and should be one of the top closers in the game.

Pitching

Year	W	L	ERA	G	GS	CG	SHO	SV	SVO	INN	H	R	ER	HR	HBP	BB	SO
1999	**1**	**3**	**2.76**	**65**	**0**	**0**	**0**	**32**	**37**	**65.1**	**44**	**21**	**20**	**5**	**5**	**44**	**99**
Career	**5**	**8**	**3.44**	**133**	**0**	**0**	**0**	**41**	**47**	**151.2**	**107**	**61**	**58**	**9**	**13**	**101**	**202**

Batting

Year	G	AB	R	H	HR	RBI	BB	SO	SB	CS	OBP	SLG	AVG
Career	**133**	**5**	**0**	**1**	**0**	**0**	**0**	**2**	**0**	**0**	**.200**	**.200**	**.200**

Fielding

Year	Posn	G	GS	TC	PO	A	E	DP	FLD%
1999	**P**	**65**	**0**	**11**	**3**	**7**	**1**	**0**	**.909**
Career		**133**	**0**	**30**	**11**	**18**	**1**	**3**	**.967**

Kevin Millwood

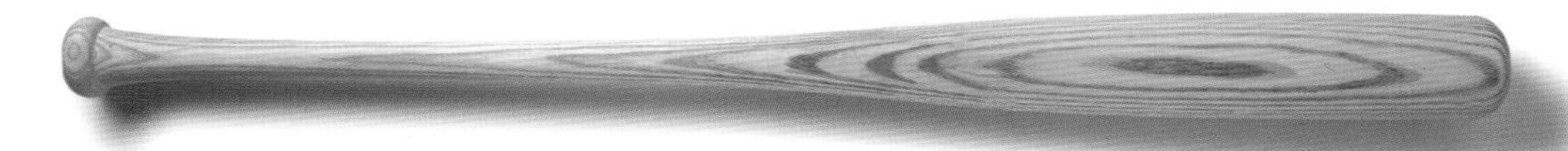

Profile

Name: Kevin Austin Millwood **Height:** 6–4 **Weight:** 220 **Throws:** Right **Bats:** Right **Position:** Pitcher **Born:** December 24, 1974, Gastonia, North Carolina **Drafted:** Selected by the Atlanta Braves in the 11th round of the 1993 free-agent draft Pre-Majors **Highlight:** Struck out 139 hitters in 1996, ranking third in the Carolina League **Personal Information:** Married on January 9, 1999, to the former Rena Stevens

"I don't know how many games Kevin went into with no-hitters in the fifth or sixth inning. It was almost a routine deal. You'd look up at the scoreboard and the other team didn't have any hits in the fifth." **Atlanta Braves manger, Bobby Cox**

Some people collect rare coins or priceless paintings. The Atlanta Braves collect ace starting pitchers. Yeah, like they needed another, right?

And the bad news for the National League is it looks this one is going to be around for a while.

On a staff with Greg Maddux, Tom Glavine and John Smoltz, 25-year-old right-hander Kevin Millwood emerged as the team's ace.

Millwood finished the 1999 season with an 18–7 record and a 2.68 earned run average in 33 starts. He led the team in wins, ERA, innings pitched (228) and strikeouts (205). Maddux, with 19 wins, was the only starter with more victories.

Millwood was second in the league in ERA, fifth in wins and eighth in innings pitched. Opposing hitters batted .202 against him.

As Maddux, Glavine and Smoltz have done so often in the past, Millwood took his game to a new level in the playoffs.

After Maddux lost Game 1 of the Division Series to the Houston Astros, Millwood saved the Braves' season with one of the best performances in postseason history. He limited the Astros to one hit—a second-inning home run by Ken Caminiti—and three baserunners while striking out eight.

"It was probably the biggest game I have pitched in and so I would have to say it is my best performance ever," said Millwood. "I think about the second or third inning I threw a few sliders and a couple of curve balls and they were pretty good and I had good control of them. From then on, I knew if I threw the right pitch and kept them guessing a little bit, it was going to be a pretty good ballgame."

Besides Caminiti, the only other Astros to reach base were Jeff Bagwell, who was aboard on Chipper Jones' error in the seventh, and Carl Everett, who followed with a fielder's choice roller.

Millwood became the first pitcher since Boston's Jim Lonborg in 1967 to throw a one-hit complete game in the postseason.

Millwood was 17–8 with a 4.08 ERA in 1998, his first full season with the Braves. He spent the last part of the 1997 season in Atlanta, going 5-3 with a 4.03 ERA.

Millwood is proof that minor league records don't mean everything. Selected by the Braves in the 11th round of the 1993 draft, he had a career minor league record of 27–31. He had losing records at four different stops, including an 0–5 mark at Class A Macon in 1994.

Millwood finally broke through in 1997, going 7–0 with a 1.93 ERA at Class AAA Richmond in 1997. He was then called up by the Braves.

Career milestones

1997 Made Major League debut, July 14

1998 Pitched a one-hit shutout against the Pittsburgh Pirates, April 14. Among National League leaders in earned run average, wins, strikeouts and opponents batting average against

1999 Named to the National League All-Star team for the first time. Among league leaders in earned run average, wins and innings pitched

Pitching

Year	W	L	ERA	G	GS	CG	SHO	SV	SVO	INN	H	R	ER	HR	HBP	BB	SO
1999	**18**	**7**	**2.68**	**33**	**33**	**2**	**0**	**0**	**0**	**228.0**	**168**	**80**	**68**	**24**	**4**	**59**	**205**
Career	**40**	**18**	**3.37**	**76**	**70**	**5**	**1**	**0**	**0**	**453.2**	**398**	**192**	**170**	**43**	**9**	**136**	**410**

Batting

Year	G	AB	R	H	HR	RBI	BB	SO	SB	CS	OBP	SLG	AVG
Career	**76**	**140**	**5**	**16**	**1**	**7**	**9**	**59**	**0**	**0**	**.168**	**.157**	**.114**

Fielding

Year	Posn	G	GS	TC	PO	A	E	DP	FLD%
1999	**P**	**33**	**33**	**35**	**13**	**20**	**2**	**0**	**.943**
Career		**76**	**70**	**70**	**25**	**42**	**3**	**1**	**.957**

Profile

Name: Scott Ryan Williamson **Height:** 6–0 **Weight:** 185 **Throws:** Right **Bats:** Right **Positions:** Pitcher **Born:** February 17, 1976, Ft. Polk, Louisiana **Drafted:** Selected by the Cincinnati Reds in the ninth round of the 1997 free-agent draft **Pre-Majors Highlight:** Made the Pioneer League All-Star team, 1997 **Personal Information:** Attended Tulane University for two years and transferred to Oklahoma State

Scott Williamson

"This is a tremendous accomplishment for the Reds' player development and scouting department."

Cincinnati Reds general manager, Jim Bowden

Career milestones

1997 Named co-Most Valuable Player for Class A Billings

1998 Split the season between Class AA Chattanooga and Class AAA Indianapolis

1999 Named the National League Rookie of the Year. Recorded 12 wins and saved 19 games for the Cincinnati Reds

Talk about a season that was right out of a storybook. That's what happened to Scott Williamson in 1999.

When the season started, not only was Williamson not on the Cincinnati Reds' 40-man roster, his name couldn't even be found in the Baseball Register, which lists 632 pages of Major League and Minor League players.

By the end of the season, Williamson was being handed the National League Rookie of the Year Award.

How's that for coming out of nowhere?

"It was really a shock," said Williamson. "It's unbelievable."

Williamson, a starter throughout the minor leagues after being drafted by the Reds in the ninth round of the 1997 draft, played a major role in Cincinnati's surprising season. He was the Reds closer most of the year, finishing 12–7 with a 2.41 earned run average, 19 saves and 107 strikeouts in 93.1 innings. The Reds battled for a playoff berth all summer and ended the season tied for the wild card spot in the National League, but lost a one-game playoff to the New York Mets.

Williamson led all National League rookie pitchers in victories, saves, relief earned-run average, relief strikeouts and winning percentage. He also was named to the National League All-Star team, the first Reds rookie pitcher to make the NL All-Star team since Ewell Blackwell in 1946.

Williamson received 17 first-place votes, nine second-place votes and six third-place votes for 118 points. He became only the seventh Reds player to win the award, a list that includes Hall of Famers Frank Robinson (1956) and Johnny Bench (1968) and franchise's most popular player ever, Pete Rose (1963). Third baseman Chris Sabo (1988) was the last Cincinnati player to earn the distinction. Right-hander Pat Zachry (1976) was the only other Reds pitcher to win it. Infielder Tommy Helms won it in 1966.

Williamson, who appeared in 62 games, allowed 54 hits and held opposing hitters to a .171 batting average.

One of Williamson's best moments came on May 27 against the Los Angeles Dodgers when he struck out six straight batters.

Williamson slumped late in the season, posting a 6.55 ERA after Sept. 1. He battled tendinitis in his shoulder and a cut on the middle finger of his throwing hand.

Williamson made it to the Reds in just his third professional season. He split the 1998 season between Class AA Chattonooga and Class AAA Indianapolis. Williamson combined to go 4–5 with a 3.73 ERA in 23 appearances, all starts. He began his professional career in 1997 at Class A Billings, where he led the league with wins (eight) and strikeouts (101) while making the Pioneer League All-Star team.

Pitching

Year	W	L	ERA	G	GS	CG	SHO	SV	SVO	INN	H	R	ER	HR	HBP	BB	SO
1999	**12**	**7**	**2.41**	**62**	**0**	**0**	**0**	**19**	**26**	**93.1**	**54**	**29**	**25**	**8**	**1**	**43**	**107**
Career	**12**	**7**	**2.41**	**62**	**0**	**0**	**0**	**19**	**26**	**93.1**	**54**	**29**	**25**	**8**	**1**	**43**	**107**

Batting

Year	G	AB	R	H	HR	RBI	BB	SO	SB	CS	OBP	SLG	AVG
Career	**62**	**7**	**0**	**0**	**0**	**0**	**1**	**6**	**0**	**0**	**.125**	**.000**	**.000**

Fielding

Year	Posn	G	GS	TC	PO	A	E	DP	FLD%
1999	**P**	**62**	**0**	**10**	**2**	**7**	**1**	**1**	**.900**
Career		**62**	**0**	**10**	**2**	**7**	**1**	**1**	**.900**

Carlos Beltran

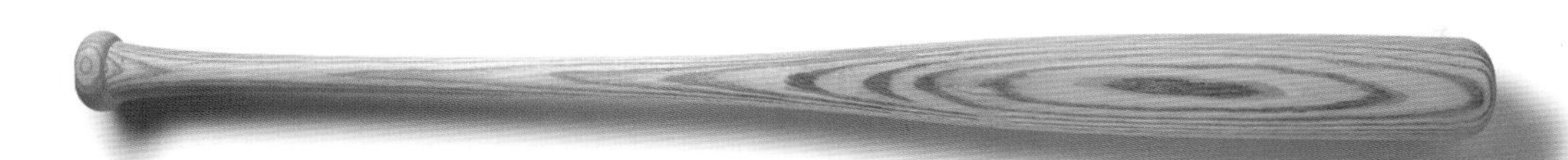

"Beltran is a heck of a player, a five-tool guy. He's one of the bright young players that's come into this league in the past five or six years." **Seattle Mariners manager, Lou Piniella**

Profile

Name: Carlos Ivan Beltran **Height:** 6–0 **Weight:** 175 **Throws:** Right **Bats:** Both **Positions:** Center Field **Born:** April 24, 1977, Manati, Puerto Rico **Drafted:** Selected by the Kansas City Royals in the second round of the 1995 free-agent draft Pre-Majors **Highlight:** Batted .278 during first professional season with the Gulf Coast League Royals, 1995 **Personal Information:** Graduated from Fernando Callejas High School, 1995

Carlos Beltran is the most exciting thing to hit Kansas City in years.

A solid all-around season earned Beltran, the Royals' center fielder, the American League Rookie of the Year honors for 1999.

Beltran had numbers most veterans would envy. The switch-hitter batted .293 with 22 homers, 108 runs batted in, 112 runs scored and 27 stolen bases. He also played well in center field with 16 assists and several good defensive plays throughout the season.

Beltran received 26 of 28 first-place votes and compiled 133 points to 45 for Seattle pitcher Freddy Garcia and 27 for Texas reliever Jeff Zimmerman.

"I feel happy because I think I deserved it," said Beltran. "I worked hard in the season and in the off-season. I put up my numbers. Every rookie, when he gets to the big leagues, wants to be Rookie of the Year. It means a lot that Kansas City gave me the opportunity to play."

Beltran led American League rookies in hits (194), multi-hit games (54), total bases (301), on-base percentage (.337), runs scored, homers and RBIs. He was second in extra base hits (56) and triples (seven). He also was second in the American League with 663 at-bats, tied for second in assists, tied for third with 10 sacrifice flies and was seventh in hits.

Beltran was the Royals' second-round pick in the 1995 draft. His fine season came at just 22 years old.

"I don't think there was ever a time this season that he didn't demonstrate he was as fine a young player who has come to the major leagues in a very long time," Royals general manager Herk Robinson said.

Beltran's numbers put him in some select company. He became the first American League Rookie to collect 100 RBIs in a season since Oakland's Mark McGwire drove in 118 in 1987. He's the first Major League rookie to do it since Los Angeles' Mike Piazza drove in 112 in 1993.

Beltran also became the eighth rookie in baseball history to score 100 runs and drive in 100 runs. He and Fred Lynn (1975) are the only two rookies to accomplish the feat since 1950.

Beltran also is already moving up in the Royals' record books. He became the third Royals player to score 100 runs and drive in 100 runs in the same season. He also became the third player in club history to record 20 homers and steal or more bases in one season.

"He seems to focus better and bear down a little more when the pressure is higher," Kansas City manager Tony Muser said. "He's one of those special-type people."

And it looks like Beltran is in for a very special career.

Career milestones

1998 Collected first Major League hit off Oakland's Buddy Groom, September 14. Registered a hit in 12 of the 14 games he appeared in for the Royals.

1999 Named the American League Rookie of the Year. Became the first American League rookie to collect 100 runs batted in in a season since Mark McGwire

Batting

Year	G	AB	R	H	HR	RBI	BB	SO	SB	CS	OBP	SLG	AVG
1999	156	663	112	194	22	108	46	123	27	8	.337	.454	.293
Career	170	721	124	210	22	115	49	135	30	8	.336	.455	.291

Fielding

Year	Posn	G	GS	TC	PO	A	E	DP	FLD%
1999	CF	156	156	421	393	16	12	3	.971
Career		168	167	466	437	16	13	3	.972

The publishers would like to thank the following sources for their kind permission to reproduce the pictures in this book:

AP Photo 149, 156/John Bazemore 64, Robert Bukaty 110, Mary Butkus 85, Paul Chiasson 154, Peter Cosgrove 75, Kevin Frayer 44, Tom Gannam 84, Morry Gash 147, Eric Gay 155, Tony Guteirrez 157, John Hayes 45, Jane Hurang 98, Bill Janscha 117, Erik S Lesser 60, Mark Duncan Michael 148, Jim Mone108, Chris O'Meara 150, Ed Reinke 144, Jim Rogash 103, Reed Saxon 158, Ron Schwane 115, Keith Srakocic 153, Pat Sullivan 107, George Widman 100, David Zablubowski 72, Ed Zurga 159

Allsport/Brian Bahr 4, 62, 73, 74, 77, 105, 121, 129, 131, 145, John Bazemore 54, Al Bello 96, 106, 124, Jonathan Daniel 18, 29, 35, 38, 39, 71, 80, 90, 91, 102, 109, 116, 125, Stephen Dunn 42, 43, 50, 99, 128, 134, 141, Otto Greule 22, 23, 48, 49, 69, 89, 133, 142, Scott Halleran 31, Tom Hauck 25, 26, 27, 68, 76, 111, 137, Harry How 40, 101, 119, 120, 130, 140, Jed Jacobsohn 17, 21, 30, 32, 36, 47, 86, 113, 138, 160, Vincent Laforet 24, 28, 37, 143, M. David Leeds 41, 59, 87, Doug Pensinger 3, 20, 46, 51, 57, 63, 88, 95, 114, David Seelig 55, 127, Ezra Shaw 33, 56, 58, 66, 67, 70, 78, 79, 82, 83, 97, 126, 132, 151, Jamie Squire 93, 94, 136, 146, Matthew Stockman 52, 53, 65, 118, 123, 135, 139, Tim Umphrey ct 152, Todd Warshaw 34, 61, 81, 92, 104, 112, 122

Corbis/Bettmann 8, 9, 10, 11, 14,15, 16, /UPI 6, 7, 12, 13

Baseball bat (20-159) provided by Jack Akers, Spartan Sports